"A profound and necessary beacon of light for Black Christian women navigating the complexities of faith, this book masterfully intertwines the narratives of Scripture with the lived experiences of Black women, addressing with great wisdom the challenges we face. Every page is a step toward healing, dignity, and a rediscovered purpose. *Church Girl* is an essential read."

—LISA FIELDS, CEO of Jude 3 Project and author of *When Faith Disappoints*

"*Church Girl* is a tour de force and the master class we didn't know we needed. Dr. Lyons isn't afraid to be countercultural or politically incorrect but is unashamedly biblical when it comes to showing God's aim for women. . . . I'll be using *Church Girl* as a tool to invest in the scores of Black women in my sphere. In the eternal words of the 90s scholar Martin Lawrence, 'You go, Church Girl!'"

—DR. ERIC MASON, pastor of Epiphany Fellowship Church
and author of *Urban Apologetics*

"In *Church Girl,* Dr. Sarita Lyons tackles, head-on, the dilemma today's Black Christian woman finds herself in as she navigates her relationship with herself, God, and the church. She challenges the world's definition of the Black woman and eloquently presents God's definition. This book is full of Godly revelation and insight that I want to chew on for years to come. *Church Girl* holds keys to identity that every Black woman needs in her pocketbook."

—NAOMI RAINE, award-winning gospel artist

"This transformative book is a journey to freedom. Dr. Lyons does an impeccable job sharing both her life story and Scripture to shine light on the dark and demonic nature of the enemy, an enemy who finds cracks in our foundations of faith in an attempt to fill them with lies and false gods and destroy those of us striving to live holy and surrendered lives unto Christ."

—JADA EDWARDS, Bible teacher, author, and women's pastor

"Through a blend of storytelling, educational insights, and the solid foundation of biblical doctrine, this book promises to reveal, heal, and uplift Church Girls of all ages. Your eyes will be opened to new perspectives, challenging you to rethink your self-perception and revitalize and redefine your Christian journey."

—TRINA JENKINS, first lady and chief minist~~ ~~
First Baptist Church of Glenard

"The wisdom, the knowledge, the res   nit-
ment to God's Word that's resulted fr   m-
passion of a one-time backslider—w   nd

maybe even a few tears. For any Black female seeking to fulfill the tremendous potential God has placed inside you, this masterpiece from Dr. Lyons is a must-read."

—CHRIS BROUSSARD, sports broadcaster and founder of the K.I.N.G. Movement

"With a blend of personal anecdotes, biblical teachings, and practical wisdom, Dr. Lyons invites readers to embrace their spirituality, reclaim their worth, and pursue their God-given destinies with courage and conviction. . . . *Church Girl* is a beacon of inspiration and empowerment, offering Black Christian women a road map to spiritual growth, personal fulfillment, and joyful living in alignment with their faith."

—STEPHANIE CARTER, first lady of Concord Church

"Dr. Sarita Lyons beautifully captures the diverse essence of Black womanhood within the Christian faith. With profound insight and a deep understanding of identity rooted in God's Word, this book is a compelling call for Black women to embrace their unique identities in Christ. A must-read for those seeking healing, transformation, and a deeper connection with their faith."

—LATASHA MORRISON, *New York Times* bestselling author of *Be the Bridge*

"*Church Girl* is the bold and beautifully written book I wish I'd had when I came to faith in my twenties. Steeped in my identity as a Black woman, I needed a clear gospel vision of my identity in Christ and sound wisdom for walking it out. With heartfelt, powerful prose, Dr. Lyons delivers. Her prophetic voice is essential in our day."

—KIM CASH TATE, author of *Cling*

"Being a Black Church Girl, I was blessed and encouraged by this book. It's honest, candid, insightful, and anointed! Dr. Lyons perfectly articulates the charge and challenge of believers to keep God's purposes, and not the ever-changing culture, in the driver's seat of their lives. Church life isn't easy, but this book will help and heal your heart."

—ERICA CAMPBELL, award-winning singer/songwriter and half of the gospel duo, Mary Mary

"Through heartfelt storytelling and insightful guidance, Dr. Lyons delves into the unique struggles and triumphs of being a Black woman of faith. With courage and candor, she tackles the complexities of societal expectations and spiritual devotion, offering a refreshing perspective on what it means to live authentically for Jesus foreal foreal. *Church Girl* is a compelling testament to the strength and resilience of Black Christian women everywhere, and it's exactly what we need."

—BRENDA PALMER, preacher and host of *Life In Perspective Podcast*

Church Girl

Church Girl

A Gospel Vision to Encourage and Challenge
Black Christian Women

Sarita T. Lyons

Foreword by Jackie Hill Perry

WaterBrook

Library of Congress Cataloging-in-Publication Data
Names: Lyons, Sarita T., author.
Title: Church girl : a gospel vision to encourage and challenge Black Christian women / by Sarita T. Lyons.
Description: Colorado Springs : WaterBrook, 2024. | Includes bibliographical references.
Identifiers: LCCN 2024000525 | ISBN 9780593601167 (trade paperback ; acid-free paper) | ISBN 9780593601174 (ebook)
Subjects: LCSH: African American women--Religious life. | Women, Black--Religious life. | Christian women.
Classification: LCC BR563.B53 L86 2024 | DDC 248.8/4308996073--dc23/eng/20240224
LC record available at https://lccn.loc.gov/2024000525

Printed in the United States of America on acid-free paper

waterbrookmultnomah.com

2 4 6 8 9 7 5 3 1

Book design by Ralph Fowler
Frontispiece © Sam D'Cruz — stock.adobe.com
Church window illustration © Chorna_L — stock.adobe.com
Heart illustration © martialred — stock.adobe.com
Glasses illustration © AGUS — stock.adobe.com

Most WaterBrook books are available at special quantity discounts for bulk purchase for premiums, fundraising, and corporate and educational needs by organizations, churches, and businesses. Special books or book excerpts also can be created to fit specific needs. For details, contact specialmarketscms@penguinrandomhouse.com.

In loving memory of the Church Girl who raised me,
Etta Mae King Taylor.
Mommy, it breaks my heart that you won't ever
hold this book in your hands, yet your fingerprints
are all over it. I couldn't have done this without you.
I'll see you soon in glory.

To the Church Girls I'm raising:
Sophia, Olivia, and Gabriella.
I love you. This is for you and the
generations that will follow.

FOREWORD

There's a diversity of bullets for which the Black Church Girl is obligated to duck. There are no hands behind the trigger, but worldly belief systems are being shot at us daily. The finger is a metaphor for the worldviews reflective of a society that is godless. The shooter is still flesh. The frameworks shot our way are fundamentally theological in the way they claim to tell us who God is. If God is the creator of all things, then the woman is his idea. And she is a good one at that. But look around for a moment at a movie, a social media clip, or the quips of a fool with a podcast mic and you'd think the female body belonged to everyone else. And that it is good only insofar as it is useful. To be a woman at all is to be a resource and a reflection. The Black woman is made in God's image, so she is helpful, resourceful, administrative, productive, etc. But she is also more than what she gives; she is worthy to be given to. This woman is an image, a testimony, a witness to the Creator God, and because of this, we are all obligated to give her her flowers. And that's not in the form of undue praise and superficial flattery but of dignity. In this we say, in word and deed, "I must honor what God himself has made."

Now back to the bullets.

The first woman put us all into a situation that only deliverance can fix because she chose to think independently of God. In that garden, in front of that tree, looking at that fruit, listening to that demon, Eve got us into some mess. And technically Adam did as the head of humanity, but either way, here we are. All of us are born using our eyes, bodies, hands, thoughts, and mouths to replicate the lie that we belong to ourselves only. Eve bit the bullet, and we're born dead in sin because of it. And before we start putting a little too much blame on Eve for our own behavior, let's fast-forward to Jesus. That God took on that flesh and went to that cross, taking the weight of our sin, absorbing God's wrath, removing our shame, and giving us his righteousness, so truth be told—there's no such thing as a Church Girl without the cross.

Being commanded to carry our own now, we still bear the marks of the battle between the world, the flesh, and the devil, primarily in the kind of life we live after removing the shrapnel. We are still dying but in a different way now. And the way I see it, Miss Dr. Sarita Lyons has given us a work that functions as an avenue for resurrection to all who know or want to know what it's like to leave the grave. Whether it's a conversation about pain, healing, rest, godliness, or community, Dr. Sarita is trying to teach Black Church Girls how to duck. Because when the pain hits, by way of church or society, from bullets aimed at the brown of your body, the curl in your crown, the simplicity of your speech, and the commitment to your Christ, do you know where your armor is? When your work or your school or your family creates an environment that feels more like Babylon than heaven, can you find your passport? Do you know where home is and how it's not made with human hands?

Remember when I talked about the flowers these women deserve? Something happens to a woman who doesn't know what she's worth: She's easily deceived. The false teachers of our day exploit this shame by centering on self more than Jesus, and when they do, can you smell the lie and call it by name? It's our duty, as women made to reflect the beauty of our Savior, to learn how to live on this side of heaven with sober minds and soft hearts. As the bullets of pain, bad preaching, fear, failure, and everything else fly above us, grazing our skin but not stealing our souls, we will remember the one who made us and made us again.

New creatures we are indeed, and that's why I'm not lying to you when I say you need this book. You need the theology, the wisdom, the instructions, the exhortations, and the challenges. You need the quick pop upside the head and the hug that follows it. It's all love when a Black mama does this, and I truly believe that for Dr. Sarita to give us this work in your hands, she obviously must love us Black Church Girls to death.

—Jackie Hill Perry

CONTENTS

Flourishing

Rescuing

There Is Good News from God for Black Women

Writing a book is a calling and is so personal, and that has been my experience with *Church Girl*. This book is birthed out of my desire to help Black women see that there is no better option for life than what Jesus provides. I want you to see your identity, beauty, worth, significance, power, and purpose through God's eyes. I want you to live well and heal from the attacks on your heart and mind that might often cause you to question, *Is God real? And if he's real, is he good? And if he's good, is he good enough for me?* I want you to be discerning about the schemes of the devil to entrap you in emotional and spiritual bondage. I know what it's like to be sinking in life and reach out for help, only to be rescued by a lifeboat that turns out to be lifeless, realizing I've grabbed hold of an illusion of truth and identity that overpromises love, healing, power, control, enlightenment, and freedom but grossly underdelivers.[1] I also know what it's like to feel strong, competent, beautiful, smart, and successful but be impotent and full of more self-deception and pride than Holy Ghost power.

This book is my love letter to Black women. Church Girls, you who follow Christ and want to take your faith seriously, this is my clarion call to you. In these pages, I offer you a relatable, biblical guide that invites

---

1. Many lifeboats are only illusions of help and rescue for Black women. They can't ultimately rescue us because of the holes in their theology, ideologies, and solutions that cause us to sink. These holes are distortions of God's Word, rejection of his will, and fantasies of counterfeit freedom, but we can't always easily see them because we aren't familiar with God's Word and we're doing whatever we can to keep our heads above water.

you to turn to the Lord, to see the majesty of Christ, to see yourself through his Word, and to celebrate with other Black women this blessed gospel vision that is the better way.

I'm a proud Church Girl today, but I haven't always lived like one. I grew up in the church and was raised by Christian parents, but there was a time in my life when I drifted from the faith and walked away from the church. This Church Girl, who almost got suspended from public school for passing out Bible tracts and having Bible study during recess, went to college and became lost in the sauce of demonic oppression and deception.

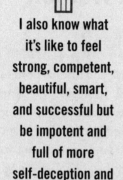

I also know what it's like to feel strong, competent, beautiful, smart, and successful but be impotent and full of more self-deception and pride than Holy Ghost power.

I cherish the years I spent attending a Historically Black College and University (HBCU). I have so many treasured memories, including lifelong friendships I made, and I know the experience helped shape me into the Black woman I am today. This was an unforgettable time in my life that I wouldn't trade for anything, but it was also a dark and difficult season I went through. It was during these college years that I began to question everything about my faith and relationship with Christ. I've often looked back since that time and wondered how I got there. But with the clarity I've gained over the years, it's my hope that my story, along with the biblical wisdom and encouragement I share throughout *Church Girl,* will help you in your faith.

In college, I had a deep desire to connect more with my cultural identity, especially as a Black woman. In my search for information and a feeling of empowerment, I became ensnared by Kemetic and Yoruba spirituality. While at first I tried to blend my Christian beliefs with these teachings and practices, combining them into a sort of syncretism, soon this newer belief system took over.

I attended lectures on ancient Africa, the New World Order, and various philosophies associated with the Black Conscious Community. I took African dance classes, engaged in meditation, and did Kundalini yoga on Sundays instead of going to church. I was reading books that rejected the legitimacy of Christ and called Black people to throw off a mind enslaved to "white Jesus" by returning to our roots and Afrocentric thinking and spirituality.

What I've discovered about deception is that there is always at least a grain of truth mixed with the lies. What is more confusing is that sometimes there may be a lot of truth with just a speck of poison, which is still lethal. I was ingesting so much new and unfamiliar information that I was initially fascinated and disoriented. Though I tried to defend the merits of my faith, I could not answer the sarcastic interrogations about the history of Christianity and the formation of the Bible from the teachers in this community. Not only did I have a shaky belief foundation, but also those I encountered were well studied, and in all honesty, the introduction to the Yoruba orisha was attractive. I didn't share what was going on with my parents; I didn't seek out a Christian friend or church leader to discuss what I was learning. I just kept diving deeper, thinking I could handle what I was being exposed to without Christian community and discipleship. My biblical illiteracy and pride fell victim to confident and well-articulated lies. Instead of being built up in my faith in Christ, I allowed the teaching about Yoruba deities to give me a sense of identity and empowerment. I was told that my male and female deities were Ogun and Oshun, and I began to put my femininity on a pedestal.

It felt amazing at the time. I thought I was so powerful, enlightened, and beautiful. And I began to believe that my Christian parents, who introduced me to Jesus, had the right intentions but incomplete information.

I realized, later on, that I was deeply mistaken and tricked. It didn't help that I was in a very vulnerable state as well. Before this period of my life, I'd had a painful church experience with male leadership that I never told anyone about, a recent breakup, and a void of not knowing my heritage very well. I felt like this new group of people understood and fulfilled my needs. Biblical illiteracy, loneliness, and pride were like doors left open to the thief's lies.[2] I was in a community of poets, artists, entrepreneurs, and friends whom I laughed with, cried with, and talked about anything and everything with, except the God of the Bible. Most of the time our fellowship was not anti-Jesus, unless I attempted to interject talk of the God of the Bible. Over time I knew that if I wanted to spend time with them, Jesus was not welcomed.

The people I was spending time with and being influenced by seemed to respect each other, both men and women. We called each other brothers, sistahs, kings, and queens. They showed me ways to naturally care for my body, dress in African garb, eat more healthily, and smudge away negativity with sage. I dabbled with tarot cards and cowrie shells. We built altars to the ancestors, bathed in honey, put a cake in a river, and buried meat in the ground as offerings to the gods. There was a lot of community, but there was no Christ. I was no match for people who rejected the Bible yet seemed to have more head knowledge about it and

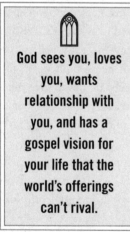

God sees you, loves you, wants relationship with you, and has a gospel vision for your life that the world's offerings can't rival.

Christianity than I did at the time. I realize now I was in one of those lifeless lifeboats and didn't know it. And I thank God that my story didn't end with me drowning in a sea of heresy. Though I was sinking, help was on the way.

One evening, while I had a spoken-word hangout at my apartment, my father called my phone, as he had so many times before to leave long prayers for my deliverance. This evening, I walked to my bedroom to take his call, but he hung up before I answered. While I was in my room, I heard someone say from the living room, "F— Jesus." It's difficult for me to recount the exact timeline and events for the rest of the night, but what I do remember is that a righ-

2. "The thief comes only to steal and kill and destroy. I came that they may have life and have it abundantly" (John 10:10, ESV).

teous indignation filled me and I started screaming, "Get out! Get out!" and proceeded to kick everyone out of my apartment. It was like a whirlwind. I wasn't thinking or feeling. I was just acting as I now believe the Holy Spirit was directing me. I grabbed a large green trash bag and started dismantling the altar for ancestor worship that I had in my room. I threw away everything that was used for demonic activity. I threw away my tarot cards, sage, candles, books, carved images, beads, jewelry, and anything else connected to witchcraft. I became sick and eventually passed out or fell asleep on my bathroom floor.

When I woke up, I could see my bed from the bathroom doorway. Under it was a New King James Version of the Bible—a Bible that I still have today—tattered, worn, and soaked with many tears. I grabbed it but didn't know what to read. I hadn't read the Bible in almost two years. I closed my eyes and flipped through pages. I guess I was praying the Lord would supernaturally allow me to land on something to help me, and boy, did he do just that. I read:

The word of the LORD came to me, saying, "Go and cry in the hearing of Jerusalem, saying, 'Thus says the LORD:

"*I remember you,*
The kindness of your youth,
The love of your betrothal,
When you went after Me in the wilderness,
In a land not sown." '" (Jeremiah 2:1–2, NKJV)

I immediately had flashbacks of me as a young Church Girl, leading Bible study, passing out Bible tracts, singing in the choir, ushering in my white nurse's outfit, attending Vacation Bible School, playing Mary in the Christmas play, praying, taking communion, sitting among the saints in the congregation, and coming out of the water feeling light shining on my face when I was baptized.

The tears began to flow. That night, I read the entire book of Jeremiah, weeping and saying sorry to God. Through Jeremiah, the Lord convicted me of my sin—my idolatry and my spiritual adultery—

but he also wooed me back to himself. He comforted me with the assurance that if I just returned to him, he would forgive and restore me.[3] I remember looking in the mirror with a mix of tears and mascara running down my face, asking for forgiveness. I also said to the Lord, "I will go wherever you want me to go, I will do whatever you want me to do, and I will say whatever you want me to say. I just ask to know you, God, like I've never known you before." The intention of my entire life was revealed and confessed in the mirror that day: I will go wherever, do whatever, and say whatever for Christ's glory. This is why you are reading *Church Girl* right now. And God has been faithfully answering my prayer to know him and fulfill my call to help others *know* him too.

I freely admit that I was the backslider, the adulterer, the silly woman, the harlot, the haughty woman, the prodigal daughter, and the fool that we hear about in Scripture. But today I am redeemed, holy, set apart, and set free by the greatest emancipator and freedom fighter in the world. The life I now have—the peace, joy, clarity about my identity, and power I received—was so simple: I just had to turn back to God. Though the specifics of my story may not be your experience, you may be able to relate to having your faith challenged and being in a vulnerable place that made you more susceptible to deception. Whether you've been affected by racism, sexism, relational disappointment, grief, or the stress and trauma of living as a Black woman in the world, I believe you, too, may have been tempted to question the relevance and necessity of trusting in an invisible God who at times feels distant and uninterested in your life. You may have at one point felt close to God, but a series of choices, concessions, and compromises left you one day looking at your life, wondering how you managed to drift so far from him. Like me, you may have experienced hurt that enticed you to look for identity, belonging, love, power, and significance outside Christ. No matter what your story is, I want you to know God sees you, loves you, wants relationship with you, and has a gospel vision for your life that the world's offerings can't rival.

---

3. Jeremiah 4:1–4.

Church Girl is the book I wish I had in college. Back then, I needed the truth and hope I'm determined to share with you that helped me weather the storms of confusion and heartache. I needed *Church Girl* to help stabilize me in a shifting secular culture and to help root my identity as a Black woman in the truth of God's Word. I needed *Church Girl* because I was unprepared to counter opposition to my faith. I needed help so that I could deal with the hurt instead of being imprisoned by the hurt. I needed the courage and conviction to stand unapologetically as a Christian when it was more popular and advantageous to follow the crowd and philosophies of the world. I needed *Church Girl* to point me to Jesus when everything around me was capturing my attention and affections.

I didn't have *Church Girl* as a resource in college, but I did have a loving God who pursued me and a family who prayed for me even when I thought their faith was antiquated and whitewashed. And I had the body of Christ—often just faithful strangers who didn't have a clue about what I was going through. God used their witness and intellectual defense of Christianity as a way to provide living water to erode my calloused heart and confused mind.

I write this book from a place of love, empathy, and urgency for Black women. The devil doesn't want you to see Jesus correctly, divide the Word rightly,[4] and embrace yourself fully as a daughter of the Most High God. There is an attack on Black women's identity, purpose, rest, hearts, and commitment to Christ. The devil's goal is to rob God of glory, and he wants to confuse you, frustrate you, and weaken you so that you won't trust God's Word or obey his will, thus getting you to forfeit the blessings of the abundant life in Christ that is your inheritance.[5] Maybe you can relate to wrestling with your faith or being overwhelmed by the weight of your sin, tempted to give

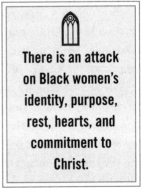

There is an attack on Black women's identity, purpose, rest, hearts, and commitment to Christ.

4. 2 Timothy 2:15, NKJV.
5. John 10:10; 17:3.

up on God, confused by the lies of Satan, weary with the evil of the world, hurt by the church, unsure of your purpose, or in need of encouragement as a Black Christian woman to keep on keeping on. If that is you, you are in good company. I pray the Lord will draw you back to himself and to the community of faith or fortify your faith and give you endurance so that you can grow, "walk worthy of the calling" (Ephesians 4:1), and experience the love, joy, peace, and strength that are part of your birthright as a new creation in Christ.[6]

What is meant by "a *gospel* vision"? I want you as a Black woman to know that there is *good news* from God for your life. My sister, putting your faith in Jesus makes everything about your life better, as you now are set apart for his kingdom purposes and are the recipient of his kingdom promises and privileges. If you yield to the transforming work of the gospel, it will influence how you think, treat your neighbors, love your friends, parent, walk in your singleness or marriage, and work, and it will improve your perspective on everything. A gospel vision for Black women guarantees that you will have the resources of heaven for a blessed, joyous, content, anointed, and sacrificial life—a life that endures and remains faithful despite the suffering and challenges that will undoubtedly come. A gospel vision for Black women says, "Don't give up, because Jesus already did the heavy lifting on the cross," and "Don't see yourself as less than, because you are a daughter of the King." A gospel vision says, "Don't be afraid to be strong as you serve the Lord in every area of life, because it's his energy that empowers you,"[7] and "Don't be afraid to be weak, because in your weakness his strength is made perfect."[8]

I believe there are three areas we can focus on as believers when we are looking to live with gospel vision: light, lens, and love. Understanding the three will help you process the themes in each chapter as you go through this book.

6. Isaiah 41:10; 2 Corinthians 5:17; Galatians 5:22.
7. Colossians 1:29.
8. 2 Corinthians 12:9.

Light

Research reveals that, of our five senses, most people (70 percent) would miss their sight the most.[9] Even more than seeing physically, God wants us to see spiritually. He provided a way for us to have spiritual sight through Christ. In Scripture, light is associated with life. When speaking of Jesus, John said, "In him was life, and that life was the light of men. That light shines in the darkness, and yet the darkness did not overcome it" (John 1:4–5). We need light from a new life in Christ to have accurate vision for our lives.

Apart from salvation, which comes only through faith in Christ, we are in a state of spiritual blindness because we can't see Christ accurately, and not seeing Christ means we can't see God.[10] When we are spiritually blind, we can't see God or learn optimally from his Word, and we ultimately reject Christ.[11] The main consequence of spiritual blindness is that people are lost and perishing.[12]

We need light from a new life in Christ to have accurate vision for our lives.

This light and spiritual sight give us wisdom. Without them, our understanding of spiritual things is compromised. Spiritual things will often look strange or be misunderstood if we still have scales on our eyes in an unredeemed state. Being saved from our sins by the work of Jesus on the cross and his resurrection is how we get this life and light we desperately need. As physical light first split the darkness at creation, so spiritual light is the only thing that can penetrate the darkness of human understanding that is obscured by sin.[13] Light is essential for

9. Hoang Nguyen, "Of the Five Senses, a Majority Would Miss Sight the Most," YouGov, July 25, 2018, https://today.yougov.com/topics/health/articles-reports/2018/07/25/five-senses-majority-would-miss-sight-most.

10. Colossians 1:15–16.

11. Romans 2:8; 2 Thessalonians 2:12.

12. 2 Corinthians 4:3–4.

13. 2 Corinthians 4:6.

our ability to accurately see anything, including God's vision for us as women.

Lens

God also cares about the lens through which we see. Our lens is our worldview. A worldview can be thought of as the comprehensive interpretive lens through which we look to understand ourselves, others, the world, and God. A worldview provides the rules we apply to make sense of what we see so we can respond accordingly. When we have a Christian worldview, we look through a Christianity-informed lens so we can see things as God intends. The primary resource that we are called to use to inform our Christian worldview is the Bible. If you go to a 3D movie, you are given special glasses to clearly view it. If you try to watch it with your 3D lenses off, you can still see, but the image on the screen isn't clear. That's what it's like to see the world, others, God, and ourselves without a biblical lens, or a Christian worldview: We can see, but things aren't clear.

There are many consequences of looking at everything through an unbiblical lens. However, when you have accurate vision, you will be able to discern truth from error,[14] you will have a clear understanding of your identity and calling,[15] you will walk in wisdom,[16] you will have a healthy fear of the Lord,[17] you won't easily be deceived,[18] and you will be more sensitive to the activity of the devil and better equipped for spiritual warfare.[19] When you have accurate vision, you will be more deeply connected to Christ's mission;[20] you will be able to suffer

14. 1 John 4:1.
15. Proverbs 3:1–6:35.
16. Hosea 14:9; James 1:5.
17. Psalm 111:10.
18. Matthew 24:24.
19. Matthew 10:16; 2 Corinthians 11:13–15; 2 Timothy 3:6–7.
20. Matthew 16:22–24.

well,[21] love well,[22] make wise choices,[23] perceive the will of God,[24] and recognize the voice of God;[25] and you will have greater confidence and trust in the Bible as the primary instruction for life.[26] Seeing through a biblical lens motivates you to pursue Christian community and discipleship, walk in the joy and peace that are found in Christ, and live more committed to God than to your personal agenda.

We need the help of the Holy Spirit to lead and guide us into all truth. Other lenses are also influencing our vision. Location, education, gender, presuppositions, culture, privilege, and pain are lenses through which we see, even if we aren't aware they are influencing our sight.

At times these lenses help us see what God wants us to see in a special and unique way that is biblically faithful. For instance, as a Black woman who is the descendant of slaves and who has experienced racism and various other forms of discrimination, like my ancestors I can read the Exodus story and clearly see that God is a just and on-time liberator, waymaker, fighter, and deliverer for me just as he was for his people when they cried out to him. Conversely, if pain and trauma become the dominant lens through which someone reads the text, that person could read the Exodus story and see God as cruel for even allowing his people to be enslaved to the Egyptians and unloving for allowing them to wander in the wilderness for forty years and giving them only manna and quail to eat. We all see through lenses. For the Christian, the goal is to have a humble awareness that we all have limitations to our lenses. My hope is that this book will provide you with helpful insights, encouragement, and tools as you continue to develop and utilize your Christian worldview in everyday life.

21. 2 Timothy 3:12; 1 Peter 4:12–19.
22. 1 Corinthians 13.
23. Ezekiel 44:23.
24. Romans 12:2.
25. John 10:27.
26. 2 Timothy 3:15–17.

Love

We also need love to see. God wants his perfect and unfailing love for us to be the tint on our lens, coloring everything we see. Whatever vision we have for ourselves must be a by-product of his love. God doesn't do anything that isn't rooted in love, as we see in Jesus's ultimate sacrifice.[27] But God doesn't just love us (action); he is love (being).[28]

Many truths, commands, and narratives throughout Scripture are hard to understand and accept if we view them apart from the tint of God's love. How do we read difficult passages of Scripture—or, as Phyllis Trible called them, "texts of terror"[29]—where women get brutally raped and killed, and still see a God we can serve and trust? How do we feel valued by God and equal to men if Scripture says, "Wives, submit to your husbands as to the Lord" (Ephesians 5:22)? The tint of God's love brings clarity and joy to passages that often make Christian women bristle. Seeing Scripture with the tint of God's love helps you presuppose his goodness, even when reading descriptive passages that reveal the evil of humanity or prescriptive passages that at first glance feel unfair.

If we are going to see correctly, if we are going to have reliable vision, we need light, the right lens, and love. We need life in Christ, we need a Christian way of seeing things as God prescribes, and we need the tint of God's love to understand that his very nature is just, perfect, and loving—which motivates all he says, does, and requires of us.

We need light, the right lens, and love to have a gospel vision for everything, including ourselves as Black women. After each chapter, I include discussion questions so you can dig deeper into these themes, whether you study on your own or in a group.

---

27. John 3:16.
28. 1 John 4:16.
29. Phyllis Trible, *Texts of Terror: Literary-Feminist Readings of Biblical Narratives* (Minneapolis: Fortress, 1984).

Rise Up, Church Girl

A Church Girl is a disciple of Jesus who has received salvation by grace alone, through faith alone, in Christ alone.[30] A Church Girl has been saved from the penalty and power of sin[31]—and will one day be saved from the presence of sin[32]—because of the finished work of Jesus Christ. A Church Girl is more than a woman who attends church services; rather, she is a member of the body of Christ who has been restored to relationship with God.[33]

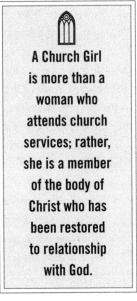

A Church Girl is more than a woman who attends church services; rather, she is a member of the body of Christ who has been restored to relationship with God.

We aren't just Church Girls in name, because our God has also called us to duty. We have been called to unashamedly represent Christ in the world and proclaim the gospel.[34] Church Girls talk back to the culture; we aren't afraid of the culture. Church Girls should feel righteous indignation when someone misrepresents God and his bride. Church Girls don't scroll dismissively past false teaching. We don't take kindly to anyone coming for the church Christ died for. We cast down strongholds. We fight with spiritual weapons.[35] We are relentless truth tellers. We love our neighbors. We fight for the marginalized. We hold up the bloodstained banner. We are clothed with strength and dignity and laugh with no fear of the future; wisdom is in our mouths, and the

---

30. John 3:13, 36; 12:26; Galatians 2:20; Ephesians 2:4–8.

31. Romans 3:24; 4:5; 5:1, 9; 8:1; 1 Corinthians 6:11; 2 Thessalonians 2:13; Titus 2:14; 1 Peter 3:18.

32. Romans 8:16–18; Hebrews 1:14; 1 John 3:2.

33. Acts 20:28; Romans 12:5; 1 Corinthians 12:27; 2 Corinthians 5:18–20; Ephesians 5:25–27; Titus 2:14.

34. Romans 1:16.

35. 2 Corinthians 10:3–4.

law of kindness on our lips.[36] We aren't afraid of cancel culture, because who can cancel what God has called? We run our race with endurance, "looking unto Jesus, the author and finisher of our faith" (Hebrews 12:2, NKJV). We bow in prayer and lift our voices in worship of the one true living God. Church Girls die daily so that we may live for Christ. Church Girls know that we are like John the Baptist and our greatest calling is to be "a voice"[37] crying out in the culture, preparing the way for the Lord. We evangelize the lost because we know we have good news to share. We aren't perfect, but we serve a God who is perfect, and we strive in his strength as we are conformed to the image of Christ.

Rise up, Church Girl, and with dignity, bear the image of our God. To do this, we must get back to the fundamentals of our faith, and we must encourage other Christian women to do the same.

The gospel makes it possible for us to have a vision of ourselves as Black women the way Christ intended. We can now . . .

See ourselves as chosen.
See ourselves as saved.
See ourselves as free.
See ourselves as restored.
See ourselves as at peace.
See ourselves as respected.
See ourselves as protected.
See ourselves as holy.
See ourselves as hopeful.
See ourselves as healthy.
See ourselves as empowered.
See ourselves as commissioned.
See ourselves as beautiful.
See ourselves as worthy.
See ourselves as loved.
See ourselves proclaiming.

36. Proverbs 31:25, NLT; Proverbs 31:26.
37. John 1:23.

See ourselves leading.

See ourselves teaching.

See ourselves thriving.

See ourselves discipling.

See ourselves healing.

See ourselves serving.

See ourselves preaching.

See ourselves prophesying.

See ourselves resting.

See ourselves worshipping.

See ourselves glorifying.

See ourselves being exactly who God wants us to be.

I'm excited to go on a journey with you from the Garden of Eden, where the first woman was created, to Golgotha, where Christ died so any woman can become a new creation. I invite you to see God's vision for your life in six specific areas:

1. Identity

2. Purpose

3. Healing

4. Resting

5. Flourishing

6. Rescuing

I conclude *Church Girl* with a love letter to the Black Church that you may be able to relate to. Undoubtedly, the Black Church raised this Church Girl, and I wanted to invite you into a celebration of the institution that has survived, thrived, and shaped so many of our Church Girl lives.

This book isn't meant to give an exhaustive answer for every concern in a Black woman's life, but prayerfully, *Church Girl* will serve as a guide to help you learn to use your gospel light, lens, and love to have a comprehensive vision for every area of your life. You may not know every detail, but you can trust that God has a plan for you. It's a good plan, Sis. It's a good gospel vision, and I'm excited to share it with you.

> When there is no prophetic vision the people cast off restraint, but blessed is he who keeps the law.
>
> —Proverbs 29:18, ESV

Church Girl

CHAPTER 1

Know Thyself

A Gospel Vision for Black Women's Identity

*God created man
in his own image;
he created him in the image of God;
he created them male and female.*
—**Genesis 1:27**

reek philosopher Socrates is widely credited for the maxim "Know thyself," which is inscribed on the Temple of Apollo in Delphi. On its face, that maxim seems good, speaking about an important kind of knowledge to have—the knowledge of the self. Many people argue that Socrates believed knowing yourself is the source of freedom, happiness, virtue, and self-improvement and is the beginning of wisdom.[1] However, that runs counter to what we are taught in Scripture: "The fear of the LORD is the beginning of wisdom, and the knowledge of the Holy One is understanding" (Proverbs 9:10). This fundamentally teaches that the fear of God[2] is the starting point for true wisdom and that to know God is true understanding. All other types of learning and knowledge (including the knowledge of yourself) are worthless unless they are

---

1. Nicholas D. Smith, *Socrates on Self-Improvement: Knowledge, Virtue, and Happiness* (Cambridge: Cambridge University Press, 2021).

2. "To fear the Lord is to stand in awe of his majesty, power, wisdom, justice and mercy, especially in Christ—in his life, death and resurrection—that is, to have an exalted view of God. To see God in all his glory and then respond to him appropriately. To humble ourselves before him. To adore him." Mark Altrogge, "What Does It Mean to Fear God?," Bible Study Tools, April 20, 2017, www.biblestudytools.com/bible-study/topical-studies/what-does-it-mean-to-fear-god.html.

first built on knowledge of God. It's vital for us as Black Christian women to have an accurate understanding of our identity. Just like the hymn many of us have sung in church proclaims, "On Christ, the solid Rock, I stand: all other ground is sinking sand."[3] How we see ourselves as Black women must be rooted in God. We don't start a quest to know ourselves with the self—we start with God. A gospel vision for Black women's identity is a call to stand on the firm foundation of Christ and discover why God made us, how he defined us, and what he has declared about us in his Word.

> A gospel vision for Black women's identity is a call to stand on the firm foundation of Christ and discover why God made us, how he defined us, and what he has declared about us in his Word.

Everyone has an opinion about Black women—who we are, what we can do, where our place is, what we should look like, and how we should show up or disappear in the world. Lessons on who we are have been taught by or caught from colonizers; culture; men; our mamas, aunties, and grandmothers; and our own grand imaginations. Some of these messages are helpful, but many are downright damaging. Throughout history, Black women have been under the proverbial microscope, being labeled, branded, classified, dissected, and defined in an attempt to erase, enslave, and at times empower us.

Historically, Black women have been assigned disrespectful and demeaning stereotypes that added to our oppression dating back to slavery, such as Mammy, Jezebel, and Sapphire.[4] Then there are more contemporary stereotypes like welfare queen, baby mama, and the angry Black woman. Some labels and identities given to Black women, on the face,

---

3. Edward Mote, "My Hope Is Built on Nothing Less," Hymnary.org, accessed March 2, 2024, https://hymnary.org/text/my_hope_is_built_on_nothing_less.

4. Carolyn M. West, "Mammy, Jezebel, Sapphire, and Their Homegirls: Developing an 'Oppositional Gaze' Toward the Images of Black Women," in *Lectures on the Psychology of Women,* ed. Joan C. Chrisler, Carla Golden, and Patricia D. Rozee, 4th ed. (Long Grove, Ill.: Waveland, 2012), 286–99.

appear to be celebratory but have proved dangerous for us to adopt. Labels such as "the strong Black woman" or "superwoman" are unhealthy. These identities teach us to grin and bear the pain of life and carry the weight of the world on our backs without showing signs of weakness or vulnerability. These supposed strength-focused identities have kept us in bondage to pretending to be okay when we aren't. "The Strong Black Woman Syndrome, which requires that Black women perpetually present an image of control and strength, is [an automatic] response to combination of daily pressures and systemic racist assaults."[5] While being called "superwoman" appears to be complimentary, it does more harm than good. For instance, when we are ascribed superhuman qualities, it encourages us to define weakness and fatigue as shameful, things to be rejected and ignored rather than embraced as symptoms and realities of the human experience. It encourages us as Black women to forfeit help and rest, two things we most need God to supply. Projecting superhuman qualities onto us as Black women invites us to see ourselves more like God than the dust he made us from. Our limitations aren't a liability; rather, they remind us to stay dependent on a gracious God.

These exaggerated and unrealistic identities have left us exhausted, ignored, used, and celebrated only for our self-sacrifice and unnecessary savior behavior. We have also adopted new ways of naming ourselves, creating identities to rewrite and more accurately retell history. In the 1960s, to beat back harmful narratives about Black people, Black women and men identified with the statement "Black is beautiful." When we were told by James Brown to "say it loud," we shouted back with cultural pride, "I'm Black and I'm proud." Black women haven't stopped listening to our elders, and thanks to Representative Maxine Waters, affectionately called "Auntie Maxine" by millennials, Black women are now unapologetically "reclaiming our time." When Black women exceed everyone's expectations in sports, academics, and entertainment, we remind the world that "Black Girls Rock!"[6] We wink at a world that

---

5. Marita Golden, *The Strong Black Woman: How a Myth Endangers the Physical and Mental Health of Black Women* (Coral Gables, Fla.: Mango, 2021), 37.

6. Black Girls Rock! (BGR) is the unapologetic mantra and movement given to all Black girls and women by its founder, Beverly Bond. In 2006, Beverly Bond, a DJ, philanthropist, and author,

wonders how we do what we do amid the many injustices we face and call the mystery of our thriving "Black Girl Magic." Black women have called themselves boss chicks or corporate baddies to honor the way they have worked to pursue entrepreneurial passions, be leaders in their industry, and use their gifts to build a table of economic empowerment and freedom in a society that seems to hand them only disrespect.

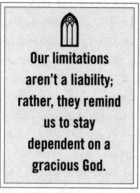

Our limitations aren't a liability; rather, they remind us to stay dependent on a gracious God.

Black women have called themselves sistahs, aunties, and mothers to emphasize the importance of extended family, and we call ourselves queens in a world that often saw us as slaves. Now more than ever, social media has been a vehicle for us to celebrate living life as Black women. With hashtags and groups—everything from Black Girls Run, Black women walk (GirlTrek), Black women read, Black women lift weights, Black women lose weight, Black women write, and Black women go to therapy (Therapy for Black Girls) to Black women (you fill in the blank)—we are unapologetically showing up for ourselves and one another. It's nearly impossible to harness a comprehensive and worthy description of what it means to be a Black woman. How do you capture what is as numerous and as individual as snowflakes and yet as wild and untamable as the wind? What do we make of the buffet of characterizations for Black womanhood?

Have you ever considered how you should define your identity as a Black woman? One thing is certain: As Black women, we have been told who we are much more than we have been asked. Let me give you the honor and favor of asking you directly: *How do you define your identity as a Black woman, and most importantly, where did you get your answer?*

By the end of this chapter, you will have a deeper understanding and

---

created BGR "to showcase empowering images of women of color." In 2010, she partnered with Black Entertainment Television (BET) to create the BGR Awards show, aimed at honoring and celebrating Black women and girls. See "About Black Girls Rock!," BGR! Network, accessed February 8, 2024, https://blackgirlsrock.com/about.

a more God-empowered answer. Our identity is the foundation of who we are, and it has a direct impact on how we think, feel, and choose to live. There is trustworthy foundational truth about womanhood, an identity bestowed by God, from which we can construct and express the diversity, beauty, and uniqueness of what it means to be Black Christian women. God didn't make us unique the way he did for us to live as if all women are the same in every way. Christ is the ultimate unifier of all Christians (Black, white, Brown, or otherwise), and as believers, we certainly should stay on brand as disciples of Jesus Christ.[7] However, God made each one of us unique, and that uniqueness provides an opportunity to show off something special about him. "Everyone who bears my name . . . is created for my glory. I have formed them; indeed, I have made them" (Isaiah 43:7).

Understanding Your Identity as a Black Christian Woman

As Black women, we aren't a monolith, and the variance within our group is special and important to God. Around his throne in heaven, with every tribe and nation, there will be Black women from Philly, Atlanta, D.C., Detroit, Dallas, Baltimore, Jacksonville, Columbus, New Orleans, Newark, Tulsa, Birmingham, New York, Chicago, California, Indianapolis, Houston, Mississippi, Charleston, London, Canada, the Caribbean, the Continent, and everywhere else around the globe. We will all be crying, "Holy, holy, holy," some with a southern twang, others with an up-north heaviness, but we will all be there in our Blackness, giving praise to God.

Toni Morrison wrote, "Cultural identities are formed and informed by a nation's literature."[8] If this is true, how much more, then, should the Christian woman have her identity shaped by the literature of God's kingdom—the Bible? For Black Christian women, the culture can't be the progenitor of our identity. God is the giver of a kingdom woman's

---

7. Ephesians 4:5–13.
8. Toni Morrison, "Black Matter(s)," in *The Source of Self-Regard: Selected Essays, Speeches, and Meditations* (New York: Alfred A. Knopf, 2019), 148.

identity, and he communicates his will in his Word.[9] This isn't to suggest that it's wrong to identify with other positive descriptors that have been curated within culture, but it's imperative that the Church Girl discerns the insufficiency and harm of any attempt to define her identity outside of God. Any positive identity or cultural nomenclature aimed at your uplifting serves only as an exclamation mark for who God declared you to be and should never contradict the blessed identity you are called to live out through Christ.

For example, no matter how well-meaning she is, it's inconsistent for a Black Christian woman to label herself as a god or goddess, because this identity is incompatible with the reality that God alone is God. While "the Black woman is God" ideology[10] is a cultural creation aimed at celebrating and elevating our gender and Blackness to divinity status to dignify and restore Black female identity, which has suffered under racist and sexist oppression, it's important to remember that though created in the image of God, we aren't God or gods. We are created, and God is the creator.[11] The same can be said for identities that, on the surface, aren't harmful. Take *boss chick*. It's perfectly fine to call yourself a boss chick when your business goals and decisions make room for Christ to be the Lord over your life. However, if being a boss chick means you are conducting your life and business on your terms, only occasionally consulting God like he's your business strategist but not your sovereign king, then the boss chick identity has moved from motivational to incompatible with being a Christian.

> For Black Christian women, the culture can't be the progenitor of our identity. God is the giver of a kingdom woman's identity, and he communicates his will in his Word.

---

9. Joshua 1:8–9; Psalm 119:5, 11; Matthew 4:4; John 17:17; Romans 15:4; 2 Timothy 3:16–17; 2 Peter 1:19–21.

10. This ideology traces back to Merlin Stone's book *When God Was a Woman: The Landmark Exploration of the Ancient Worship of the Great Goddess and the Eventual Suppression of Women's Rites* (New York: Harcourt, 1976).

11. Genesis 1:1, 26–27.

To understand our identity is to know that our Blackness and womanness matter to God and aren't incidental. In America, we've been implicitly—and at times explicitly—taught to funnel our existence and experiences through whiteness as the normative paradigm. We've often had to translate the Christian experience for ourselves as we read books not written by us, to us, or about us. We've had to ingest teachings, illustrations, discipleship, and community in ways that haven't always been relatable to Black women. It doesn't mean that those Christian teachings or practices weren't biblical or even that they were done with malicious intent, but the testimony of many Black women is that church life hasn't always been contextualized so we feel seen, known, valued, and loved.

We've always faced our circumstances with faith in a God who loves us and brings deliverance wherever we need it in our lives. Our survival and thriving have always depended on Church Girls holding on to these truths: God made the Black woman. God died for you, redeemed you, and endowed you with power and purpose. God gave you an identity that only he could give, and you are called to show off the glory of Christ by showing up in life fully as a Black woman. Church Girl, you are just as much blessed and highly favored as anyone else in the body of Christ. It's our honorable task as Church Girls to humbly and passionately search out and celebrate our identity, which undoubtedly dignifies us and glorifies God.

Going Back to the Beginning for a Gospel Vision of Our Identity

Who am I? When Black women have attempted to give an honest answer, our own disorientation in the West, far from our original homeland, has rendered us much like someone recovering from a brain injury. As Black women, our long-term memory is damaged, and we are fighting to make sense of fractured family trees while still charting a course forward with courage and joy. But is our disconnection from Africa the only cause of our inability to confidently answer this question about our identity?

All identity questions force us to consider who we are and who made us. Black women are known for proudly naming the women who came before us. I love to say I am the great-granddaughter of Carrie Davis, Ruby King, and Emaline Cobbs. I love to say I am the granddaughter of Blanche Virginia King and Ruby Taylor. I am grateful to be the daughter of Etta Mae King Taylor. Connection to our maternal ancestors fills us with delight, and the farther we can go back, the more we stick out our chests with pride. These names also provide clues about our identity. We are blessed if we have in our possession pictures and details of their lives. We love to search old photographs of our foremothers, staring into their faces, picking out their noses, their eyes, their profiles, and the unique way they hold their hands, and matching those characteristics to ours. We love to see ourselves in them, but make no mistake—if they are living, it brings them great joy to see themselves in you. Even if you are adopted or have difficulty tracing your biological maternal roots, you can name the women who were like mothers, who raised you, cared for you, combed your hair, bought you clothes, fed you, and told you that you were beautiful and could be anything you wanted to be. We honor the women who discipled us, pointed us to Jesus, and mothered us in the faith. We all can name a mother who was integral in our natural and spiritual identity formation, and if you walked closely with them for some time, I'm sure some of their spiritual DNA and personality has rubbed off on you.

> **We honor the women who discipled us, pointed us to Jesus, and mothered us in the faith.**

You are their legacy. You are the evidence that their lives mattered, that they survived and had an impact that in some beautiful way will persist even after they take their last breaths. Bearing witness to those women gives us strength and endurance for the journey of life. If they could make it through slavery, segregation, Jim Crow, the Freedom Rides, and domestic work, we can make it too. If they could survive the abuse, abandonment, glass ceilings, and single parenting, we can survive too. But for the Black Christian woman, does our road map to identity stop there, with our ancestors?

The Black Conscious Community has told Black people that to know ourselves, we must *Sankofa*[12] —that is, we must go back and get the truth of who we are. We are encouraged to go back to our roots, go back to the wisdom, spirituality, teaching, and ways of being of our ancestors and indigenous tribes in Africa for insight into the self. To understand the self, we must in a way *Sankofa*, but for Black Christian women to truly understand our identity, we should go back further than the world encourages us to travel. We must journey back further than southern plantations lined with weeping willows stained with the blood of strange fruit. We must go back further than the Caribbean islands where sand beaches and sugarcane plantations tell the story of our resistance. If we want to understand our identity, we must go back further than the pyramids or the University of Sankoré. We must go back further than the shores of Gorée Island before so many of us were stolen from African nations where we once ruled as kings and queens. If we want to know our identity as Black Christian women, we must *Sankofa* as far back as the Garden of Eden, where a woman named Eve was made by God.

Only God can solve the mystery of identity. Only God can authoritatively and perfectly tell us who we are and how we should live. Our ability to see and receive his divine plan for our lives is the springboard from which we can safely launch into the world, knowing who we are. From there, we can confidently clothe ourselves with the colorful and textured layers of identity and personality that rightfully belong to us. Formation at creation instructs our destination. It's in the garden that we see God do something amazing with dirt and a rib that was the genesis of who we are.

---

12. *Sankofa,* meaning "go back and fetch it," is Twi from the Akan people in Ghana and is used in the proverb "It is not taboo to fetch what is at risk of being left behind." This is often symbolized by a bird turning its head backward. The word refers to African people going back to the beginning for the truth. It's broken down as *san* ("return"), *ko* ("go"), *fa* ("look, seek, and take"). See "Sankofa: Embracing Past Lessons for a Brighter Future," Ayeeko, October 24, 2022, https:// ayeeko.africa/blogs/blog/sankofa-sankofa-symbol-and-meaning; "About Sankofa," Stockton University, accessed February 8, 2024, www.stockton.edu/sankofa/about.html.

Identity formation must start with discovering where, when, and why God formed the first woman.

If you want to truly know yourself, if you want to discern your purpose, you must first go to the garden, the womb of human creation, the original meeting place between God and humanity. What happened in that garden has had life-and-death implications not only for Black women but also for all humankind. Identity formation must start with discovering where, when, and why God formed the first woman. It's this woman, who would be expelled from the garden with the name Eve, that is our first mother, and she has a lot to teach us if we have ears to hear.

The Creation of Woman

Perhaps you've never heard the details of the creation story, or you've caught bits and pieces of the Eden account but are still unfamiliar with how they relate to Black women's identity. Maybe you know the Genesis story backward and forward but have missed an array of identity implications for your life. I pray I can tell it in a way that is faithful, fresh, and maybe even a little funny—Lord knows we could all use a good laugh, especially because this garden story gets downright frightful real quick. But the treasures we can mine about our identity are incalculable and foundational for how we see ourselves.

Eve spent her entire sinless life being called "woman" and is introduced to us in the second chapter of Genesis as God's good solution to man's aloneness. After God created the entire world by the words of his mouth, he then got close and personal to form his human creation, which would be the *imago Dei*.[13] Adam had been formed by God out of the dust of the ground and became a living being when God literally "breathed the breath of life into his nostrils" (Genesis 2:7). Ladies, can we just take a moment to imagine what manner of man Adam must have been since

13. Genesis 1:26–27.

he was formed from the ground by God? Let me be honest—I always pictured Adam as Philip Michael Thomas from the 1980s show *Miami Vice*. Surely God didn't sculpt him sloppily, and can we agree Adam was probably fine? I can't imagine that this man would have been inarticulate or fearful. To say he was strong and brilliant is an understatement. He had to be organized, meticulous, and creative, especially given all the naming of animals and stewarding of creation God called him to do.

Yet no matter how handsome and genius you can imagine Adam to have been, when God saw him working, God said, "It is not good for the man to be alone. I will make a helper corresponding [suitable] to him" (verse 18). God saw a need in the man, and his loving and wise response was to meet that need without a conversation with Adam. God didn't say to him, "It looks like you could use some help. I'm thinking about making a woman. How do you feel about that?" God didn't ask him for input: "Do you want a blonde or a brunette? Would you like her to be tall or short? Do you want a woman who is good with numbers, or would you prefer a reader? Do you want a woman who has great domestic skills, or would you like her to be artsy and able to sing you to sleep? Or would you like a woman to stimulate your mind with her poetry? Do you want a talkative woman or a subdued, mysterious woman? An adventurous, extroverted woman who says everything that's on her mind or an introvert whose social battery runs low but who will keep you on your toes?"

That's how amazing God is—he knew man. God knew what man needed. God didn't engage Adam to build a woman in the garden like children build a bear at the mall. God fashioned the woman based on his sovereignty. Although Adam was created by God, he was insufficient in his ability to even recognize his need for help, nor did he have the capability to dream up a reasonable request to meet his own need. Church Girl, one of the treasured aspects of your existence is that you were God's idea, God's creation, and God's design and made for God's purpose. He made you to bring goodness and completeness to humanity. He wants you to remember that he is the author, builder, and sustainer of your life.

Then God just knocked the man out and went to work. God performed the first surgical procedure in the middle of a garden, removing one of Adam's ribs, the very substance that covered and protected the delicate life-sustaining organs of man (lungs and heart). Adam unknowingly contributed (a rib), but he didn't create. From man's rib, God formed someone like him but distinct from him, who would be another glorious image bearer called to rule and reign.[14] God didn't give us too many details, but we do know that when Adam woke up from his divine anesthesia, standing right before his eyes was someone unlike anything else God had created. Can't you picture Adam wiping the sleep from his eyes while trying to make sense of something he didn't recognize?

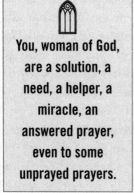

You, woman of God, are a solution, a need, a helper, a miracle, an answered prayer, even to some unprayed prayers.

Maybe he was drowsy from surgery and initially thought it was another animal that God wanted him to name, but at some point, she came into clear view, and what Adam beheld was far from an animal but not exactly like him. She was softer than Adam, she was more beautiful than Adam, and she was shaped significantly different from how he was shaped (*amen,* somebody). Did he see a woman that looked like Pam Grier, Beverly Crawford, or Grace Jones? Did she look like Lupita Nyong'o, Viola Davis, Halle Berry, Halle Bailey, or Adut Akech? Or did she look like you? Can you imagine your first mother? You should try, because it's important for you to see her and see yourself in her.

Then, before this woman had a chance to utter one word to reveal her brilliance, before she could lift one finger to aid him in the stewardship of the garden, before she proved why she would be the glorious means through which Adam would be fruitful and multiply, Adam knew he had been blessed by God! Adam had to have been blown away by this woman, who was the answer to a prayer he hadn't even had the wisdom to pray. Adam never knew he needed anyone, yet he responded to seeing this woman as if he had longed for her from the beginning.

14. Genesis 1:26–27; 2:21–22.

Do you see what this story is saying? You, woman of God, are a solution, a need, a helper, a miracle, an answered prayer, even to some unprayed prayers. God, in his infinite wisdom and benevolence, created because he knew a man needed, a world needed, a generation needed, a church needed, *you*. God knows the worth of your identity because he alone gave it to you. You didn't even earn it yourself; your value can't depreciate with time or circumstances; you are marked with the image of God and were born because he wanted you born. The hope is that people around you, like Adam, will recognize your beauty and worth, too, but regardless, my sister, know it for yourself!

Notice what happened next in the creation story. Upon gazing at this masterpiece from God, Adam cleared his throat and prophetically declared (cue Etta James), "This at last is bone of my bones and flesh of my flesh; she shall be called Woman, because she was taken out of Man." The text continues on to tell us, "Therefore a man shall leave his father and his mother and hold fast to his wife, and they shall become one flesh" (Genesis 2:23–24, ESV).

Adam was in the Spirit! He saw this woman and began to prophesy. Prior to this, at no other point in his existence had we heard him say anything. We can reasonably assume that he had said something since creation, but in the first two chapters of Genesis, we see only God speaking to Adam and Adam responding to God through actions of obedience. Yet in this passage we have the first recorded words of Adam that God wanted us to hear. They are poetic and prophetic in response to the arrival of this amazing woman. Do you see the impact this woman had on Adam? God made the entire ocean, and you never hear Adam saying anything about its massiveness. God made mountains and lightning, tigers and lions, the sun and moon, yet we don't get one quote from Adam about the beauty and magnificence of those things. God even gave Adam life-and-death instructions about the tree of the knowledge of good and evil,[15] and even then, there isn't one record of Adam asking a follow-up question or commenting on the gravity of such a command. But now we hear him talking! He was saying, "She is different from me

15. Genesis 2:15–17.

but from me; I will name her woman." Knowing, understanding, and relating to the first woman are critical for us because her life prior to sin is the direct expression of God's desire and created intention for all women. Don't miss that. Whether married, single, widowed, divorced, with child, or never having birthed a child, we all are inextricably connected to this woman. She is one of our mothers. We have in Genesis 2 the template, the blueprint, the picture, for womanhood. Through the first woman, we are to understand the most important aspects of our identity—that we are needed, wonderfully and specially created, called to kingdom duty, and equal with man in the eyes of the Lord.

You Were Created to Have Equality with Men

Women and men are image bearers of God.

> Then God said, "Let us make man in our image, according to our likeness." . . .
>
> So God created man
> in his own image;
> he created him in the image of God;
> he created them male and female. (Genesis 1:26–27)[16]

These two verses make up one of the most humbling passages in Scripture to me, especially given what we now know about how man and woman failed the temptation in the garden and the blood sacrifice Jesus would pay for our redemption. The idea that the Godhead (the Father, Son, and Holy Spirit) would decide to make humankind in their image and likeness is mind blowing. To be an image bearer of God is to uniquely and profoundly resemble him in nature, character, and spirit, so much so that when we encounter people, they see and experience something about God. He gave us the ability to show up in the world and show him off.

When I was growing up, people would see me and say, "I see your

---

16. *Man* in this context means *mankind*, both woman and man.

mother and father in you," because I looked like them and because I came from them, but I wasn't either of them. I am me. At the moment of salvation, you received the indwelling of the Holy Spirit, who helps you in your sanctification. With sanctification, you are becoming more than an image bearer; you are embarking on the lifelong process of looking less like your natural self and beginning to look (act) more like Jesus.

The Bible teaches us that God gave the man and woman he created not only the glorious gift of being his image bearers but also a blessing to ensure they could fulfill the other callings he had in store for them. God called both man and woman to be fruitful, to multiply, and to fill and have dominion over the earth.[17] Not only do we see male and female image bearers as having equal value and worth, but also this subsequent call reveals equality between the man and woman as they co-rule the earth.

A clear picture of equality doesn't end there. God's choice to form the woman from man's rib is theologically important. To emphasize this point, one commentator said of the material used in the creation of woman, "[she was] not made out of his head to top him, not out of his feet to be trampled upon by him, but out of his side to be equal with him, under his arm to be protected, and near his heart to be beloved."[18] The woman is built by God with the same bone and flesh of Adam, which persuades Adam to rightly identify their equality—"Bone of my bone and flesh of my flesh"—but also to notice and honor their undeniable differences by calling her "woman" (Genesis 2:23).[19]

You Were Created to Be a Helper[20]

In Genesis 2:18, we learn the important reason God created woman and her unique identity in relation to man: "The Lord God said, 'It is not

---

17. Genesis 1:28.

18. Quoted in R. Kent Hughes, *Genesis: Beginning and Blessing* (Wheaton, Ill.: Crossway, 2004), 60.

19. Parts of this section are informed by a chapter I wrote in Eric Mason's *Urban Apologetics.* For further reading, see Sarita T. Lyons, "Black Women and the Appeal of the Black Conscious Community and Feminism," in *Urban Apologetics: Restoring Black Dignity with the Gospel,* ed. Eric Mason (Grand Rapids, Mich.: Zondervan Reflective, 2021).

20. Significant portions of this section were taken from Lyons, "Black Women," 144–45.

good for the man to be alone. I will make a helper corresponding to him.'"

Of all the callings God gave women, one of the most unwelcomed and unappreciated is the distinction of being called a "helper." Christian women often cringe when they read that woman was specifically created to be a help to man, as if we are mere slaves or seasonings for their lives. But my sister, to loathe this calling only proves ignorance to the beauty and power we are called to walk in.

In verse 18, God decided to make a necessary companion for man, but the next verses don't detail the creation of woman; rather, they describe how God brought all the animals to Adam so he could name them. Andreas and Margaret Köstenberger reflected on the intention behind this order of events:

> What's going on here? Most likely, God is leading the man through a process of understanding, helping him to realize that he needs a counterpart, human but different, with whom he shares the image of God and can exercise representative rule through the procreation of offspring. In verse 20, then, the same phrase recurs once again: "no suitable helper was found for him."[21]

Through Adam's naming of the animals, God "led the man to see that none of the animals could meet his need for companionship. What is more, we see that the woman's creation isn't man's idea; it's an act of divine grace."[22]

In the Old Testament, the Hebrew word *ezer* ("helper") appears twenty-one times. Twice in reference to Eve (Genesis 2:18, 20), three times in reference to Israel's appeal for military help (Isaiah 30:5; Ezekiel 12:14; Daniel 11:34), but the other sixteen times, it's referring to God himself.[23] There is no inferiority in the term *ezer*. It shows us

---

21. Andreas J. Köstenberger and Margaret E. Köstenberger, *God's Design for Man and Woman: A Biblical-Theological Survey* (Wheaton, Ill.: Crossway, 2014), 33–34.

22. Köstenberger and Köstenberger, *God's Design,* 34.

23. The sixteen references to God as the helper of his people are in Exodus 18:4; Deuteronomy 33:7, 26, 29; Psalm 20:2; 33:20; 70:5; 89:19; 115:9–11; 121:1–2; 124:8; 146:5; Hosea 13:9.

woman's ability to help the way God does, contribute with military-like strength, and be a rescuer. What a powerful piece of our identity! We can draw strength from the matriarchs in the faith and use them as examples of how to live out this powerful calling.

As I shared in the chapter I wrote in *Urban Apologetics,* here are examples of *ezer* women from the Old and New Testaments:

- Midwives Shiphrah and Puah defied the order of Pharoah and refused to kill the baby boys born to Hebrew women (Exodus 1:15–21).

- Jochebed put her son Moses in a basket on the riverbank to save his life (Exodus 2:3–4).

- Zipporah, the wife of Moses, performed a circumcision (male duty) to save her husband from God's wrath (Exodus 4:24–26).

- The daughters of Zelophehad appealed to Moses to receive their father's inheritance. Their appeal benefited other women and changed the law of the nation (Numbers 26:33; 27:1–11).

- Rahab, a known prostitute, strategically helped the Israelite spies by hiding them in her home. She also used her negotiation skills to help save her family (Joshua 2:1–21; 6:17, 25).

- Deborah was in influential woman. She was used by God as a prophet, judge, and military strategist who organized the battle plan against Sisera and took the honored place beside the military leader Barak in battle. Deborah was also the wife of Lappidoth (Judges 4:1–14).

- Ruth, a widow and pagan woman, refused to leave her mother-in-law Naomi and instead cared for her and took her God as her own. She was a diligent worker and had noble character that caught the attention of Boaz (Ruth 1–4).

- Abigail, wife of Nabal, intervened to save her household from being killed by David and his men because of her foolish husband's actions (1 Samuel 25:3–35).

- Huldah, a prophet, was asked to interpret the book of the law by the high priest Hilkiah and King Josiah. Her interpretation led to religious reform in Judah (2 Kings 22:11–23:25).

- Joanna, Susanna, Mary Magdalene, and many other women helped Jesus's ministry by giving financially (Luke 8:2–3).

- Mary Magdalene was the first person Jesus called to proclaim the good news of his resurrection to the other disciples (John 20:16–18).

- Lydia was a businesswoman who provided a meeting place in her home and gave money for the new Christian church in Philippi (Acts 16:11–15, 40).

- Priscilla and her husband, Aquila, were tentmakers and co-workers in ministry with Paul, planting churches. The church in Ephesus met in their house, and she and her husband taught Apollos and corrected his doctrine. They also risked their lives for Paul and experienced persecution (Acts 18:24–26; Romans 16:3–5).

- Phoebe was a deacon and benefactor for gospel ministry. She was trusted by Paul to deliver his letter to the church in Rome (Romans 16:1–2).

- Mary, Tryphaena, Tryphosa, and Persis were Paul's helpers and co-laborers in ministry. They were described as women who "worked very hard in the Lord" (Romans 16:6, 12).

- Junia, who co-labored with Paul in ministry, was imprisoned for the Gospel and commended among the apostles for her faithfulness and character (Romans 16:7). She and her husband Andronicus "were among the first generation of Christian apostolic leaders."[24]

24. Nijay K. Gupta, "Junia, the Female Apostle Imprisoned for the Gospel," *Christianity Today,* March 23, 2023, www.christianitytoday.com/ct/2023/march-web-only/junia-female-apostle-paul -fellow-prisoner-preaching-gospel.html.

- Euodia and Syntyche were co-workers in ministry with Paul who were commended for contending for the gospel (Philippians 4:2–3).

- Lois and Eunice, Timothy's grandmother and mother, taught Timothy the ways of the sacred scriptures and were known for their great faith (2 Timothy 1:5, 3:14–15).[25]

You Were Created to Have Influence for Good, Not Evil (Genesis 3:6)[26]

One of the ways *Merriam-Webster* defines influence is "the power or capacity of causing an effect in indirect or intangible ways."[27] As women, we can use our influence for good—to support and encourage our husbands, friends, and faith leaders; spread the gospel; and point people to God. How you steward your influence can be a type of help.

It is undeniable that the first example in Scripture of a woman's influence is a negative expression. However, it nonetheless shows just how powerful her influence is. Despite the clear command that God gave Adam about not eating from the tree of the knowledge of good and evil, the Bible tells us that after the woman listened to the counsel of the serpent, she ate the fruit and then gave it to her husband, and he ate it.[28] Can you believe that? Adam said nothing. There was no rebuke, no rejection, and no running by Adam. Instead of spiritual leadership, Adam was eating the fruit too. She gave him the fruit and he ate it. We cannot deny that it reveals God gave woman influential power. What should we take from this? Church Girl, you have power, but how are you going to use it?

We often talk about who has power and who doesn't, but we rarely discuss how to wield it. Power in the hands of the wise and godly is good; power in the hands of the fool and ungodly is not—they're bound to

---

25. Lyons, "Black Women," 144–45.

26. Significant portions of this section were taken from Lyons, "Black Women," 145–46.

27. *Merriam-Webster*, s.v. "influence," accessed February 29, 2024, www.merriam-webster.com/dictionary/influence.

28. Genesis 3:6.

misuse and abuse it. How can we steward the gift of power responsibly? I believe we can learn important lessons from some of our favorite superhero movies. In these movies, when the hero first discovers their powers and is learning to use them, we often see the inadvertent chaos the person causes, a lot of times involving destruction of property. But then they find a mentor who understands their powers and can help them learn ways to use these powers for good.[29]

That's what Church Girls need: mature women in the faith guiding us on stewarding this power of influence well. I believe the church and other Christian woman have misunderstood and misused the power of influence God gave us. Perhaps this has resulted in men in the church making unfair conclusions about women. Having power is a weighty responsibility, and both men and women in various contexts have access to power and are capable of misusing and abusing it.

The question we must ask ourselves is *What am I filled with?* Or another way of saying it is *What am I under the influence of?* When a person drives drunk, they are charged with a DUI. This is a very serious crime because it puts the driver and everyone else on the road at risk. When we are filled with alcohol, our reflexes are diminished, and our abilities to think clearly, steer straight, and focus are worsened. As we seek to steward our superpower of influence, it's imperative we remember that whatever fills us controls us. God tells us to not be drunk with wine, and to apply this to our lives more broadly, anything that fills, intoxicates, dominates, and controls us can be substituted for wine: a substance, a state of mind, information, an ideology, a belief, an emotion. Church Girl, are you being filled with God's Spirit, or are you being filled with false teaching, anger, hopelessness, the love of money, foolishness, carnality, bitterness, fear, or pride? When we are filled with God's Spirit, we can all be found guilty of an LUI—living under the influence of God.

How do we ensure that we are being filled with the Holy Spirit? We have to draw near to God, get in the presence of the Spirit through our worship, get in community where the Spirit is being exalted, get in the Word of God, sit under sound biblical teaching, listen to music that ush-

---

29. Lyons, "Black Women," 146.

ers us into worship, pray, confess and repent of our sins, and, most importantly, surrender and submit to what God has called us to do. We must do this over and over again, because we can't be filled with one "spiritual sip." I mention these things not as legalistic practices or a rigid spiritual checklist but rather as some of the daily habits of grace that the disciple of Jesus Christ is called to. This is the life of the Church Girl who walks in step with the Spirit. While the Holy Spirit dwells within every believer, he can be grieved when we rebel against God,[30] and his activity and productivity within our lives can be quenched.[31] As women, if we allow this to take place, we forfeit experiencing the fullness of the Spirit's work and power in and through us and limit our ability to be women with godly influence. When filled with the Spirit, we allow him to fully occupy and control every area of our lives so that our actions are fruitful, our thoughts are sound, our motives are pure, and our influence as women glorifies God.

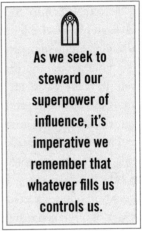

As we seek to steward our superpower of influence, it's imperative we remember that whatever fills us controls us.

Eve's ultimate redemption reminds me of a scripture God used to comfort my heart during a very difficult season of illness I suffered as a result of some of my own poor lifestyle choices: "I will not die, but I will live and proclaim what the LORD has done. The LORD disciplined me severely but did not give me over to death" (Psalm 118:17–18). You may be able to recall times when you experienced the discipline of God for your own unhealthy or disobedient decisions. But Eve's ability to be used by God wasn't destroyed, and neither is yours.

Those who are redeemed by Christ inherit the right to eternal life. Our unrighteousness is cleansed by the blood of Jesus, and we are made holy through his perfection.

30. Ephesians 4:30.
31. 1 Thessalonians 5:19.

Thankfully, the first misuse of a woman's influential power was not where the story ended for her. That's good news for you, Church Girl. We all sin and at times struggle to steward the gifts and callings God has given us, but that doesn't have to be the end of our stories. Misusing our influence doesn't disqualify us from being used by God in the future, because he is faithful to forgive us if we repent. We must humble ourselves and be teachable under the tutelage of the Holy Spirit and Christian discipleship so that we can effectively walk in our "superpower." Just like superheroes in movies, we must be trained to steward our influence well. In Hebrews 12:11, the writer tells us, "No discipline seems pleasant at the time, but painful. Later on, however, it produces a harvest of righteousness and peace for those who have been trained by it" (NIV).

The woman's story did not end when sin entered the world. God had a plan for her to produce a blessed harvest of righteousness by calling her to be a life giver even after she was a co-conspirator in death entering the world. God wants to do the same through you! Church Girl, your power of influence is an important tool in God's redemption plan. I ask you: What harvest of righteousness will you allow God to produce through you, as you use your influence for his honor and glory?[32]

You Were Created to Be Free

We see that, from the beginning, woman was created and defined by God. She was created to be an image bearer of God, have equality and co-rule with man as they filled the earth, be a helper, and use her influence for good. Woman is God's idea. Woman is God's creation. From the beginning, woman was declared "very good" by God (Genesis 1:31). Woman was made for a specific purpose, without any design input or negotiation from man. Woman was created as the solution for the lack of human community,[33] and she was the inspiration for the first recorded

32. Lyons, "Black Women," 147.
33. Genesis 2:18–22, 24.

human speech.[34] It's in this fundamental identity that God has called you and me to find joy and mission and to agree with him that we are very good.

But here is the tricky part. Even with all we know about the importance of the first woman, we must face the reality that she wasn't immune to the serpent. The woman was given many identity markers, and one of them was freedom. The highest expression of love is the ability to be free to choose, even to choose wrongly. God's love frees you to reject and hate him while he keeps on loving you. In fact, our first mother is the only woman who ever walked the earth free from sin. Though Eve listened to the serpent, disobeyed God, and fell with the man,[35] she wasn't created fallen; she was created free. *Free* is a beautiful God-given identity for women—one that he wanted us to have in the garden and one that he still wants us to have today. The gospel message is that, through a relationship with Christ, we can walk in our God-designed identity as free women.

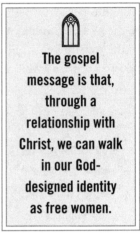

The gospel message is that, through a relationship with Christ, we can walk in our God-designed identity as free women.

There is so much talk of freedom in our culture because Black women haven't always been free. When it comes to fighting for the rights of women—or even when it comes to the culture's philosophies about self-actualization and autonomy—it seems the highest aim of life is to be free. There are so many marches, books, and lectures on how unfree women are and how to fight for freedom. Being unfree is a painful product of the Fall, but the truth is, the woman God made was free from the beginning. Freedom for women isn't a feminist idea; it's God's idea. The world wants you to believe that true freedom is living however you

34. Genesis 2:23.
35. Genesis 3:1–7.

want, while living according to God's standards is considered bondage. However, sin, not God, puts us in bondage.[36] The Lord *made* the first woman—as he makes all women who are in Christ—free.[37]

The one critical difference between a biblical view of freedom and the world's definition of freedom is that our freedom is a call to live on God's terms, not our own.[38] Freedom for the Christian woman is gained, first, through a relationship with Christ and, second, through submission to the perfect lordship of a loving, just God. Man and woman were free in the garden, but they had boundaries established by God. God wants you to know that your identity as a free woman is actualized in your willingness to honor his boundaries and commands. My sister, you are truly free when you obey him.

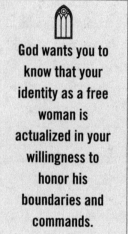

God wants you to know that your identity as a free woman is actualized in your willingness to honor his boundaries and commands.

The first woman's identity was free. The woman had a mind to think, emotions to feel, a heart to contemplate, a will to choose, and ears to hear. She was so free she could hear a voice that wasn't God's and follow it. While our first mother used her freedom to disobey God and brought sin into the world, through Christ and the help of the Holy Spirit, we can make another choice every day. The great gift of freedom must be handled responsibly. The good news is that if we obey God, live for him, and allow him to rule and reign in our lives, we will get the blessed opportunity to feel the peace and power of what it really means to be a free woman and share it with other women. Free women free women.[39] We can become great emancipators in the earth. We will, both socially and spiritually, like Harriet Tubman, lead other women through under-

36. John 8:34.
37. John 8:36; Romans 6:6–7.
38. Titus 2:11–12; 1 John 3:4–10.
39. Adapted from Pricelis Perreaux-Dominguez of Full Collective, where she sold merchandise that read "Free people free people." See "Our Mission + Vision," Full Collective, https://wearefullcollective.com/about-full-collective.

ground railroads, fighting the ungodly oppression of women in the world and fighting demonic oppression by pointing people to Christ, the greatest liberator.

If the Son sets you free, you really will be free. (John 8:36)

A Gospel Vision for Your Identity

Having a gospel vision for your identity starts with knowing and accepting that God made you and therefore he alone has the right to tell you who you are. You can't know yourself apart from knowing God. He first established your identity at creation, and he gave you some similar traits and callings to those of men, but you also have some traits that are unique. Like your first mother in the garden, you are uniquely created to be a helper, an influencer for good, and free within the boundaries God established. The creation of woman—and of your life—was not an afterthought but a needed and beautiful addition to bring balance to the world and to show off something special about God's glory. Even after sin, God had a plan to redeem humanity and use you and all women to be a witness for Christ who brings restoration to the fallen world.

Discussion Questions

 LIGHT: God made you and gave you your identity at creation.

1. Why is it important whom we allow to define us as Black women?

2. Who or what has most shaped your identity as a Black Christian woman?

3. Why does God have the ultimate right and authority to give us our identity? How satisfied are you with what God said from the beginning? What is a struggle to embrace, and what do you joyously embrace?

4. What is one area of God's unique design of woman discussed in this chapter that you want to lean into more as you walk out your identity as a Church Girl?

👓 LENS: The Bible should be the lens through which we fundamentally understand our identity.

1. Have you ever imagined yourself or another Black woman as a daughter of Eve? Why or why not? What influence does your answer have on how you identify with God's vision for womanhood from the beginning?

2. How does the biblical account of the creation of woman not align with some of the world's narratives of Black women's identity?

❤️ LOVE: God's love for you is evidenced by his care in creating woman.

1. How is God's love for you on display in how he made woman?

2. What are some things you now love more about yourself and other Black women after thinking about God's intention for women?

CHAPTER 2

Girl, Why You So Pushy?

A Gospel Vision for Black Women's Purpose

*Adam named his wife Eve, because she would
become the mother of all the living.*
—Genesis 3:20, NIV

I remember the first time I was called "pushy." I was a sophomore at Florida A&M University (FAMU) and had been tasked with completing a journalism project with a guy from Miami, whom I'll call Darnell. I knew Darnell was from Miami because he introduced himself as "Big D from the Bottom," and I'd been at FAMU long enough to know "the Bottom" meant the southern part of Florida. Together, we had to shoot and edit film for a segment called "Man on the Street." We had to create a concept, find an interview location, and put a package together in just a few days. Simple, right? Not so much.

It was like pulling teeth to meet with Darnell to work out all the details. I wanted to schedule a time we could sit down together to get a complete vision of what we wanted to accomplish and map out a fun and engaging idea that would guarantee us an A for the project. I knew there was going to be a problem when Darnell took my number and said, "I gotchu, Shawty. I holla." From our initial conversation, it was clear that Darnell was uninterested and that his approach was the exact opposite of mine. I believe his words were "Be chilly, Philly, and let it flow." *Be chilly, Philly?* Can you feel the internal eye roll I gave him? He also told me he wasn't available to edit film on Friday night because he was going to a party and he didn't do work on weekends. That certainly would have been nice to know on Wednesday since the assignment was due on Monday.

With no cellphones or texting in the early nineties, I could only call and leave multiple answering machine messages on Thursday, trying to connect with him. Some of you will remember that, in the nineties, people would pick their favorite songs and record them as their voice-mail greetings. I had to endure listening to his answering machine's greeting—the non-clean version of rap group 2 Live Crew's song, with Uncle Luke and company yelling in my ear, "Pop that coochie, baby . . ." I was disgusted.

Darnell and I finally met on Sunday. However, before we began to plan the shoot that was set to take place at Governor's Square Mall in Tallahassee, he took a moment to offer me some unsolicited feedback. I will never forget his words, wrapped in his distinct Dade County accent, as he folded his hands and leaned forward like he had been paid big bucks to drop life-transforming pearls of wisdom on me. He said it so confidently with a half grin as he licked his lips, like LL Cool J revealing his gold fronts: "You sexy, red, but you hella pushy."

I wish I could clearly articulate all the thoughts that swarmed through my head. My chest began to burn. There were many things problematic about what Darnell said to me, from calling me sexy to calling me red, which was short for "redbone" because I was light-skinned. However, if I'm honest, of all his objectifying and inappropriate descriptions of me, the one that hit me the hardest was "pushy." I hadn't even made it out of my teens, and my hard work, my enthusiasm to do well, my unwilling-ness to fail, my focus, and my courage to hold someone else accountable to do what was right were being called "pushy." It felt like a curse word to my soul. If I hadn't had that assignment due in just a few hours, maybe I would have responded in a more deserving way, a more Philly way, but instead, I did what many Black women are conditioned to do when we are disrespected. I kept a straight face, pretended that what he had said didn't hurt me, and kept on *pushing*.

I'm sure you as a Black woman know that feeling when other people, particularly men, deflect from their own insecurity by minimizing you and finding ways to bring you down instead of celebrating you, supporting your efforts, or being inspired to do more themselves. Many times, when you are classified as "pushy," you are being critiqued instead of encouraged, and ultimately, what is good about your focus and tenacity is recharacterized as something bad.

When we see something godly and great about Black women, we should fan the flame, not smother it. While we'd like to believe only men need that reproof, that isn't true. As women, we must be careful that we aren't enviously smothering other Black women's fire. We must be committed to calling out sexism as well as exposing any insecurity living in our own hearts that could hurt or hinder another Black woman. No one should ever throw water on a Black woman's God-given purpose. The world and the church need Black women's Spirit-controlled fire.

I remember the day God helped me reframe that verbal assault and reclaim being "pushy" as something to cherish as a God-given purpose while I was meditating on the narrative of Genesis 3. This chapter tells us that after man and woman sinned by eating from the tree of the knowledge of good and evil, God cursed the serpent and assigned consequences for their disobedience. Before God sacrificed an animal to make clothing to cover the man's and his wife's nakedness,[1] "Adam named his wife Eve, because she would become the mother of all the living" (verse 20, NIV). *Eve* can also mean "full of life" or "life giver." The woman who had used her influence to encourage the man to join her in disobeying God was now named "the mother of all the living." Her name is in harmony with the prophecy God spoke about putting hostility between her seed and the serpent's seed.[2] Eventually, her seed would be Jesus, who would be born to crush the head of

Her name, "life giver," is a hopeful and redemptive picture that Satan's plan to kill, steal, and destroy won't win in the end.

---

1. God killing an animal to cover Adam and Eve (Genesis 3:21) is also a foreshadowing of what he would later do to provide their ultimate redemption and to cover the debt of sin.
2. Genesis 3:15.

Satan by dying on the cross and being raised from the dead. Her name, "life giver," is a hopeful and redemptive picture that Satan's plan to kill, steal, and destroy won't win in the end. This woman, who had used her life to participate in being a life taker, would become a life giver and receive redemption through her future seed, Christ. The redemption of Eve and her assignment to be a life giver revolutionized how I understood my purpose and what it means for you and me to be pushy women.

Church Girl, you have been called by God to be a life giver, whether by birthing children or by bringing to life any divinely ordained purpose he has put in you. Just as our gift to have influence can be used for good or evil, I believe the same is true of our tendency as women to be pushy. Being pushy is in fact a beautiful way in which God has wired us as life givers; however, like influence, being pushy must be under the Spirit's control. Being pushy women doesn't give us license to be jerks, insufferable, unkind, individualistic, controlling, or bad team players, but rather, we are to steward our pushy inclination to bring forth life in multiple ways and in various seasons for God's glory.

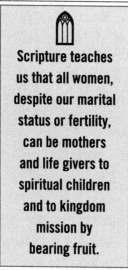

Scripture teaches us that all women, despite our marital status or fertility, can be mothers and life givers to spiritual children and to kingdom mission by bearing fruit.

Don't be easily discouraged if you or others identify that trait in you. Instead, ask God to teach you how to use this trait to give rather than take life, to guard your heart, to walk in wisdom, and to be willing to correct any offense or misuse of your life-giver call. I wish I'd had this clarity when I was nineteen years old sitting in front of Darnell, because I could have said, "Don't you ever call me sexy or red again. My name is Sarita, and yes, I am pushy; that's what life givers do." Absolutely, women are pushy. What do you expect from women, who are called to be life givers? It's what women who are pregnant with purpose do—we push!

Being a life giver is much more than being a woman who gives birth to a physical baby, though God has indeed uniquely designed women with wombs to be the carriers and birthers of human life. Mothers have the honored privilege of bringing other image bearers into the world who should be raised to fear God and represent him in the earth. However, God hasn't called every woman to have the specific purpose of birthing biological children. But he has called every woman be a life giver. Scripture teaches us that all women, despite our marital status or fertility, can be mothers and life givers to spiritual children[3] and to kingdom mission by bearing fruit.[4]

You aren't alone in your purpose to push. We have been pushing since the beginning of time. I want to celebrate and introduce you to some amazing African and Black women pushers and life givers who had God's hand on their lives. I pray that the stories of how they became life givers will inspire you to keep pushing and give birth to your purpose too.

Perpetua and Felicitas (Circa 182–203)

In the year 203, the passion of Perpetua and Felicitas was a beautiful and painful example of Christian sacrifice and courage for the gospel. These two women found their purpose in birthing kingdom mission by dying for the faith. If you live in the West, where we enjoy more religious freedoms than our sisters in other parts of the world, I'm sure you don't often consider a woman's purpose in Christ involving a gruesome death for the gospel, but martyrdom is in fact the way Perpetua and Felicitas showed us how to push through persecution and share in Christ's suffering. Though we may never be physically martyred for the faith, if we care about sharing the gospel in a world that is hostile to Christ, we should expect to suffer like him as we act as midwives, pushing the spiritually dead toward him to be born again.

Perpetua was a married noblewoman from Carthage in modern-day Tunisia, Africa, who had recently had a child and was nursing.[5] Felicitas,

---

3. Psalm 113:9; Matthew 12:49–50; John 19:26–27; Romans 16:3; Titus 2:3–5.
4. John 15:1–8.
5. Jerome Gay, Jr., *The Whitewashing of Christianity: A Hidden Past, a Hurtful Present and a Hopeful Future* (Chicago: 13th & Joan, 2020), 116.

whom we know less about, was Perpetua's servant and was pregnant at the time of her imprisonment. She prayed to deliver her child before her martyrdom.[6] She gave birth to a son shortly before going to her death. Perpetua kept a diary, some of the earliest writings we have from a Christian woman, which were later published as *The Passion of Saints Perpetua and Felicity*. While in prison, Perpetua's father, who was frantic and wanted to save his daughter's life, visited her and tried to convince her to renounce Christianity to save her life. Perpetua responded to her father, "I cannot be called anything other than what I am, a Christian." While in prison, the women were baptized and were instrumental in their prison warden being converted to the faith.[7] These women pushed to proclaim Christ in the face of persecution, and this eyewitness account of their final moments in the arena is heart gripping:

> They were stripped and wrapped in nets, and when they were thus brought out the people were shocked at the sight, the one a graceful girl, the other fresh from childbirth with milk dripping from her breasts. So they were brought back and clothed in loose gowns. First Perpetua was tossed [by the beast]. She sat up and drew her torn tunic about her, being more mindful of shame than of pain.[8]

Perpetua was dignified even in death. It's reported that she stood up in the arena after being thrown by the beast and asked to "retie her hair, for loose hair was a sign of mourning, and this was a joyful day for her."[9] Until recently, almost all the artwork depicting these two women have them appearing as white women. However, as Jerome Gay, Jr., wrote,

6. Camille Lewis Brown, *African Saints, African Stories: 40 Holy Men and Women* (Cincinnati: Franciscan Media, 2008), 71.

7. "Joy in the Face of Suffering: Saints Perpetua and Felicity," Basilica of the National Shrine of the Immaculate Conception, March 7, 2020, www.nationalshrine.org/blog/joy-in-the-face-of -suffering-saints-perpetua-and-felicity.

8. Vincent J. O'Malley, *Saints of Africa* (Huntington, Ind.: Our Sunday Visitor, 2001), 43, quoting Donald Attwater, *Martyrs: From St. Stephen to John Tung* (New York: Sheed & Ward, 1957), 28.

9. George Moore, "Finding Black History in Church History: Remembering the Martyrdom of Perpetua and Felicitas," Jude 3 Project, February 25, 2021, https://jude3project.org/blog/finding blackhistory, quoting Justo L. González, *The Story of Christianity*, vol. 1, *The Early Church to the Reformation*, rev. ed. (New York: HarperOne, 2010), 99.

One of the many hurtful aspects of whitewashing is how it presents the Christian faith and history inaccurately. Many Black and Brown people have responded to this by assuming that Christianity was only received by Black people during slavery; therefore they've drawn the conclusion that Christianity was not a faith that Africans embraced prior to the Trans-Atlantic Slave Trade. . . . This is historically inaccurate. . . . Black African men and women . . . lived and died for Yeshua long before the slave trade.[10]

Perpetua and Felicitas are two such women who should be correctly understood to be North African women who were martyred for Jesus Christ. Additionally, in a publishing world that has often overlooked Black women, we should celebrate that Perpetua, an African woman, was one of the first Christian women writers. We are thankful for her diaries, which tell her powerful story and spur us on to be fearless witnesses for Christ.

We would all do well to survey our own lives and ask, *What am I willing to lose for the sake of Christ to fulfill my purpose as a life giver?* How can you start or continue in your purpose to share the message of the gospel, which will point others to new life in Christ Jesus? Do you envision your purpose as merely individualistic, laced with selfish ambitions, affording only personal gains of happiness, security, wealth, and pleasure? Are you as a Black Christian woman, like these two sisters, willing to die to yourself for Jesus, or does the fear of being uncomfortable or canceled take precedence in your life? Scripture shows us that the persecution of the early church energized the faithful and caused the spread of the gospel.[11] We aren't trained much to think this way today, but I want to encourage you to not avoid suffering for the faith, in whatever way it may come.[12]

While you may not be thrown to the beasts in an arena, you may be thrown into uncomfortable conversations where you are called to share truth and a Christian perspective on difficult topics. You may not be

10. Gay, *Whitewashing of Christianity,* 108–9.
11. Luke 21:12–13; Acts 8:1–8; 11:19–24.
12. 1 Peter 4:16.

crucified, but you may endure ridicule for being an example of holiness and walking upright in a crooked world. You may not be burned at the stake, but you may catch smoke for standing on God's Word uncompromisingly, challenging doctrines of demons and false teachings, prophetically calling your family, friends, co-workers, and neighbors to repentance, and telling the world Christ is the only way to life everlasting.

May we, in the face of much suffering and persecution, count it a worthy purpose to push through suffering for Christ and give birth to the gospel. In what were likely some of her final words, Perpetua turned to her brother and another Christian convert watching them being tortured and said, "Stand fast in the faith and love one another. And do not let what we suffer be a stumbling-block to you."[13] Praise God for these pushy women who birthed a testimony of unflinching faith and commitment to Christ through their lives and deaths!

Monica of Hippo (Circa 331–87)

Monica of Hippo may not be a household name among Black Christian women, but she should be. Monica was raised near the city of Carthage, where she would suffer in an arranged marriage to a pagan man who was unfaithful and abusive.[14] Historians consider Monica's greatest weapons to have been her patience and prayers. After she had prayed many years for his salvation, her husband converted to Christianity on his deathbed. But that wouldn't be the end of her heartache; the eldest of her three children resisted Christ for many years.

While you may not know Monica, you are most likely familiar with her eldest, a wayward son turned church father. Yes, Monica of Hippo was the mother of the North African stalwart church father and writer of *Confessions*—Augustine of Hippo. Prior to Augustine's conversion, he jumped between Stoicism, Manichaeism, Pythagoreanism, various women, and criminal activity. He ran from the gospel message and his

13. Quoted in Brown, *African Saints,* 74.
14. Brown, *African Saints,* 14.

mother's pleadings to turn to Christ.[15] However, his mother refused to give up on her son and followed him from city to city, praying for him to be saved. I don't know about you, but that sounds like a pushy woman to me—a mother being persistent in prayer for the salvation of her son. The woman who gave Augustine life also pushed in her prayers so that he could have new life in Christ. Augustine eventually gave his life to Christ and was baptized in April 387, and Monica died soon after. She was able to see her most fervent prayer answered. Augustine was known to have said that his mother "had borne him twice: first in the flesh, and afterwards in the spirit. . . . The second childbirth was perhaps far more painful than the first."[16]

Some of us who are mothers may know the heartache of loving children who don't love the Lord or who are drifting from their Christian upbringing. We can feel powerless to have any influence to change their eternal fate. Let Mother Monica be an enduring example that prayer changes things and we should never give up praying for our children, no matter how hard they run from God. May we as women—mothers of natural and spiritual children, aunties, sisters, and friends—be that unwavering and pushy in our prayers for the salvation of our families, our communities, and the world.

> May we as women—mothers of natural and spiritual children, aunties, sisters, and friends—be that unwavering and pushy in our prayers for the salvation of our families, our communities, and the world.

PUSH is a well-known acronym among many Black Christian women that stands for "Pray until something happens." Black women know the power of persistent prayers. No one can outrun our pushy prayers. Some of the greatest men and women in the faith are those who, like Augustine, had someone who loved them enough to pray for them to have a life

---

15. Brown, *African Saints*, 14.

16. Brown, *African Saints*, 17, quoting Léon Cristiani, *Saint Monica and Her Son Augustine*, trans. M. Angeline Bouchard (Boston: Pauline Books and Media, 1994), 97.

that pleased the Lord. When we dare to be undaunted and believe that Jesus has the power to give life and transform, deliver, heal, and redeem lives, we will commit to being pushy and persistent in prayer. Someone will be so glad that you, like Monica of Hippo, prayed for them.

Rebecca Protten (1718–80)

Rebecca Freundlich Protten has the distinguished honor of being called "the mother of modern missions." Rebecca was born into slavery on the island of Antigua and was mixed race, having an African mother who was impregnated by her European enslaver.[17] When Rebecca was seven years old, she was kidnapped or sold and taken to St. Thomas, where she was enslaved by a Dutch family.[18] When she was twelve years old, her enslaver died and his family granted her freedom.[19] Once free, she set out to find out more about Christianity.[20] She converted to Christianity after meeting Moravian missionaries and served faithfully as a missionary after that. Though her primary ministry was to enslaved African women, her relationship to the Moravian missionaries afforded her opportunities to preach and hold various leadership positions within their church.[21] While there is little documentation on Rebecca's life, we have testimonials about her in the writings of those who knew her and a handful of personal letters that have survived.

Before the age of twenty, Rebecca was "a preacher and a mentor, a provocateur and a prophet, determined to take what she regarded as the Bible's liberating grace to people of African descent."

She broadcast her message . . . to the slave quarters deep in the island's plantation heartland, where she proclaimed salvation to the

---

17. Lilian Ortinau, "Rebecca Protten (1718–1780)," Black Central Europe, accessed February 9, 2024, https://blackcentraleurope.com/biographies/rebecca-protten-lilian-ortinau.
18. Jon F. Sensbach, *Rebecca's Revival: Creating Black Christianity in the Atlantic World* (Cambridge, Mass.: Harvard University Press, 2005), 31–32.
19. Ortinau, "Rebecca Protten."
20. Sensbach, *Rebecca's Revival,* 36–37.
21. Ortinau, "Rebecca Protten."

domestic servants, cane boilers, weavers, and cotton pickers whose bodies and spirits were strip-mined every day by slavery.[22]

Plantation owners became increasingly agitated and violent in response to Rebecca's teaching for fear that she would stir an uprising among their enslaved people. They terrorized Rebecca and those she taught with violent intimidation. But her evangelizing couldn't be stopped. Authorities switched tactics, arresting Rebecca and her first husband, Matthäus, on trumped-up charges of having an unlawful marriage. She was given an opportunity to make a deal for her release if she would only testify in a manner that she thought was blasphemous. Instead of compromise, Rebecca remained in a prison hole for fifteen weeks, was fined her entire fortune, and was told she would be forced to return to enslavement. By God's grace Rebecca and her husband were released, and she reflected on her experience:

> The Savior has shown me his eternal love. . . . He has shown me how full of mercy he is. So I will no longer love myself, but give myself willingly to him, with body and soul, to do his will. I have prayed to him that if there was a drop of blood in me that did not want to be obedient to him, for him to reveal it to me and take it away and I have a great hunger after the souls.[23]

Her words of self-denial and determination to serve God should be encouraging. Our present-day desires around purpose aren't all bad, but too often, our focus can turn to achieving riches for personal comfort, creating content to gain followers, taking personality tests to determine what we should be doing with our lives, or standing in line so someone can prophesy our purpose to us. A surrendered and selfless life like Rebecca's doesn't happen by accident. You can begin to cultivate a similar heart in your own life in several ways:

---

22. Sensbach, *Rebecca's Revival*, 3.
23. Quoted in Sensbach, *Rebecca's Revival*, 131.

1. Pray, and obey the admonishment to "seek first the kingdom of God and his righteousness, and all these things will be provided for you" (Matthew 6:33). The more we pray for God's help and for understanding his will, the more we reinforce the truth that our lives aren't our own—we belong to God. Prayer keeps us close to the source of wisdom and provision so that we are less tempted to depend on ourselves or our own wisdom for our needs. Rebecca's prayers were largely focused on her purpose to evangelize the lost, not on personal gain or protection. Ask yourself, *If God were to answer my prayers, would only my life change or would the world change?*

2. Take the call to make disciples seriously. Rebecca's life was marked by being on mission for God. In your everyday life, ask the Lord to make you sensitive to open doors to share the gospel and to help you notice women he may be calling you to walk alongside and teach the ways of Christ.

3. Don't be deterred by suffering. Rebecca suffered much in her life, but it never took her off mission. In fact, it fueled her determination. We know that suffering is a part of not only the human experience but also the Christian life. However, when you and I suffer, we too often let it sideline us indefinitely instead of using those experiences as motivation to share with others the hope of a future where pain will be no more.[24] If God allowed it, he intends to use it. We often give birth to something great from the place of our pain. Other women need to hear your stories, so don't let your suffering silence you. You may discover a new mission field where you have greater empathy for and connection to other hurting women when you push through your pain and let God use your suffering for his glory.

Rebecca remained committed to the mission of sharing the gospel until the very end. As one writer noted,

---

24. Revelation 21:4.

She'd sown the seeds of Afro-Protestantism in the Americas that began in the West Indies and still reverberates throughout the African-American Christian community today.[25]

Rebecca was a life giver of the highest order. She was committed to Jesus and resolute in ministering to the enslaved and to women of both African and European descent. This Christian woman, who walked in her purpose as a life giver, left us a legacy to follow as her life personified the words of Paul: "I consider my life of no value to myself; my *purpose* is to finish my course and the ministry I received from the Lord Jesus, to testify to the gospel of God's grace" (Acts 20:24).

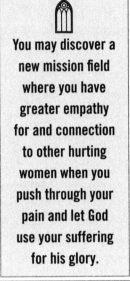

You may discover a new mission field where you have greater empathy for and connection to other hurting women when you push through your pain and let God use your suffering for his glory.

Church Girl, I challenge you to survey your life and consider whether it reflects that what you most care about is living completely surrendered to the Lord and on mission to help others have encounters with Christ. If not, would you consider praying and asking the Lord to reset your priorities so that you will find ways in your day-to-day life to begin to add making disciples to your to-do list?

Sara Lucy Bagby Johnson
(1843–1906)

I haven't fully processed why Sara Lucy Bagby Johnson's story has tugged at my heart the way it has, but it's undeniable that I'm glad I stumbled upon this Black woman. With many historical Black women life givers,

---

25. Kathleen Rouser, "Rebecca Protten: A Zeal for Taking the Gospel to Slaves," Heroes, Heroines, and History, March 21, 2019, www.hhhistory.com/2019/03/rebecca-protten-zeal-for -taking-gospel.html.

it can be difficult to gather information with sparse records. Yet we know that Sara Lucy was the last person to be prosecuted under the Fugitive Slave Act and was returned to her enslaver after escaping via the Underground Railroad.[26]

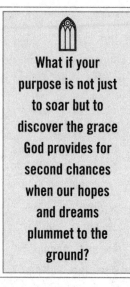

What if your purpose is not just to soar but to discover the grace God provides for second chances when our hopes and dreams plummet to the ground?

Sara Lucy was born in the early 1840s and purchased by John Goshorn in 1852 for six hundred dollars before she was given as a gift to his son William Scott Goshorn in 1857.[27] Sara Lucy managed to escape, ended up in Cleveland, Ohio, and got a job as a domestic. Some reports claim that she ran away because she was pregnant and didn't want her child born in slavery.[28] Goshorn traveled there on January 16, 1861, to reclaim her. She was arrested at the home of her employer, jeweler Lucius Benton. After a short trial and a failed attempt by abolitionists to purchase her from Goshorn, she was soon taken back to Wheeling, Virginia. But her story didn't end there. During the Civil War, Sara Lucy was rescued and freed by a Union officer, then married a Union soldier named George Johnson in Pittsburgh and later returned to Cleveland.[29]

Sara Lucy died in 1906 after complications from a fall. She was buried in an unmarked grave in Cleveland for more than one hundred years, until locals learned of her story and rallied to honor her with a tombstone.[30] The inscription on her tombstone reads, "Unfettered and free."

26. The Fugitive Slave Act, which was passed in 1850, was a federal law that declared that enslaved people were property and must be returned to their owners if they ran away. See Michelle A. Day and Joseph Wickens, "The Arrest and Trial of Lucy Bagby," Cleveland Historical, accessed February 9, 2024, https://clevelandhistorical.org/items/show/517.

27. Day and Wickens, "Arrest and Trial."

28. John Stauffer, "Fear and Doubt in Cleveland," *New York Times,* December 22, 2010, https://archive.nytimes.com/opinionator.blogs.nytimes.com/2010/12/22/fear-and-doubt-in-cleveland.

29. Day and Wickens, "Arrest and Trial."

30. Dave Davis, "Headstone for Unmarked Grave of Sara Lucy Bagby Johnson: Whatever Happened To . . . ?," Cleveland.com, November 21, 2011, www.cleveland.com/metro/2011/11/a_headstone_for_the_unmarked_g.html.

Unfettered means released from restraining or inhibiting force, and isn't that what we Church Girls, like Sara Lucy, want?[31] To have the ability to live without restraint and without being stifled by the force of an enslaver and the force of the law? While she wasn't the only Black person who experienced slavery, then freedom, then being legally returned to a life of slavery, the idea that she was the last is striking.

I think about what that train ride back to the plantation must have been like for her. Reports indicate that she was punished severely upon returning to her enslaver and gave birth to a child who wouldn't be free.[32] After experiencing being paid for work, she was now bound and forced to work for nothing. If you push hard once to give birth to a new life, do you have it in you to push again? I believe many Black women can relate in a multitude of ways to fighting, scraping, and running to some form of freedom, only to experience a demoralizing setback that dashes their hopes and dreams. Yet Sara Lucy pushed through capture, through trial, through the ride back to Wheeling, through torturous punishment, through labor to give birth to a child she couldn't protect, through the pain of despair, and she still had enough pushiness in her to give birth to hope. We know she had hope, because she lived. For many of us, giving birth to the hope of a better day is proof that we are life givers.

What if your purpose is not just to soar but to discover the grace God provides for second chances when our hopes and dreams plummet to the ground? What if your purpose is to give birth to a testimony that you can rise *again* like a phoenix, just like Sara Lucy? What purpose is still calling your name after multiple setbacks? Are multiple miscarriages, a failed business, broken relationships, divorce, roadblocks in education, reoccurring sickness, or depression and anxiety dragging you down again? Is a sin or addiction that you experienced victory over in the past attempting to rear its ugly head in your life and drag you back to slavery? Is the death of another loved one bringing the unwelcomed gift of grief just when you thought you couldn't spare another tear? Church Girl,

31. Collins, s.v. "unfetter," accessed February 9, 2024, www.collinsdictionary.com/dictionary/english/unfetter.
32. Stauffer, "Fear and Doubt in Cleveland."

what disappointment is God calling you to push through to live another day? What is the devil telling you that you can't overcome . . . again? Though I have no proof that Sara Lucy was a Christian woman who walked with God, we can be certain that he was providentially at work in her life, if for no other reason than to leave us an example of endurance. If you can relate to the hardship of setbacks and disappointments as you try to live out your life's purpose, then it was worth it for me to share Sara Lucy's story.

> You may not be the first to do something great, but maybe you can be the last to sit on your gifts and ignore your call to be a life giver.

Many Black women are celebrated for being the first, but we can celebrate Sara Lucy for being the last—the last person to have to return to a life of slavery. You may not be the first, but maybe your purpose is to be the last. What if your legacy is that you were the last person in your family to struggle with shame? What if you are the last woman in your family to be in an abusive marriage? What if you are the last Black Christian woman who ever was afraid to share the gospel with others and live unapologetically as a Christian? You may not be the first to do something great, but maybe you can be the last to sit on your gifts and ignore your call to be a life giver.

Maybe Sara Lucy's story is so compelling to me because I've discovered that one's purpose is rarely a destination but more often the journey of climbing mountains, walking through valleys, failing, falling, and bruising knees. The call is in the pushing to get back up when life knocks us down, which takes supernatural faith and hope. The Lord wants to meet us in our disappointment and breathe his life and strength into us. Remember Sara Lucy's legacy, "Unfettered and free," and remember the words of Paul: "I am sure of this, that he who started a good work in you will carry it on to completion until the day of Christ Jesus" (Philippians 1:6). My sister, keep living, keep believing, and keep finding the will to push, and push again, and again and again.

Nannie Helen Burroughs (1879–1961)

At the National Baptist Convention in 1900, Nannie Helen Burroughs, then secretary to the Foreign Mission Board, began her meteoric rise on the national scene when she shook the church and challenged male church leadership with her speech titled "How the Sisters Are Hindered from Helping." She compellingly argued for women to have their voices, leadership, and missions work valued, supported, and unleashed from male control. While Nannie was never accused of mincing words, her convention speech is a master class on discretion in rebuke, fearlessness in conviction, and focus on the ultimate mission of the church. Her words are wise, biblical, and challenging:

> We come not to usurp thrones nor to sow discord, but to so organize and systematize the work that each church may help through a Woman's Missionary Society and not be made poorer thereby. It is for the utilization of talent and the stimulation to Christian activity in our Baptist churches that prompt us to service. We realize that to allow these gems to lie unpolished longer means a loss to the denomination. For a number of years there has been a righteous discontent, a burning zeal to go forward in his name among the Baptist women of our churches and it will be the dynamic force in the religious campaign at the opening of the 20th century. . . . We realize, too, that the work is too great and laborers too few for us to stand by while like Trojans the brethren at the head of the work under the convention toil unceasingly.[33]

Notice the language that Nannie used next in her speech. Do you see her clear understanding of a woman's call to be an *ezer,* the military agent of help, as God himself is a helper to his people?

33. Nannie Helen Burroughs, "How the Sisters Are Hindered from Helping" (speech, National Baptist Convention, Richmond, Va., September 13, 1900), https://awpc.cattcenter.iastate.edu/2019/09/26/how-the-sisters-are-hindered-from-helping.

We come now to the rescue. We unfurl our banner upon which is inscribed this motto, "The World for Christ. Woman, Arise, He calleth for Thee." Will you as a pastor and friend of missions help by not hindering these women when they come among you to speak and to enlist the women of your church? It has ever been from the time of Miriam, that most remarkable woman, the sister of Moses, that most remarkable man, down to the courageous women that in very recent years have carried the Gospel into Tibet and Africa and proclaimed and taught the truth where no man has been allowed to enter. Surely, women somehow have had a very important part in the work of saving this redeemed earth.[34]

Seeing how Nannie grew up and what she overcame will help you appreciate how God can call you as a Black Christian woman from difficult circumstances and give you a purpose to change the world. Like Nannie, you might just start with the church. Born in 1879 in Orange, Virginia, Nannie lived in poverty with her family and experienced loss early when her sister and father passed away. She was raised by her mother, Jennie, a former slave who later moved to Washington, D.C., in hope of better opportunities. Nannie was a great student and had the honor of being taught by Mary Church Terrell, one of the founders of the National Association of Colored Women. Along with Nannie's experiences with racism and sexism, she was denied opportunities to teach in the D.C. school system believing colorism was the likely reason.[35]

This experience as a dark-skinned woman whose mother was a domestic worker and whose father was a poor preacher gave her greater empathy for wage-earning women and respect for Black culture. She knew from experience that dark-skinned girls from impoverished working families were typically marginalized, undervalued, and excluded from activities and opportunities.[36] She once wrote a column in a news-

---

34. Burroughs, "How the Sisters."

35. Jasmine L. Holmes, *Carved in Ebony: Lessons from the Black Women Who Shape Us* (Minneapolis: Bethany House, 2021), 56–57.

36. Bettye Collier-Thomas, *Jesus, Jobs, and Justice: African American Women and Religion* (Philadelphia: Temple University Press, 2010), 128–29.

paper called "Not Color but Character," where she said, "Many Negroes have colorphobia as badly as white folk have Negrophobia. . . . Color is not a badge of superiority of mind nor soul."[37] In addition to advocating "for black civil rights, and . . . for poor and working-class black women, [Nannie] served for over fifty years as the corresponding secretary and president of the Woman's Convention, Auxiliary to the National Baptist Convention."[38] Jasmine Holmes reflected on Nannie's life, saying, "Nannie Helen Burroughs's accomplishments are staggering by any estimation. The woman never stopped."[39]

Nannie was a quintessential life giver. Though she never married or birthed children, she was the mother of many missions and organizations aimed at improving the lives of women. She reminds us Church Girls that we don't have to be married or have children to give birth to something beautiful and important. She pushed efforts that undeniably changed the lives of many Black women for the better. She founded the Women's Industrial Club of Kentucky and the National Association of Wage Earners, helped mobilize the International Council of Women of the Darker Races, served on the executive committee of the Baptist World Alliance, wrote a recurring column for *The Courier,* and served as the editor of *The Worker* magazine.[40] Perhaps one of her most beloved initiatives, however, was giving birth to the National Training School for Women and Girls in 1909. The school operated under the Woman's Convention of the National Baptist Convention, and its aim was to help every student become "the fiber of a sturdy moral, industrious and intellectual woman."[41] Nannie "championed the respect and dignity of working women,"[42] honoring domestic work and workers and defying narrow constructions of the middle class's idea of true womanhood, saying, "We are not less honorable if we are servants. Fidelity to duty, rather

37. Quoted in Collier-Thomas, *Jesus, Jobs, and Justice,* 133.

38. Collier-Thomas, *Jesus, Jobs, and Justice,* 129.

39. Holmes, *Carved in Ebony,* 59.

40. Holmes, *Carved in Ebony,* 59–60.

41. Quoted in "Trades Hall of National Training School for Women and Girls," National Park Service, last updated November 13, 2020, www.nps.gov/places/national-training-school-for-women-and-girls.htm.

42. Betty Livingston Adams, *Black Women's Christian Activism: Seeking Social Justice in a Northern Suburb* (New York: New York University Press, 2016), 44.

than the grade of one's occupation is the true measure of character." She also said, "[Servants are] too honest, industrious and independent . . . to be debased by idleness. [They] have character enough for queens."[43]

Nannie Helen Burroughs teaches us the honor of being a servant and encourages us to measure our greatness and excellence by our work ethic and faithfulness to whatever endeavors we pursue. Positions, titles, salaries, and worldly prominence aren't what make us great; we should be known by our character.

Her methods and philosophies often resulted in her being referred to as the female Booker T. Washington. Instead of complaining when life is hard or quitting when doors are shut in our faces, we should follow in the footsteps of Nannie Helen Burroughs, who pushed through poverty, racism, sexism, and colorism. She pushed movements, she pushed the church, she pushed buttons, and she pushed her people. She also pushed Christian values and used her understanding of her faith to defend others and to hold people accountable to truth and justice. Until the very end of her life, she was a doer, a pusher, and a life giver who wouldn't be denied.

May her life and words inspire you to live out your purpose as a life giver: "What we need are mental and spiritual giants who are aflame with a purpose."[44] Do you know how you become a mental and spiritual giant? You do the things that help you grow. You abide in Christ, become a student of God's Word, observe and learn the culture you are called to live in, serve others, develop a fearlessness to say and do hard things that comes from first fearing God, and hang around other women who are giants to learn their ways. Nannie is just one mental and spiritual giant you can learn from, but find others who will set your purpose aflame and cheer you on as you give life. Consider, What is one specific area where you can become a life giver in your family, church, and community? How might those places begin to come alive for God's glory if you put your hand to the plow and push like Nannie?

43. "The Colored Woman and Her Relation to the Domestic Problem," quoted in Adams, *Black Women's Christian Activism,* 44–45.

44. Nannie Helen Burroughs, "Unload the Leeches and Parasitic 'Toms' and Take the Promised Land," c. 1933, Archives of Women's Political Communication, Iowa State University, accessed February 10, 2024, https://awpc.cattcenter.iastate.edu/2019/09/27/a-celebrated-speech-by-a -celebrated-woman.

The World May Not Know Their Names, but You Do

We all have our personal stories of heroes and life givers that we need to honor. Some of these life givers, like the women we've learned about, have made a lot of good noise as they birthed businesses, ministries, missions, and movements against tremendous opposition and adversity. However, you don't have to change the world or have your name in a history book to be a life giver. Many women who deserve to be honored, like you and many women you know, have quietly and faithfully given life to their places of work, families, churches, and neighbors.

For me, it's my beautiful, resilient mother, Etta Mae King Taylor, who quietly loved me, nurtured me, and raised me to fear God and use my gifts for his glory as she worked as a public school English teacher and served at our church. She demonstrated what it looked like to be a godly wife, mother, and woman. She sacrificially poured her life into me as she fought cancer and a host of other illnesses. Through her delicious cooking, hospitality, generosity, commitment to education, and consistency in teaching me the Scriptures, my mom will always be the greatest life giver I know next to Jesus. I saw what few others saw: a wife, mother, grandmother, and sister who pushed to give life despite her limitations. Since my mother's death in January 2024, I've seen the power of a life giver's legacy. My mother was sick for a long time, so when she died, she didn't have life insurance because no one would insure someone as sick as she was. But my mother left me a far greater inheritance than money. Her words, wisdom, and wealth in Christ have been passed down to me. Her joy in life, her strength and sensitivity, her comedic nature, her ability to thrive in adversity, her commitment to the Lord and her family, and so much more are what she deposited in me that death cannot steal. I'll spend the rest of my days pushing to be a life giver who reflects that she ran her race well. In her honor, I'll be making eternal deposits in my home, the church, and women all over the world.

Sister Martina Lambert, the woman who discipled me, has also always been a life giver for me. She's spent time with me like I was her own flesh and blood. She's given life to my ministry by affirming my call and giving me my first opportunity to preach at her women's ministry. She's opened her home, her heart, and her Bible to help mature my faith in Christ. She's spent hours just loving me, caring for my family, gently reproving me when I needed correction, and pushing me to be everything God called me to be.

> **The hidden figures who modeled being life givers for you need to be encouraged and told that their labor wasn't in vain.**

These women and many more have been life givers for me, and I'm thankful. Though their names aren't in lights and they aren't known around the world, I know them, and I hold their lights and pushiness within me.

Who are the life givers and the pushy women who have shaped you? Who are the quiet life givers who remind you in simplicity and obscurity that you can be a life giver of great worth? If you are able, I implore you to connect with them, honor them, and let them know how thankful you are for their impact. The hidden figures who modeled being life givers for you need to be encouraged and told that their labor wasn't in vain.

A Gospel Vision for Your Purpose

A gospel vision for your purpose is rooted in the truth that God called your foremother Eve to be a life giver and he has also called you to do the same. To be a life giver in the fullest sense is not only to raise biological and spiritual children to love God but also to give life by doing fearless, sacrificial, world-shaping things (like the women we talked about in this chapter), as well as simply obeying God faithfully in the daily rhythms of life in your job, your church, and your home. Where you bring truth, love, care, compassion, and commitment to Christ without compromise, you are being a life giver for God's glory.

Discussion Questions

 LIGHT: God gave you your purpose as a life giver.

1. How do we see the gospel at work in Eve and all women called to be life givers?

2. Have you ever been called "pushy"? How did that make you feel and respond?

LENS: We should reframe what it means to be a pushy woman and celebrate all pushy women who give life for God's glory.

1. How is being pushy as a life giver a calling, not a curse or character flaw, for Black women?

2. Who are some women pushers from Scripture and in your own life who inspire you to fulfill your purpose as a life giver too?

LOVE: God loves us so much that even when we sin, we don't lose our purpose to give life.

1. Just like Eve, you don't need to have led a perfect life to have your God-given purpose intact. How have you experienced redemption and God preserving your purpose?

2. Which life giver from this chapter most inspired or challenged you? What lessons are you taking from her life to fulfill your purpose to push and be a life giver?

CHAPTER 3

All My Life I Had to Fight

A Gospel Vision for Black Women's Hurt and Healing in the Church

The LORD is near the brokenhearted;
he saves those crushed in spirit.
—**Psalm 34:18**

For many Black women, Sofia, played by Oprah Winfrey in the movie *The Color Purple,* personifies our pain and frustration with the fight we've been in, it feels like, from birth. One of her character's famous quotes is "All my life I had to fight."[1] It's a statement that speaks to a fight you probably can relate to. As Black women, we often find ourselves contending with people in our families, in our jobs, in the political landscape, and in the church. I'm sure you've had experiences when you felt like you had to fight for respect, love, agency, dignity, peace, the freedom to be great without being despised, and the freedom to be weak without being discarded.

Unfortunately, many Black women can personally empathize with Sofia and her well-known speech from the movie: "A girl child ain't safe in a family of men. But I ain't never thought I'd have to fight in my own house. I loves Harpo. God knows I do. But I'll kill him dead before I let him beat me."[2] Oftentimes, Harpo is someone they know, someone they

1. *The Color Purple,* directed by Steven Spielberg (Burbank, Calif.: Warner Bros., 1985).
2. *The Color Purple.*

trust, someone they love, and at times, it's someone in the church, or an entire system.

Despite hearing the cliché "The church is a hospital for sick people," most people have a reasonable expectation that the church isn't perfect but that it should be a haven where—from the pulpit to the back pew— there is mutual respect, love, protection, and grace to grow in Christ. However, for some Black women, this hope of a spiritual haven has instead felt like a Harpo, where abuse of power, gaslighting, invisibility, silencing, and exclusion are confusingly co-mingled with acts of kindness, words of love, community service, Spirit-filled worship, and talk of God. Like Sofia with Harpo, many Black women genuinely love the church, yet we often have deep cognitive dissonance around loving people who have harmed us. Perhaps that's one reason church hurt hurts so bad. The love for Harpo is real and deep.

There is nothing more destabilizing and disorienting than loving someone or something that brings you harm. Church hurt is additionally more painful because, whether realistic or not, we often have higher expectations for the people of God. Like the character Sofia said, "I ain't never thought I'd have to fight in my own house," and no Christian woman wants to fight in her house or God's house. It's too easy for Black women to be labeled under the unfortunate stereotype that we are angry, aggressive, hard to get along with, and eager to fight. The fuller story shows the truth, depth, and righteousness behind why we fight and what we're fighting for. While Sofia's physical fight jumped out at us on-screen, it embodied our long spiritual,

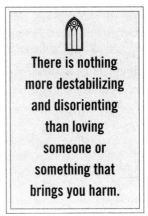

There is nothing more destabilizing and disorienting than loving someone or something that brings you harm.

mental, and emotional struggle—a fight for respect, love, agency, dignity, peace, and the freedom to unclench our fists and relax our shoulders, to be safe in the household of faith.

Unlike the character Sofia, though, we aren't vowing to—nor am I suggesting that the solution is to—kill Harpo. But maybe in our attempt to survive our church hurt, something else has died. Could it be that we've let the broken system or the broken person who hurt us kill our trust, our attendance, our willingness to serve, our confidence in Scripture, our unity, and, in the worse cases, our relationships with God? How have Black women been hurt in the church—how have you been hurt? Let's go there and name it, because you can't heal what you don't name and you can't fix what you don't face. But more than calling the hurt out, we must also seek God for the wisdom to begin doing something about church hurt in a way that honors him and will ultimately heal us *and* the church.

Let's seek the gospel of Jesus for the light, lens, and love we need to heal and change—not just for ourselves but for his church. My hope is that truth and compassion will unite us and help us name the hurt, consider how the gospel encourages us to deal with church pain, and discover some practical beginning steps for us to take for real healing and lasting change.

This topic is of such importance that I've divided it into two parts. This chapter (part 1) focuses on naming and defining some of Black women's experiences. We are so diverse and come from such an array of backgrounds that I wanted to make space to not rush through naming these hurts and how we experience them. Part 2 focuses on healing from church hurt. In the next chapter, I will cover considerations for optimizing your healing journey with some practical steps and suggestions.

What Is Church Hurt?

Church hurt has become such a loaded phrase that as soon as you hear it, you can instantly think of a personal experience or know someone who can. Church hurt is real, and for those who have experienced it, you know that it can leave wounds on your mind, family, and faith. It's important to also recognize that not all church hurt experiences are the same. This short but loaded catchphrase can be used to represent a range of experiences from "I've been damaged" to "I disagreed with something, and they didn't see it my way." I like the definition Pastor

Jerome Gay, Jr., used in his book on the subject: "*Church hurt* refers to the pain inflicted by religious institutions, their members, and/or their leadership—a pain that distances sufferers from their communities and sometimes from God."[3]

Despite the range of church hurt experiences and unmet expectations, it's imperative that we as Black women feel seen in our difficult task of speaking up and working to hold others accountable when we are injured. You, like many other Black women, may have had the difficult task of courageously levying charges against your offenders. Perhaps you've made yourself vulnerable to scrutiny and cross-examination and even experienced retribution for speaking up, only to see those who harmed you walk free with no consequences, continuing to serve, being honored members of the congregation, and in some cases continuing to pastor a church.

When you hear "church hurt," what do you think and feel? Using the checklist below, what words or phrases resonate with you regarding church hurt? If you are a Black woman in leadership, do you have experiences of being accused of church hurt that make your views on it more layered?

> **Despite the range of church hurt experiences and unmet expectations, it's imperative that we as Black women feel seen in our difficult task of speaking up and working to hold others accountable when we are injured.**

☐ Sad   ☐ Fearful
☐ Abuse   ☐ Angry
☐ Shame   ☐ Bitter
☐ Silenced   ☐ Resigned
☐ Alone   ☐ Unfair

3. Jerome Gay, Jr., *Church Hurt: Holding the Church Accountable and Helping Hurt People Heal* (Bellingham, Wash.: Renown, 2022), 5.

- ☐ Complicated
- ☐ Misunderstood
- ☐ Failure
- ☐ Sin
- ☐ Ignored
- ☐ Powerless
- ☐ Crime
- ☐ Unmet Expectations
- ☐ Unexpressed Expectations
- ☐ Why Me
- ☐ I'll Be Fine
- ☐ Left the Church
- ☐ Broken Trust
- ☐ Blame
- ☐ Tears
- ☐ Embarrassed

- ☐ I Hurt Someone
- ☐ Forgiveness
- ☐ Shock
- ☐ Nothing Will Change
- ☐ Spiritual Attack
- ☐ Lies
- ☐ Leadership
- ☐ Rebellion
- ☐ Power
- ☐ Immaturity
- ☐ Triggered
- ☐ Members
- ☐ Overexaggerating
- ☐ Lack of Accountability
- ☐ Used

Throughout this chapter, we will give voice not just to the hurt we've felt but also to the hurt we've dealt. I believe the church would be on a better path to real healing if we talked and cried about both. As a member and leader in the church, I've witnessed and personally been on both sides of the church hurt equation. I've been hurt by leaders and parishioners. And I've caused hurt to leaders and parishioners, which I deeply regret and have repented of to God and to the people I'm aware I injured. I've lost copious amounts of sleep after being deeply injured by both men and women in the church. Despite the popular narrative, it's not only men who hurt Black women in the church. In my years of experience in ministry, I've seen so many women who were hurt by other women. Again, to use *The Color Purple,* it was another Black woman, Celie, who told Harpo to beat Sofia. Celie had been abused by men, and she was now encouraging a man to abuse another woman.

It's imperative that we balance our journeys of healing with boldness and humility. It's okay and necessary to see yourself as a victim when you indeed are one. It's not healthy to normalize disrespect, abuse, or silence or to diminish and ignore your suffering. However, it also doesn't help us to see ourselves only as victims, because we all are more like David than we realize. We have Uriahs, and we have Sauls—we cause hurt (plot against and murder), and we get hurt (become hated and hunted). Even still, God called David "a man after my own heart" (Acts 13:22). God's love, mercy, and grace are big enough and powerful enough for us, both the hurt and the hurters.

When you understand this, it helps you embrace another hard truth: God loves the person who hurt you in the church, even though he doesn't condone their offense. God loves the person you may hate. God loves the person you are trying to forget, distance yourself from, slander, sue, bring charges against, and maybe rightfully send to jail. He loves them and you. Ultimately, he wants to bring you and them healing and, in many cases, restoration as an extension of the salvation, reconciliation, and healing he provided for us on the cross. That's a hard pill to swallow, but making peace with this is sometimes the first step in your healing journey. God loves you and your offender. God wants to heal everyone who is broken, even the one who broke you.[4]

> There is hope for your healing from church hurt. What may shock you the most is that both the blessing and irony of being a part of God's family are that sometimes the hurt and the help are all in the house.

My deepest prayer is that we will not only talk about the problems but also allow the gospel to light a path to a place of healing for our hearts, our relationships, and our fractured faith. This isn't an easy journey of healing that I'm inviting you on—it isn't a journey that can be spelled out with a simple one-size-fits-all ten-step plan—but there is hope for your healing from church hurt. What may shock you the most is that both the blessing and irony of being a part of God's family are that sometimes the hurt and the help are all in the house.

4. Romans 5:6–10.

How Are Black Women Hurt in the Church?

From my personal experience, reading, and anecdotal data collected from my years of counseling, leading in church, serving, and ministering to women, I've compiled this list to represent more obvious categories as well as hurts we don't often name. I hope I've captured many of the categories of hurt you can relate to as a Black woman.

I want to encourage you to name the hurt for yourself. Please add to what I've written and share your own testimonies of hurt and healing in safe communities. I believe it's important to tell your stories so that other women don't feel alone; so that the church can listen, lament, and learn in hope of changing; and, most important, because your hurt deserves a witness. Your life, pain, and path to healing matter to the Lord.

I also want to affirm that I know, like you may know, many churches that are loving, mobilizing, valuing, protecting, and growing from the life, faithfulness, sacrifice, and wisdom of Black women. There are many church leaders and members of various congregations who are grateful to God for our presence, gifts, love, leadership, wisdom, and faith. If you are a Black woman who can read this chapter and say, "None of this is my experience in church," you, my sister, are in the minority. I hope you will take this time to thank God and let your leadership know how much you appreciate them.

In the next chapter, I will explore some ways we can begin to heal from church hurt, but first, let's give language to the hurts we've endured, and with God, we'll start to find our way to healing.

We Are Hurt When We Are "Mis-seen"

Being mis-seen for Black women is a complicated mix of being invisible on one hand and overseen on the other. To be mis-seen is to never be thought of, listened to, or believed while being relegated to a lower status than our rightful place as image bearers of God. This may seem strange because women in most Black churches make up between 70 and 90 percent of the congregation.[5] How could we ever be invisible? When we're part of a culture that at times sees our physical presence, our problems, and our bodies but disconnects them from the totality of the intrinsic value of our personhood, we're at risk of being mis-seen. Let me break this down further.

Mis-seen as Invisibility

Black women sometimes feel scanned in the church but not seen, particularly Black women in white or more diverse spaces. Diminished visibility equals diminished perceived value. When we are mis-seen, we aren't seen as valuable contributors to the life of the church; we aren't seen as women who can lead, teach, organize, cast vision, develop ministries, add value in the creative spaces of the church, and just be an overall asset to God's house versus a liability.

> I know, like you may know, many churches that are loving, mobilizing, valuing, protecting, and growing from the life, faithfulness, sacrifice, and wisdom of Black women.

Interestingly, based on conversations I've had, one of the consequences of being mis-seen is being overlooked relationally. Diminished value affects Black women's perceived attractiveness and availability for marriage. If you are a Black woman who worships in a space where you are looked down on, talked down to, underutilized for kingdom mission, voiceless, and ignored by leadership at best, how attractive can you be to potential suitors? Are Black women seen and celebrated in churches as "a good thing" that can bring a husband "favor from the LORD" (Proverbs 18:22)? A church culture's implicit biases toward Black women are likely seen and

---

5. Tiffany Thomas, "The Legacy of Women in the Black Church," *Christianity Today,* February 11, 2016, www.christianitytoday.com/women-leaders/2016/february/legacy-of-women -in-Black-church.html.

felt by others and, unfortunately, adopted as a lens through which Black women are viewed.

Mis-seen as Overseen

When Black women are pathologized more than praised, condemned more than consulted, eaten up in sermons instead of esteemed, used more than honored for our usefulness, and tolerated more than valued as thinkers, our mis-seenness takes the form of our being overseen since damaging stereotypes are perpetuated of our being loud, thirsty, rebellious, damaged, uncooperative, and insubmissive. Black women can't win in spaces where there is a current of disrespect flowing through the heart of the church. In some churches, the stated or unstated beliefs are that Black women aren't good parents if we aren't stay-at-home moms, we aren't special until we've married, we aren't beautiful until we've thinned our thickness and calmed our curves and straightened our hair, we aren't godly until we've shut our mouths, and we're lazy if we aren't highly educated and achieving according to the world's standards. Ironically, when we do achieve, we are often judged as being too much or not needy enough for men.

Black women are judged for being single, divorced, or single parents without even being asked how men's choices potentially put us in this state. If we are in a church culture where we can't show up in the diverse and beautiful ways that we do and be seen as flourishing in Christ, we will continue to be unfairly judged and essentially unwanted.

We Are Hurt When We Are Discipled in Whiteness

The invisibility problem Black women contend with in faith spaces is exacerbated by whiteness. We are taught that salvation affords us the opportunity to come "out of darkness into [the] marvelous light" (1 Peter 2:9), but many Black women experience being overtly or covertly discipled out of Blackness into "the marvelous white." *Whiteness* is different from white people. Whiteness is a mindset, an ideology, a way

of seeing the world that centers, elevates, and standardizes white supremacy above everything. Many Black women are discipled into whiteness in
predominantly white churches where the
ways of white women are normalized as the
standard not only for womanhood but also
for godliness. When "biblical womanhood"
is defaulted to a white-woman archetype,
everything that is Black is associated with
something that is wrong, not quite sanctified enough, unqualified, undignified, and
needing transformation and upgrading by
whiteness.[6] Our God-given personalities
and passion in how we speak, worship, raise
our children, work, wear our hair, and dress
are often labeled as ungodly because they
are frequently outside the norm of white
acceptability.

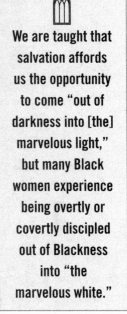

We are taught that salvation affords us the opportunity to come "out of darkness into [the] marvelous light," but many Black women experience being overtly or covertly discipled out of Blackness into "the marvelous white."

Research on intersectionality and Black
women reminds us that, in this country,
white men are considered the prototypical
man, white women are considered the
prototypical woman, and Black men are considered the prototypical
Black person. So Black women are viewed as adequately representing
neither Blackness nor womanhood, thus rendering us "metaphorically
invisible."[7] That is a staggering conclusion given that "the 'typical' Christian of the twenty-first century is not a white man [nor a white woman

6. Historically, character traits that have been upheld as a reflection of godliness are often
stereotypes of a white southern woman or "the Victorian true woman"—"one 'who, through
Christ, blesses man and helps make his home a joy and life a privilege.' White ministers described
this ideal woman as 'pliant . . . adapted [by nature] to meet man's wants . . . feminine . . . soft,
tender and delicate.'" Delores S. Williams, *Sisters in the Wilderness: The Challenge of Womanist
God-Talk* (Maryknoll, N.Y.: Orbis Books, 2013), 109.

7. David Miller, "Intersectionality: How Gender Interacts with Other Social Identities to Shape
Bias," The Conversation, February 4, 2016, http://theconversation.com/intersectionality-how
-gender-interacts-with-other-social-identities-to-shape-bias-53724.

nor a Black man] but an African woman."[8] Discipling Black women in whiteness can show up in many ways, such as these:

1. Always using white images of biblical characters.

2. Not teaching about the presence of women of color in Scripture.

3. Not including Black women theologians and scholars in church curriculum.

4. Not recognizing cultural differences as equally godly and valuable, thus allowing white supremacy, not Scripture, to define biblical femininity.

5. Placing the expectation on Black women to educate white people about racism on demand, for free, and without a care for the consequences to our mental, spiritual, or physical health.

6. Encouraging Black women to shrink because we are seen as lacking gentle spirits—the Sapphire stereotype.

7. Prioritizing one-on-one discipleship, where it's often a white woman discipling a Black woman but rarely a Black woman discipling a white woman. White Christians prefer one-on-one discipleship, while Black Christians typically prefer communal or group discipleship, mentorship, and study.[9]

8. Rejecting Black women's presentation in worship, teaching, leadership, voice tone, mannerisms, confidence, appearance, and the variety of other ways we show up.

---

8. Vince L. Bantu, *A Multitude of All Peoples: Engaging Ancient Christianity's Global Identity* (Downers Grove, Ill.: IVP Academic, 2020), 2.

9. A Barna study revealed that Black Christians "preferred group-based discipleship to one-on-one . . . while white Christians favored being discipled on their own." Black Christians are "four times more likely than white Christians to list study groups as 'very important' to their spiritual development." Additionally, the "group mindset" for mentorship and spiritual development is a core feature in Black communities. Kate Shellnutt, "How Black and White Christians Do Discipleship Differently," *Christianity Today*, January 13, 2017, www.christianitytoday.com/news/2017/january/how-black-white-christians-discipleship-differently.html. I will add that group discipleship is the prevailing model seen in Scripture.

9. Exalting stay-at-home moms over working moms or home-schooling over sending children to brick-and-mortar schools, which discounts how many Black women have prayerfully considered how to honor God and remain virtuous as they make personal choices to mother and provide for their families or to offset the difficulties systemic oppression has imposed on their lives and livelihood.

10. Encouraging Black women to buy into the lie of Christian nationalism, be deaf to the needs of other Black and Brown people, deny the impacts of race and class, declare that "all lives matter" when we are burying Black bodies after state-sanctioned lynching, or strip off Black culture and diasporic Christian ways of faithfully living, musing, and flourishing for the glory of God.

> **We also don't have to lay down our Blackness as we pick up our crosses. As Black women, we must honor the supremacy of Christ.**

Whiteness is church hurt wherever it lives. If you ever find yourself in a context where your Blackness is despised or your unique expressions of Christianity are excluded, it's important to remember that, "despite the persisting association of the Christian faith with Western culture/whiteness, Christianity has always been a global religion that spread from Jerusalem in every direction."[10] Know, my sister, that God intended for your Blackness to beautifully represent Christ throughout the world and in your local church.

We can correct the effects of being discipled in whiteness by actively decentering whiteness and by having "conversations about colorism, anti-blackness, anti-indigenous sentiments and embodied solidarity among mi-

---

10. Bantu, *Multitude of All Peoples,* 3.

nority communities."[11] This includes creating, seeking, and appreciating the communal and intergenerational discipleship that has been a staple in our heritage and Black church history and having conversations around Black womanhood, Black women theologians, Black women in leadership, Black parenting, and Black love.

Decentering whiteness doesn't mean centering Blackness but centering Christ. We don't tear down white supremacy by erecting Black supremacy; Christ is supreme above all.[12] But we also don't have to lay down our Blackness as we pick up our crosses. As Black women, we must honor the supremacy of Christ without diminishing or minimizing the bodies and unique lives God gave us to image him. God made you, Black woman, and you are good, like everything he made. If what he created and called good is unwelcomed, you should go where everything and everyone he made is welcomed and celebrated.

We Are Hurt When We Are Harshly Criticized

Black women, like all people, need truth with grace as we are being sanctified into the image of Christ. We deserve to be seen for more than our sins or areas of needed growth, and we are hurt by harsh, critical, and condemning engagement. Some of us have experienced the church criticizing more than discipling, equipping, and encouraging us. When we are treated as if nothing we do is ever right or good enough, it is demoralizing, makes us hyper-self-conscious, and leaves us feeling unsafe and unwelcomed.

Like everyone else, we aren't perfect, and we need truth. But not being perfect doesn't give anyone the right to keep us under the proverbial microscope of judgment, where we are dissected and picked apart. Being a part of a healthy church community doesn't mean we are exempt from being challenged, especially when we exhibit patterns of sin-

---

11. Juliany González Nieves, "Building a Longer Table: Decentering Whiteness in Our (Re) conciliation Conversations," Legacy Disciple, July 30, 2019, https://legacydisciple.org/index .php/2019/07/30/building-a-longer-table-decentering-whiteness-in-our-reconciliation -conversations.

12. Colossians 1:15–20.

ful behavior and attitudes that don't reflect a heart submitted to Christ. Godly correction is an act of love that should be respected.[13] However, being a part of a healthy church community should mean leaders also humbly welcome grace-filled critique and correction from Black women without responding with retribution, like blackballing us from ministry or caricaturing us as problem women because we dared to speak up.

We Are Hurt When We Are Abused

Black women deserve to be emotionally, spiritually, and physically safe. We deserve to be protected, believed, and defended, but we haven't always felt that way in God's house. There are several behaviors that have wounded Black women for which the church must confess and repent, such as mishandled domestic violence reports where women were asked to share blame with the people who abused them, were given scriptures and counseled to stay submitted in abusive relationships, were discouraged from going to the police, or were told that their abusers should be "won over without a word."[14] The church must also confess and repent of allowing leaders and laymen to be sexual predators, covering up abuse, blaming and shaming victims, and turning a blind eye to women's suffering by forgoing accountability and church discipline.

We have been hurt in the church when leadership abuses their power and takes advantage of us sexually. This can happen as an outgrowth of a counseling relationship in the church where there are no checks and balances, the counselor is not trained in managing transference and countertransference issues that arise, and the power differential in the relationship extinguishes a woman's ability to say no or perceive the sexual advances as wrong. Sexual abuse can also occur in the form of harassment through inappropriate comments about a woman's appearance, objectification of a woman's body, and inappropriate or explicit talk, texts, or social media messages that can function as a type of grooming.

I've never forgotten the numerous times a pastor or other leader was

13. Hebrews 12:5–11.
14. 1 Peter 3:1–2.

sexually inappropriate with me. I've been kissed on the mouth by a leader when rising from prayer at the altar. While in college, I was asked by a pastor if I would take a bath with him. I've been groped and looked at lustfully. I've heard inappropriate comments about how my body looked or how lucky any man who was with me would be. I know I'm not alone in any of these experiences. We know when we are being harassed, and we can sense when something is off. Sometimes we strike back in anger; sometimes we tell; but most times, like I did, we freeze in shock and embarrassment, then wonder what we must have done to "invite" that gross treatment. It's a disgusting and belittling feeling when someone who holds himself out as a man of God behaves this way toward us.

> **Black women deserve to be emotionally, spiritually, and physically safe. We deserve to be protected, believed, and defended, but we haven't always felt that way in God's house.**

In addition to the sexual abuse, another injury occurs when other men and women cover for the abuser and gaslight or retaliate against the victim. Too often, a leader's lifestyle of fornication and abuse of power is a long-standing known fact that the leader's handlers, and even sometimes family, turn from and look the other way. This silence leaves many women vulnerable to being victims and blamed for a leader's offenses. When other leaders preach at the abuser's church and conferences and support their ministry, it creates secondary hurt and often disappointment at the leaders who knew but stood by, said nothing, and financially gained from the relationship.

As Black women, we've experienced various forms of spiritual abuse by having the Word of God weaponized against us to manipulate, intimidate, and control us. We've been blasted by sermons from "bully pulpits" to rebuke us or deliver personal angry messages to us that should have happened in private conversations pursuing biblical reconciliation. We don't come to church to be degradingly lectured or shamed by misogynistic comments that might be said from the pulpit or at meetings couched in jokes. Fear about our safety and growing distrust can cause us to disengage from the church in ways that reduce our ability to connect with and trust men or church leaders. The insidious ways emotional and spiritual abuse operates often mean the abuse lasts much longer than instances of sexual abuse and goes undetected, except by the person experiencing it, and even then, sometimes the victim doesn't have language to name the hurt they are enduring. Abuse by a leader in the church is so confusing and damaging because there is an assumption of the leader's goodness, trustworthiness, rightness, and untouchability. The abuse of Black women thrives in environments where secret keeping is the culture, man is an idol, and "Do not touch my anointed ones or harm my prophets" (1 Chronicles 16:22) is misused to excuse abusive behavior.

We Are Hurt When We Are Treated as Theologically Uninterested

For centuries our culture has believed that the STEM professions should be reserved for boys and that girls are better suited for liberal arts or home economics. Some Christian spaces are no better, demonstrating they don't believe intellectual spiritual pursuits are in women's wheelhouse. However, not only are we as Black women flocking to our Bibles, but we are also graduating from seminaries. Perhaps you, too, are writing books and curriculum, teaching, preaching, and pursuing God with all your heart on a large platform or just faithfully in your home, community, business, job, and local church. Black women are also one of the fastest-rising demographics of more highly educated,[15] business-starting/entrepreneurial,[16] well-read groups.[17] We desire intellectually challeng-

15. Rachaell Davis, "New Study Shows Black Women Are Among the Most Educated Group in the United States," Essence, October 27, 2020, www.essence.com/news/new-study-black-women -most-educated.

16. Donna Kelley, Mahdi Majbouri, and Angela Randolph, "Black Women Are More Likely to Start a Business than White Men," *Harvard Business Review,* May 11, 2021, https://hbr .org/2021/05/black-women-are-more-likely-to-start-a-business-than-white-men.

17. Philip Bump, "The Most Likely Person to Read a Book? A College-Educated Black Woman," *The Atlantic,* January 16, 2014, www.theatlantic.com/culture/archive/2014/01/ most-likely-person-read-book-college-educated-black-woman/357091.

ing Christian studies and books and deep biblical engagement. We need the church to support and encourage us in this pursuit of God.

Women's ministry shouldn't just be focused on craft making, shopping trips, recipe swaps, and home management talks. There is nothing wrong with those events; in fact, many women need those skills (some younger generations were never taught), and such events create beautiful opportunities for women to relax and bond. My point, however, is that ministry to women should be balanced and that the previously mentioned activities aren't all that women should be driven toward. We are hurt because there isn't space for us to learn topics like systematic theology, Bible study methods, apologetics, and church history. We also don't typically have readily available access to conferences, teaching materials, and leadership development, and when many of us graduate from seminary, too few of us have places or positions to bring our education and willingness to work within our local churches.

We Are Hurt by a Perceived Hierarchal Relationship Status

Marital elitism and single servitude continue to hurt us. While marriage is a beautiful gift from God, I also know that if the Lord hasn't called a woman to marriage, it shouldn't be viewed as a character flaw. We don't say that it is, but the way some churches treat married and single women may communicate something very different. If you are a single woman, you are no less important or more in need of sanctification than married women.

Marital elitism is when marriage is seen as the supreme evolution of the human experience. This sends the message that if you aren't married, you have more maturing to do and that singleness is a mark of God's dissatisfaction with your life. Single women may be talked down to or treated like the workhorses of the church, as if their lives, jobs, commitments, and time aren't as valuable as a married woman's. Married women are even sometimes given preferential treatment for leadership or disciple-maker roles.

Single women, especially those who live alone, often have basic needs that aren't considered by the church (snow shoveling, assistance when they are sick or need care at home, meals, household repairs, etc.). However, I've seen the church readily send out Meal Train sign-ups for married women after they give birth. The church brings food over or helps families when they are in financial need but rarely steps up this way for a single woman.

We all have busy and demanding lives riddled with strife, grief, spiritual warfare, and various other forms of suffering. We all deserve support, respect, care, and permission to rest when needed. Ultimately, these hierarchal structures around marital status hurt both single and married women as they teach us to each view our value based on our relationship to a man, give married women a false sense of superiority or spiritual maturity, and diminish the power of both callings to be useful in God's kingdom. Additionally, the enemy uses this tension to sow seeds of discord and create a wedge between married and single women that shouldn't exist. As women, we are called to support and learn from one another, as God used both married and single women throughout Scripture.

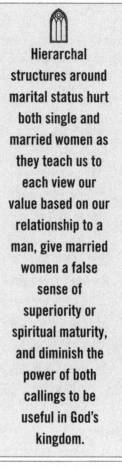

Hierarchal structures around marital status hurt both single and married women as they teach us to each view our value based on our relationship to a man, give married women a false sense of superiority or spiritual maturity, and diminish the power of both callings to be useful in God's kingdom.

We Are Hurt When Our Gifts Aren't Discerned, Developed, and Deployed

The Bible tells us that the Holy Spirit decides which gifts people should have and distributes them as he wills.[18] It also teaches that the body (the church) is called to appreciate its need for the diverse gifts, receive the various members of the body with their gifts, and equip all people, in-

18. 1 Corinthians 12:11.

cluding women, for the work of ministry.[19] When both men and women are seen as having gifts from the Spirit that are crucial to the health, growth, and unity of the body of Christ, the church functions as God intended it to function.

However, the lack of appreciation, reception, and equipping of Black women's gifts in churches has been the source of much hurt. We've been shut down and shut out of ministry and comprehensive service within the church based on gender, race, and status to the detriment of the flourishing of the local and global church.

> When both men and women are seen as having gifts from the Spirit that are crucial to the health, growth, and unity of the body of Christ, the church functions as God intended it to function.

While we may not all agree on how Scripture articulates limits and freedoms for women in ministry, as there are scholarly arguments for various positions,[20] we shouldn't let this create disfellowship and disunity. We can support, encourage, and love one another despite some of our theological differences. I encourage you to ask questions and study to discern whether church practices that limit the authority of women reflect biblical faithfulness, though they are unpopular in the culture and contradict our personal preferences, or whether the limits are extrabiblical prohibitions functioning as hideouts for sexism cloaked in complementarianism. It's painful that so much division has arisen over this issue, and I take great offense on behalf of many of my sisters when people callously injure and demonize other Black women who don't arrive at the same conclusions but are committed to faithfully serving the Lord and are bearing much fruit.

19. 1 Corinthians 12:12–31; Ephesians 4:11–16.
20. See James R. Beck, ed., *Two Views on Women in Ministry*, rev. ed. (Grand Rapids, Mich.: Zondervan, 2005).

We Are Hurt When We Are Used and Discarded

The sad irony of Black women being used and discarded is that it shows our gifts, impact, and contributions are necessary and build up the church just like those of our brothers. However, we are often rendered powerless despite our work and left unseen, uncredited, and unpaid. Black women who have the desire to be seen, given credit, and paid run the risk of seeming "un-Christian" in light of the scriptures that point to God's opposition to the proud and the admonishment to not be selfishly ambitious.[21] I don't want to discard the importance of those scriptures, but too often in church culture, the only people being seen, receiving attribution, holding power, and getting paid are the men. Our church history tells us that women have been the backbone of the church for years. These same women have labored and watched men take the credit, money, and positions because of their egos, not biblical reasoning.

Black women have reported proposing a ministry idea, doing research, spending their own money to help advance it, and doing the behind-the-scenes grunt work, all to have their entire idea co-opted and then given to a man with less experience or knowledge. In some cases, women have been asked to train men to take paid jobs for the work the women were previously doing as volunteers. A man is often needed to be the face of the ministry, even if it's a woman who designed and implemented it. A man is most often given credit for the success, and then the woman is told "thank you" behind the scenes, if at all. When women are used and not considered worthy of respect, the practice of taking from women without gratitude, attribution, or honorable pay feels natural and right, but that shouldn't be the case.

We Are Hurt by "Sister Cliques"

Many Black women have been hurt by the difficulty of finding a path into established friendship groups at churches, especially when they are new

21. Philippians 2:3; James 4:6–7.

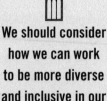

We should consider how we can work to be more diverse and inclusive in our friendships and more intentional about learning from and living among others who are different from us.

members or when groups form and remain in silos. When friendship cultivation is stressful because of closed relational cliques, Black women feel alone and disappointed that the church hasn't lived up to its claims of offering healthy biblical communities for them to grow and be loved in. When groups of women fellowship only with their same type of Christian women, whether it be by race, status (marital, financial, able-bodied, educational, etc.), or age, it immediately others people and creates divisions. This doesn't discount the benefit of sometimes spending time with women in similar age groups or other life circumstances for relatability and support. However, as Church Girls, we should consider how we can work to be more diverse and inclusive in our friendships and more intentional about learning from and living among others who are different from us. This practice will guard our hearts against pride and the sin of partiality that can so easily divide us and injure our neighbors.

We Are Hurt by the Absence of Brother-Sister Relationships

Many churches lack the knowledge, teaching, and practical training to disciple members on how men and women should have healthy non-sexual relationships and function as brothers and sisters. Most churches have marriage and singles ministries that focus on men and women healthily relating to one another in a covenant or dating context. These ministries are helpful but limit the discussion and discipleship focus. When conversations come up about relationships between men and women, too often those relationships are romanticized, courtship and marriage are discussed, and the gift of being brothers and sisters in Christ is completely ignored. Not only are Black women hurt by the amputation of this type of relationship, but the entire family of God is also hurt when we have no imagination, encouragement, or skills on how to function as brothers and sisters *first*. When our status as siblings in Christ isn't at the forefront of our minds, women are more easily objectified for their physical attributes, judged on their quality as "wifey material," or avoided, demonized, and unassisted with normal life needs that a brother would naturally show up to help his sister with. Our brothers can also be objectified if women view and praise them only for their potential to protect, provide, procreate, and parent.

> **When we conceptualize men and women only as lovers, no one learns how to be siblings and everyone loses someone from the opposite sex whom God intended to be a great friend and family member.**

There is also a mentality that sexualizes all interactions. Instead of finding more ways for us to come together in mixed-gender community, have fun, communicate on a range of topics, and do life together, men and women are shuffled apart. Too often, married men and women are viewed as off limits for friendships with singles as if no one in the body has an ounce of self-control, which is a fruit of the Spirit.[22] Sure, we must walk in wisdom and have boundaries, but we stifle the church when we don't celebrate the family of God and help both men and women function as healthy brothers and sisters, and it particularly hurts Black women, who typically and historically bear the negative stereotypes of being loose, fast, sexually promiscuous, and temptresses. When we conceptualize men and women only as lovers, no one learns how to be siblings and everyone loses someone from the opposite sex whom God intended to be a great friend and family member.

22. Galatians 5:22–23.

Reading about church hurt may have brought up several different reactions and emotions. First, you may be rejoicing over feeling seen. Despite hurt being a difficult reality for so many Black women, there is great comfort in not feeling alone and in having our painful experiences acknowledged.

Second, you may feel angry, overwhelmed, and sad because this section brought up uncomfortable memories for you. I want to encourage you to sit with those feelings and know they are okay. You don't have to rush past them or wish them away. Your hurt and grief deserve every tear shed and every deep breath you had to take to read through this section. Honor that discomfort by noticing it and just letting it be. If you need to phone a friend, do so, because you don't have to work through your pain alone.

Third, some of you may be thinking, *I was aware of some of these hurts but never considered others.* That's a great place to be. While not every hurt or every variation was represented in this section, prayerfully, this stirred your heart with more questions, empathy, and commitment to ask other Church Girls to tell you their stories.

Fourth, you may be someone who is realizing for the first time that you've caused hurt to another Black woman, whether through your silence, gaslighting, criticism, judgment, or unwelcoming attitude. If you feel any conviction, God is at work in your heart, and it's a beautiful act of grace. Just repent. Repent to God and repent to the one you know you injured. It may seem like water under the bridge, but you can never go wrong being humble and saying sorry. Jesus died for all hurt—the hurt we feel and the hurt we've caused. Thank you, Lord, for grace.

Before moving on to part 2 of this section on hurt and healing, please take a moment to journal or discuss these questions with others:

1. Which reaction group(s) do you find yourself in after reading this chapter? Is there another category to describe where you are?

2. Which hurt(s) resonated the most with you, and why? What hurt have you experienced that wasn't named?

3. What did you discover about yourself from doing the church hurt checklist?

4. Who are your Sauls and Uriahs?

5. What is your reaction to the statement "God wants to heal everyone who is broken, even the one who broke you"?

CHAPTER 4

Breaking Free

A Gospel Vision for Black Women's Hurt and Healing in the Church

LORD my God, I called to you for help,
and you healed me.
—Psalm 30:2, NIV

Healing from church hurt is a process that will look different for each Church Girl. What worked for one may not work for you, and it's impossible to predict when you will confidently be able to say, "I've been healed," or even what healing will look like for you on this side of heaven. What I can say is that Jesus's mission statement in Luke 4 tells you that he came not only to bring you healing from your sin but also to touch and transform every area of brokenness and pain you may be experiencing. Jesus said he was anointed and came "to preach good news to the poor . . . to proclaim release to the captives and recovery of sight to the blind, to set free the oppressed, to proclaim the year of the Lord's favor" (verses 18–19). So, my sister, if your church hurt has left you in need of good news, the gospel has that. If

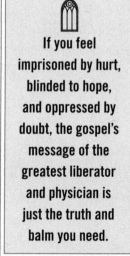

If you feel imprisoned by hurt, blinded to hope, and oppressed by doubt, the gospel's message of the greatest liberator and physician is just the truth and balm you need.

you feel poor, as if you've lost everything dear to you, the gospel can help you recover what you need. If you feel imprisoned by hurt, blinded to hope, and oppressed by doubt, the gospel's message of the greatest liberator and physician is just the truth and balm you need.

Baggage, Bandages, and Bondage

Before we get into specifics about the path to healing, I want to review three things to be aware of for our healing process.

Baggage

In her song, "Bag Lady," recording artist Erykah Badu told women that dragging heavy emotional baggage through life would hurt our proverbial backs and cause us emotional harm, and church hurt baggage can have a similar effect. Church hurt baggage is the unintentionally accumulated weight that we carry into life and other church experiences. It usually doesn't serve us in the end, but we relentlessly hold on to the emotional stuff to remind us to stay vigilant, keep our guard up, and self-protect. It makes sense, but it doesn't make things better. Baggage can change how we function in relationships with others—keeping people at a distance, lacking openness and transparency, being paranoid about the motives of people who are demonstrating kindness, avoiding social situations, and rejecting help because we believe no one can be trusted. Church hurt baggage can also affect us emotionally in various ways, such as increased depression, anxiety, hopelessness, hypersensitivity, and anger.

We don't often handle our baggage with care. Some of these behaviors can morph into bitterness, processing pain with others can turn into gossip, speaking up about a horrible situation at one church can turn into defaming all churches, calling out one unrighteous leader can turn into categorizing all leaders as bad, and warranted distrust of some people can turn into distrust of God. We can't help it if we've been injured; it's not our fault. However, when we don't heal well and we have difficulty parting with pain, we can unconsciously sentence ourselves to a life of dragging around our hurts, narratives, emotions, and beliefs about people, places, and God, like a bag lady who carries her belongings wherever she travels. Remember the admonishment of the writer of Hebrews to "lay aside every weight, and the sin which so easily ensnares us, and . . . run with endurance the race that is set before us" (12:1, NKJV).

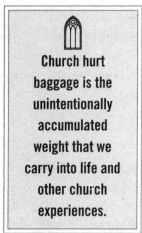

Church hurt baggage is the unintentionally accumulated weight that we carry into life and other church experiences.

The good news is that the Holy Spirit is your strength and Jesus is your burden bearer. Those of you who feel like you are carrying heavy and unhelpful baggage from church hurt, go through your bags. To go through your emotional bags, you must be willing to *stop, investigate,* and *strategize* so that you don't get paralyzed by pain and can keep moving.

I remember one day I went on a hike with friends, and I kept feeling this sharp pain in my back. I knew I needed to stop and look, but I didn't want to fall behind the group of women I was hiking with, so I kept going, trying to tough out the pain. I kept suffering, and my attitude on the hike changed. I complained as we climbed. I was mad at everyone who appeared so comfortable, taking on the rough terrain with excitement. I couldn't wait for the hike to end. I didn't notice the waterfall; I didn't notice the beautiful leaves; I had no idea what the ladies were laughing about—I was in a tunnel of pain. Pain has a way of distracting us from what is good all around us. I remember being frustrated that no one asked me if I was okay, that no one checked on me or noticed I was struggling, but I was pretending to be fine.

Finally, I couldn't take it anymore, and I said, "Hold on, y'all; I have to stop. Something is scratching my back." Everyone gladly stopped and said, "Oh no, how can we help?" I sat down, looked through my backpack, and discovered a safety pin that had come unclasped and was poking through my bag into my back. That small pin was causing a lot of pain, and all I needed to do was stop, investigate, and close the pin.

I know what you may be dealing with is far more painful than a safety pin poking through a backpack, but the point is this: If you are in pain, you should take some time to *stop, investigate* the source of the pain, and *strategize* how to deal with it so you can safely keep moving forward without emotional agony. Interestingly, since I walked for so long with the open safety pin sticking my back, once I corrected the problem, my back was still a little tender but nothing like it was before. You may still be emotionally tender, even though you are actively addressing the pain and on a healthy path of healing. You don't have to carry around heavy bags of unaddressed pain. I implore you to *stop, investigate,* and *strategize* to improve the quality of your life and lay aside that weight.

Bandages

Jesus is my doctor, He writes down all of my 'scriptions,
He gives me all of my medicines in my room.[1]

Scripture assures us that Jesus "heals the brokenhearted and binds up their wounds" (Psalm 147:3, NKJV). Just one touch from him is all we need, but when healing isn't instantaneous, Jesus also has amazing grace and offers diverse bandages as paths to accomplish healing. Bandages help stop serious cuts from bleeding out and keep germs from getting into open wounds so they can heal. Bandages also hold in place healing balm or ointment on wounds. Depending on how bad the injury is, sometimes bandages help set broken bones by keeping the area immobilized until the fracture can fuse back together. But bandages aren't permanent.

In most cases, the first bandage in our healing journey is acknowledging the hurt and grieving. Lament is an important biblical step in healing. The book of Lamentations proves that God wants us to make room to lament. But we don't stop with the bandage of lament. Some bandages will look like professional or biblical counseling. Some bandages will involve using spiritual practices like meditating on God's Word, em-

---

1. "Come On in My Room," Hymnary.org, accessed February 29, 2024, https://hymnary.org/text/come_on_in_my_room.

bracing solitude, fasting, praying, joining community support groups, and retreating with other women for peace and renewal. Some bandages will look like taking a break from a particular local church and being ministered to and cared for at another church as you sort through your feelings and experience. Some healing bandages will look like going through conflict resolution with a layperson or leader, with others lending accountability because they are committed to your healing, not covering up a failure or scandal.

Some bandages may require more in-depth trauma work or psychological intervention, especially if a church hurt experience has surfaced prior trauma and unhealed pain. Sometimes the bandage is just stepping down from a ministry you lead or serve in for a period as you heal, and other times the bandage is simply receiving a genuine apology from an offender and seeing fruit of repentance—observable and measurable change over time. Some bandages may be engaging in restorative practices on your own or with a community of healthy sisters. Other times those bandages may require you to transition entirely from a particular church if you've identified spiritual abuse and an unwillingness on the leadership's part to discuss these matters and move toward accountability, repentance, and change.

> You don't have to carry around heavy bags of unaddressed pain. I implore you to *stop, investigate,* and *strategize* to improve the quality of your life and lay aside that weight.

With physical bandages, there are different ones to accommodate the type and severity of the injury sustained. We should consider it the same for the wounds we receive in the church. Not all wounds need the same bandages, but all hurts need to heal. The prophet Jeremiah assures us that when we apply a bandage, we are in fact cooperating with God's desire to put bandages of healing on us: "I will apply a bandage unto thee, and I will heal thee of thy wounds, saith Jehovah; for they have called thee an outcast" (Jeremiah 30:17,

Darby). Seek the Lord for the types of bandages he wants to apply to your life.

Bondage

When we wear bandages perpetually, we are no longer healing well, since wounds that don't have a chance to air out often fester, causing infection. We can become dependent on our bandages in unhealthy ways, just like someone whose bones are malformed and brittle from not removing the boot, getting off the crutches, and courageously facing physical therapy. We can become like people who can't see themselves facing life without medication or without the process of venting and rehashing their hurts with their therapists but never taking the advice on how to move beyond those things. Like when wounds are bound too long, we can become septic, sensitive, overreactive to any touch, and wounded all over again—our bandages become bondage. When we are in perpetual bandages that turn into bondage, we function like mummies in a horror movie. Our movements are restricted, our voices are muffled, no one can see or experience us apart from our bandages, and we aren't living fully. God has called us to use bandages to heal and return to life with our minds and hearts intact, able to live well among others, not to be defined by our wounds.

Healing is different for everyone. You may not heal at the speed or in the way someone else thinks you should. So if you aren't healed and healthy, please don't pretend to be. Don't feel pressured to rush your process and unwrap your bandages prematurely, but know that the goal is healing, restoration, and revival of self, community, and faith. God's kingdom mission should be helped, not hindered, by your recovery. Ask God to help you discern whether brokenness, pain, and the effects of church hurt have become an unhealthy lifestyle and an adopted maladaptive identity that have shut down your entire life. Neither our offenders nor the enemy should have power over us to keep us bound when Christ came to set us free. Ask Jesus to help you get free.

If you need help unwrapping yourself from the bandages that have turned into bondage, know that Jesus will send help in the form of other sisters who have been where you are or other healthy church leaders and communities that will love you, value you, respect you, and give you space to heal. Even though no person or place is perfect, the community of God is called to "bear the infirmities of the weak" (Romans 15:1, Darby).

Steps Toward Healing

As you pray and receive help from God, here are more steps you can take toward healing.

Take Time Out or Get Out, but Don't Leave the Faith

I mentioned earlier that sometimes a bandage we need to apply is time away from leading or serving in a particular ministry as we heal. We may even need to take Jordan Peele's advice and *get out* of situations and churches so detrimental to our safety and sanity.[2] I want to offer ten suggestions for taking time out or leaving a church:

1. Take advantage of any options or systems within the church to handle crises, make reports of abuse, or follow their pathways for restoration. Sometimes leaving isn't the best or only option. It's natural to want to get away from people and places where injury has happened, but that's not always the needed response. Part of the Christian experience is embracing that disappointment and hurt will happen among the body of Christ, just like in any human relationship. The difference is that the church, more than any other place, should have the tools, power, and desire to use heaven's resources to heal and restore unity. When possible, before leaving, give the house a chance to work things out as the family of God.[3]

2. *Get Out,* directed by Jordan Peele (Universal City, Calif.: Universal Pictures, 2017).
3. I understand that some situations may require your immediate exit for safety reasons. I'm not encouraging anyone to remain in an unsafe environment where they are physically, emotionally, or

2. Tell someone from the church; don't leave without a trace. Even having just one trusted person that will be able to account for your safety is helpful. Discuss limits on what that trusted person can share. You may be fine with them discussing your reasons for leaving, or you may prefer to do that on your own at a later time. This way, your advocate or friend will be able to represent you well while maintaining your confidence.

3. Be careful of talking only to biased people. When we don't like someone or some place, we tend to seek out other people who will quickly agree with us and share the same negative opinions. I get it; I've done it too. It makes sense, especially when we are hurting, in that it helps us not feel alone and validates our feelings and experiences. However, that strategy may not be as helpful for your healing as you think. A person or group may have negative sentiments toward the same individual or church, but it may not be a similar experience, and you have no idea which point on their own healing journey and maturation you've entered. Additionally, you are communicating with only one side of the story, which can be clouded by a variety of factors.[4] My counsel is to be intentional about having balanced and unbiased people speak into your life as you heal. True healing happens in environments that are full of wisdom and love, are God fearing, and encourage you along a path to biblical reconciliation and peace.

4. Find a supportive Christian community or another place of worship you feel comfortable in to continue your faith practice. Avoid isolation at all costs.

5. Consider writing a letter to the church leadership explaining your need to take time away or reason for leaving. Be open to

---

spiritually abused or under threat. Even in the worst of cases, it's my prayer that churches will have structures and systems in place to handle injuries. Many times our wounds aren't life threatening; therefore, I'm encouraging you to give church protocols for help and healing a chance.

4. Proverbs 18:17.

possibly talking to one person in leadership in case they have follow-up questions or even just want to lend support and prayer. There are often many people who care and want to be available to you during your difficult time. Leaving a church doesn't mean every member or leader must be avoided forever. Sharing what you experienced is also helpful for churches eager to make change and address problems within their congregations. People can't fix what they don't know about. While some churches cover up problems, other churches may not know.

6. Find another faith leader or counselor to process some of your experiences with. This can dispel the myth that all leaders are the same, give you a different perspective, provide helpful next steps for healing and moving forward, and validate your painful experiences. Church hurt is so destabilizing that many times the victim doesn't trust their own mind and feelings. Having someone affirm that what you experienced was wrong or help bring clarity will protect you from minimizing or self-blame.

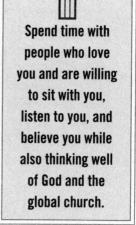

Spend time with people who love you and are willing to sit with you, listen to you, and believe you while also thinking well of God and the global church.

7. Spend time with people who love you and are willing to sit with you, listen to you, and believe you while also thinking well of God and the global church. Finding rest in the arms of someone who you know is anti-God, anti-church, and anti-Christianity is not only unhelpful but also hurtful, as this person won't view God, his Word, or the church as places for healing, truth, and restoration. When your heart is tender, it's important to be with people who love you and Jesus.

8. Educate yourself on church hurt, and find other women who are in process and building healing communities. This helps give language and understanding to what you've experienced. Many people, unfortunately, have been through what you've been through, and experts in various fields have studied, treated, and written on the subject. Become a student of your pain, not just a responder.

9. Consider people of peace at the church you are taking a break from or leaving. Too often, well-meaning people who weren't the cause of your hurt can get swept into an overall negative pile with the people who actually caused injury. You may not be ready to connect or share with a lot of people, but strive to see individuals for who they are. There may be leaders, friends from your small group, the person who was always so friendly and attentive, or other people you can stay connected to. This will guard your heart against the enemy's desire to cause you to project pain and offense onto places and people where they don't belong.

10. Prioritize reading your Bible, praying, worshipping, meditating on God's Word, and taking care of your spiritual needs. The devil would love nothing more than for our church hurt to stop us in our sanctified tracks. It's imperative to press into the Lord even more and allow his Word, love, character, and gospel to soothe and sustain us. Remember, God wants to work through your hurt with you.

Healing is spiritual warfare. As mentioned above, the enemy has plans for your church hurt that don't involve your healing or God's glory. We know that the "thief comes only to steal and kill and destroy." But as Jesus told us, he came that we "may have life and have it in abundance" (John 10:10). The context of this verse is referring to the false teachers and religious leaders who opposed Jesus, but the spirit behind that activity certainly is the devil. Church hurt is a form of spiritual warfare where the devil's goal is always more grievous and dangerous than giving you a needed break or healthy exit from a church. Consider what the devil may be attempting to rob you and God of because of your church hurt. The devil always wants to snatch away the Word of God from you.[5] He wants you to distrust God.[6] Perhaps most of all, he wants to steal your faith in God.[7]

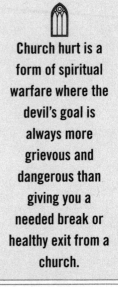

> Church hurt is a form of spiritual warfare where the devil's goal is always more grievous and dangerous than giving you a needed break or healthy exit from a church.

While Satan would like to destroy God's church, Jesus has already barred him from doing this.[8] So instead, the devil tries to take out individual members, causing them to question God, forsake the gathering of the saints, avoid reconciliation, be deceived by false teaching, compromise their witness, abandon the mission of the church to make disciples, sow seeds of discord among the family of God, and ultimately reject that the gospel of Jesus Christ is true. This is the plan of Satan, and he will cunningly use the fiery darts of church hurt to rob God of glory and sift you from the family of faith or the faith altogether.

Don't let the failures of people cause you to see God as a failure. It's okay to leave a place, but don't leave Christ. Trust that the Lord wants to continue to grow your faith and help you flourish as a member of his kingdom in a healthy, but not perfect, church.

Rightly Define Your Painful Experience

Right now in church culture, we are experiencing a rising tendency to call every disagreement, relational irritation, or church conflict a trauma

---

5. Mark 4:15; Acts 20:28–30.
6. Genesis 3:1.
7. Ephesians 6:16; 1 Peter 5:9.
8. Matthew 16:18.

or spiritual abuse. As a clinician, I know that two people can experience the same event and have completely different reactions. However, our use of the terms *trauma* and *spiritual abuse* to describe everything negative we experience at the local church is often overstating the reality. It's important to distinguish between *church hurt, trauma,* and *spiritual abuse.* These three terms are often used interchangeably, but they in fact mean different things. We've previously defined *church hurt,* but let's review *trauma* and *spiritual abuse.* The American Psychological Association defines *trauma* like this:

> Any disturbing experience that results in significant fear, helplessness, dissociation, confusion, or other disruptive feelings intense enough to have a long-lasting negative effect on a person's attitudes, behavior, and other aspects of functioning. Traumatic events include those caused by human behavior (e.g., rape, war, industrial accidents) as well as by nature (e.g., earthquakes) and often challenge an individual's view of the world as a just, safe, and predictable place.[9]

The definition for *trauma* appears broad enough to capture an array of painful experiences, including church hurt, but Kaytee Gillis presented another perspective:

> A word that [was] once rarely uttered outside of clinical discussions, "trauma" is now freely deployed by armchair psychologists all over social media. With so many throwing out words such as "trauma," and its cousin, "triggered," many argue that the true meaning of the word has been watered down, to the detriment of those who've truly experienced trauma.[10]

---

9. APA Dictionary of Psychology, s.v. "trauma," American Psychological Association, last updated April 19, 2018, https://dictionary.apa.org/trauma.
10. Kaytee Gillis, "Why Is Everything About Trauma Lately?," *Psychology Today,* June 5, 2023, www.psychologytoday.com/us/blog/invisible-bruises/202305/why-is-everything-about-trauma-lately.

Christian clinical psychologist Dr. Diane Langberg said,

Spiritual abuse involves using the sacred to harm or deceive the soul of another. . . .

When we use God's sacred Word in a way that harms another, commanding them to do wrong, manipulating them, deceiving them, or humiliating them, we have spiritually abused them. We tell them, "God says," but we don't reflect the character of the God whose words we use. We twist God's words in order to coerce, to manipulate.[11]

Our healing is affected by the use or misuse of our definitions of our experiences. There are times when we call something "no big deal" when it is in fact trauma and spiritual abuse that deserves our full attention and healthy proactive response. Other times we call church hurt *trauma* and see offenses against us in such an exaggerated and unhopeful way that we don't leave room for biblical reconciliation that could lead to deeper relationships with others and spiritual growth.

One concern is that we have lost sight of the fact that we live in a fallen world. Though we are saved, we still have the propensity to sin, and brothers and sisters in the faith will at times disagree, have anger toward one another, rebuke sharply, and cause offense.[12] However, how we respond to those things is key and determines whether we are working toward unity, maturity in the faith, healing, and peace. If we are minimizing dangerous abusive situations, compromising core doctrinal issues that rightly should cause division, or catastrophizing smaller relational hurts and infractions that are bound to happen when we do life with other humans, we are adding insult to injury.

We can't put out a seven-alarm fire with a glass of water, and we shouldn't extinguish birthday candles with a fire hose. When we understate a problem, injury and unhealthy systems are likely to continue, but when we overstate a problem, we give an exaggerated response that

11. Diane Langberg, *Redeeming Power: Understanding Authority and Abuse in the Church* (Grand Rapids, Mich.: Brazos, 2020), 127.

12. Acts 15:36–41; Galatians 2:11–14; Philippians 4:2–3; Philemon 1:8–22.

misses a gospel opportunity for personal and community healing to take place. In either case, long-term damage to people and the witness of God is at stake. Sometimes an unhelpful classification of a problem and response is more dangerous and injurious than the original injury.

I want to encourage you with these four points as you process your experiences:

1. Ask God to help you see the problem and solution accurately over time. Like with any injury, the initial shock of an experience may cause us to misdefine it. We should be open to revisiting it, processing it with God, and praying for insight, wisdom, and clarity. This act of humility—to ask God for wisdom[13]—doesn't mean we ignore or distrust our feelings; rather, it keeps us dependent on an all-knowing God for understanding and revelation about our feelings.

2. Get counsel and assistance from diverse and healthy Christians to help you navigate the waters of church hurt, trauma, or spiritual abuse. Counseling will also help you connect the dots in your possible history of trauma and its influence on your church experience.

3. Journal. Write down your experiences so that you have documentation. Writing is also a means of airing out the soul. Writing helps us clearly see the source of our unpleasant feelings, own our experiences, process emotions we have about ourselves and others, and recognize patterns. It also reduces stress and alleviates some of the pressure in our minds from ruminative thoughts or emotional flooding.

4. Record yourself talking through your experiences. Some of us are verbal processors and find talking through things unscripted much easier than writing (I'm like this). While talking to others is helpful, we may feel the need to edit ourselves or feel self-

13. James 1:5–8.

conscious about sharing some details, especially as we are trying to sort through our memories. People who have experienced trauma often have problems with their memory that can, at first glance, make them look untrustworthy in their storytelling.[14] Recording yourself without a time limit or pressure to get everything perfect can be helpful in processing your story. Also, going back to listen to yourself over time can bring clarity and encourage self-empathy.

Discerning a Healthy Community for Healing

There is an African proverb that says, "If a child doesn't feel the embrace of the village, it will burn it down to feel its warmth." This proverb emphasizes the need of people, particularly the most vulnerable among us, to feel love and acceptance from their communities. Healthy Christian communities don't leave the hurting out in the cold; rather, they embrace those who are hurting and isolated, and they obey the call to wrap their warm arms around those who are in pain.

While getting counseling may be what more of us need for recovering from church hurt, a psychologist has acknowledged that "deep healing and connection can be found outside of the therapy room" and "trauma heals in healthy relationships where one is seen, heard, validated, and respected."[15] People hurt us, but people also heal us. We see this profoundly displayed in Mark 2:2–5 with the men who tore up tiles on a roof and lowered a paralyzed man down to where Jesus was because they couldn't get to him through the crowd. A community carried the disabled man to Jesus by any means necessary because they were invested in his healing as if it were their own. Here are a few descriptions of how healthy community should function and respond to your need for healing:

14. "How Trauma Can Impact Four Types of Memory [Infographic]," National Institute for the Clinical Application of Behavioral Medicine, 2017, www.nicabm.com/trauma-how-trauma-can-impact-4-types-of-memory-infographic.

15. Adrian A. Fletcher, "The Healing Power of Community and Connection," *Psychology Today*, April 13, 2022, www.psychologytoday.com/us/blog/keeping-it-real-and-resilient/202204/the-healing-power-of-community-and-connection.

1. Healthy communities take your healing personally. The people who carried the paralyzed man to Jesus acted with such intense determination, as if they needed healing for themselves. But perhaps that is the point. Healthy communities understand that they are only as strong as their weakest, most vulnerable members. Galatians 6:2 admonishes us to "carry one another's burdens; in this way you will fulfill the law of Christ."

2. Healthy communities will break down barriers to get you the help you need. We see in Mark 2, in dramatic fashion, the community not letting a crowd or lack of easy access deter them from getting the paralyzed man the help he needed. Healthy communities will problem solve with and for you when you can't think straight or when you don't have the energy or will to do it for yourself. They will scale a wall, tear up a roof, and break through other barriers to help you. You must allow your community to say "We gotchu" and go into action to help you. That might look like helping you find counseling, putting together resources for your therapy, helping you set up appointments with church leaders, or just coming to get you because you need to get out of the house, get something to eat, and have fun. "Two are better than one because they have a good reward for their efforts. For if either falls, his companion can lift him up; but pity the one who falls without another to lift him up" (Ecclesiastes 4:9–10).

> A sign you are in a healthy community is that they will do everything they can to help you but they realize no one can help you like Jesus can.

3. Healthy communities know the best thing they can do for you is take you to Jesus. The four friends in Mark 2 didn't stage an intervention or wear out the paralyzed man with chants of "Get up; you can do it." They knew his condition required the Great

Physician. Our friends and family are often amazing support systems when we are healing from church hurt, but healthy communities recognize their limitations and will take you to the One who has no limitations. A sign you are in a healthy community is that they will do everything they can to help you but they realize no one can help you like Jesus can. This may look like washing you with the Word, praying, anointing you with oil, exhorting you through godly counsel, ushering you into worship, and encouraging you to go back to church. Healthy communities should always be known for carrying you to Jesus, and guess what? He may perform the healing you need because of their faith, not yours. Mark 2:5 says, "*Seeing their faith,* Jesus told the paralytic, 'Son, your sins are forgiven.'"

Learn to Make Healthy Appeals for Justice

Advocacy for yourself and others can be a helpful part of your healing journey and at times an important intervening step before hurt happens.

> **Advocacy for yourself and others can be a helpful part of your healing journey and at times an important intervening step before hurt happens.**

If you've experienced rules or practices from the church that you believe to be unjust, you should get acquainted with the daughters of Zelophehad, whose story is told in Numbers 27. These five women were from the tribe of Manasseh. At the time of their father's death, the law required that any inheritance from a father must pass to his sons. However, Zelophehad didn't have any sons, only the daughters. The text doesn't tell us how these five women felt, although we might surmise that they were upset or disappointed that their dad's property, and ultimately his name, would be "taken away from his clan" (verse 4) and they would be denied a right to his land. We don't know about their personal conversations or strategy sessions, but we do know what they did and the results.

This brief narrative provides a wise example of how to speak up, models what healthy leadership looks like when it's challenged or confronted with a complaint, demonstrates the love and compassion of a holy God for women, and shows the power and purpose of speaking up and the influence women's voices had on an entire nation.

Choose the Right Approach (Numbers 27:1)

> *The daughters of Zelophehad approached. . . . These were the names of his daughters: Mahlah, Noah, Hoglah, Milcah, and Tirzah.*

Notice we don't see them gossiping in the neighborhood or among the other tribes about how unfair the law was. We don't see them talking bad about the leadership. In fact, God's response certainly doesn't reflect that the five daughters did anything sinful because they thought the law was unfair. We see them draw near to Moses and the rest of the leaders. The Hebrew word *qarab* used in this verse means "to draw near."[16] *Qarab* is also used when depicting a servant of God drawing near to him for help, comfort, direction, and protection.[17] When we believe something unfair has happened, whom we ultimately draw near to, whom we should approach for recourse, is God. When we make an appeal, let's draw near to the Lord for help and humbly draw near to the person or people he has given authority to shepherd us.

Show Respect for Authority and Leadership (Numbers 27:2)

> *They stood before Moses, the priest Eleazar, the leaders, and the entire community at the entrance to the tent of meeting.*

---

16. "Strong's H7126—Qārab," Blue Letter Bible, accessed February 12, 2024, www.blueletterbible.org/lexicon/h7126.
17. Exodus 40:32; Deuteronomy 5:27; Ecclesiastes 5:1; Psalm 65:4; 119:169.

We see that the women respected and submitted to their leadership and went straight to the people God put in charge. Their heart posture toward their leaders mattered. Scripture admonishes us, "Obey your leaders and submit to them, for they are keeping watch over your souls, as those who will have to give an account. Let them do this with joy and not with groaning, for that would be of no advantage to you" (Hebrews 13:17, esv).

Appeal Based on Integrity and Fairness, Not Entitlement (Numbers 27:3)

Our father died in the wilderness, but he was not among Korah's followers, who gathered together against the LORD. Instead, he died because of his own sin, and he had no sons.

Their father didn't engage in a rebellion against Moses, and their inheritance was tied to their father's name. They made their appeal based on the good reputation of their father, who was loyal to the Lord. They approached not with entitlement or with selfish motivations but with humility. Even if this was a strategy to move the hearts of the leaders, it showed discretion and wisdom.

Give Leadership a Chance to Hear You Out and Respond (Numbers 27:4)

Why should the name of our father be taken away from his clan? Since he had no son, give us property among our father's brothers.

They didn't assume that things couldn't change just because they had never been done that way and because there was a law preventing them from obtaining the land. The daughters gave the leaders an opportunity to empathize and change. We often say, "You do not have because you do not ask" (James 4:2), and the example of the daughters of Zelophehad demonstrates that, despite how things look, the culture of the church, or the rules that are in place, there is wisdom in humbly approaching leaders and asking for what you hope to receive.

Pray That the Leaders Will Be Wise and Consult God (Numbers 27:5)

Moses brought their case before the LORD.

Moses heard their appeal and decided to consult the Lord. Just like the daughters of Zelophehad approached (*qarab*) the leaders with their request, now Moses was approaching (*qarab*) God for direction. This is a word for all leaders. Moses didn't quickly tell the daughters, "It's always been done this way" or "I'm the pastor, and these are the rules; deal with it." He acted with great humility and said he would ask the Lord what he should do. Can you imagine how much healthier our churches would be if leaders had this humble and wise disposition? We see that Moses recognized that all wisdom and authority didn't stop with him and that his purpose as a leader was to go to God,[18] and that's what he did for the daughters of Zelophehad.

Trust the Lord to Answer (Numbers 27:6–11)

The LORD answered him, "What Zelophehad's daughters say is correct. You are to give them hereditary property among their father's brothers and transfer their father's inheritance to them. Tell the Israelites: When a man dies without having a son, transfer his inheritance to his daughter. . . . This is to be a statutory ordinance for the Israelites as the LORD commanded Moses."

The Lord told Moses that the daughters were correct in their appeal. However, the Lord told Moses not only to give Zelophehad's property to his daughters but also to change the law for everyone moving forward.

This is a powerful story about advocacy, about the process of speaking up when you believe there is injustice—going to leaders, leaders going to God, and trusting God to answer. Not only did their appeal change their circumstances, but it also brought about a change for the commu-

18. Exodus 18:19.

You don't have to stay silent in the face of injustice or be afraid to make an appeal for change.

nity. As a Church Girl, you don't have to stay silent in the face of injustice or be afraid to make an appeal for change. In fact, your voice may be the impetus for God to move and change the community at large. Certainly, not all leaders will listen, humbly go to God, or change rules and positions, but have faith that if God is calling you to speak, then he will go before you. Sometimes we may make multiple appeals, like the persistent widow in Luke 18; other times we may simply pray, patiently wait for God to act, and take the posture of Jesus, who "entrusted himself to the one who judges justly" (1 Peter 2:23).

Speak to Jesus, Who Hears You

Your healing requires that you speak honestly to God. When we are hurting, we may tell a friend how we feel; we may tell a therapist or a stranger, but until we talk to God for real, we won't experience the full freedom we need. Psalm 34:18 tells us that "the LORD is near the brokenhearted; he saves those crushed in spirit." Jesus said, "Come to me, all of you who are weary and burdened" (Matthew 11:28). When you don't go to Jesus and talk honestly about your broken heart, you are hiding your heart from the only person who can heal it. We often hide our hearts and refuse to speak truthfully with God about our feelings because we believe feelings are bad (they aren't), suppressing feelings and faking are Christian virtues (they're not), God will hear us but won't help us (he will), or God can't handle our deep, agonizing, and complex thoughts and feelings (he can). God already knows what you are thinking and feeling anyway,[19] so why not tell him yourself? Esau McCaulley wrote in his book *Reading While Black,* "Traumatized communities must be able

19. Psalm 139:1–4.

to tell God the truth about what they feel. We must trust that God can handle those emotions."[20] God welcomes and wants us to honestly share how we feel as an act of trust and intimacy. African church father Athanasius said, "Most of Scripture speaks to us; the Psalms speak *for* us."[21]

My suggestion for you is that if you don't know what to say or feel uncomfortable honestly talking to Jesus, try praying the Psalms until you can form your own words, but the words in Scripture are always enough. In fact, the Psalms may be the key to unlock your mouth and move your heart toward God.

In the Psalms we see people talking honestly with God about all sorts of difficult thoughts and feelings, such as anguish and lament, anger, grief, vengeance, loneliness, betrayal, injustice, desperation, discouragement, and hopelessness.[22]

Search the Psalms to help communicate your heart to God. God doesn't require pretty prayers, just honest prayers. The

> **When you don't go to Jesus and talk honestly about your broken heart, you are hiding your heart from the only person who can heal it.**

gospel's promise is that Jesus's blood closed the gap between you and God; you now have been brought near.[23] Don't let your pain separate you from God. Your healing happens not when you hide your heart but when you pour it.[24]

20. Esau McCaulley, *Reading While Black: African American Biblical Interpretation as an Exercise in Hope* (Downers Grove, Ill.: IVP Academic, 2020), 126.

21. Quoted in "Journal ~ Psalms," YouVersion, accessed March 4, 2024, www.bible.com/reading-plans/11200-journal-psalms.

22. Psalms 13; 32; 34; 86 (anguish and lament); 7; 35; 69; 109 (anger); 1; 16; 73; 112; 119 (grief); 35; 64; 109; 137 (vengeance); 25; 73 (loneliness); 41; 55 (betrayal); 7; 10; 58; 94 (injustice); 3–4; 28; 130; 141–143 (desperation); 13; 22; 42; 77 (discouragement); and 88 (hopelessness).

23. Ephesians 2:13.

24. Psalm 62:8.

Focus on Jesus, Who Sees You

Whenever I've had painful medical interventions I needed for healing, without fail, my doctor has told me to focus on something positive or beautiful during my procedure. Sometimes they've even had a cheesy painting of a beach on the ceiling for me to stare at. Where we put our focus during the pain and healing process makes a difference. During your healing, focus on Jesus—see the God who sees you.[25] Nourish your soul with the truth that Jesus loves and values women. Sometimes you can feel so alone and unseen in your hurt, but there is one who always sees you. Here are just a few beautiful reminders from Scripture:

- Jesus went through Samaria to reveal himself as the living water to a woman at a well.[26] My sister, Jesus will go to great lengths to set up an encounter with you so that he can satisfy your thirst.

- Jesus saw and protected a woman whom men attempted to stone for adultery. He forgave her sins and called out the men's judgment of her in light of their own need for forgiveness.[27] Jesus sees your sin, but he also sees how others are sinning against you, and he will intervene and protect in his own way.

- Jesus saw women as his disciples who supported his ministry from their own possessions.[28] He sees you as valuable to his kingdom mission despite the church hurt.

- Jesus saw the poor widow who offered all she had and used that moment to teach his disciples a lesson on faith.[29] He sees your sacrifice and desire to be faithful in the midst of your church hurt.

- Jesus saw the widow at Nain in her son's funeral procession, had compassion on her, and raised her son from the dead.[30] Jesus sees

25. Genesis 16:13.
26. John 4:4–26.
27. John 8:2–11.
28. Luke 8:1–3.
29. Mark 12:41–44.
30. Luke 7:11–17.

your grief and loss and wants to restore what feels lost to church hurt.

- Jesus saw the woman in the synagogue who was bent over by Satan. He called her to come to him, declared freedom over her life, and touched her and brought healing after eighteen years of suffering. He even rebuked the religious leaders who were angry that he healed her on the Sabbath.[31] My sister, God isn't afraid to touch you when others have ignored and rejected you, and no matter how long you've suffered, the One who is Lord will heal you and set you free in front of your adversaries if you will have the faith to come to him.

Jesus saw women and called men to see women too. When a religious leader was indignant with the woman pouring expensive oil over Jesus's feet and washing them with her tears, he could see only a sinner. But Jesus kept his eyes on the woman while he asked the man a question: "Do you see this woman?" Jesus rebuked him for mis-seeing the woman and for his own lack of love for him.[32] Church Girl, like this woman, you are seen in ways others won't often see you. But Jesus will rebuke people who mis-see you and your love for him. Like this woman, keep showing your gratitude for how Jesus has saved and forgiven you.

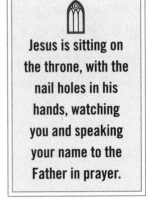

Jesus is sitting on the throne, with the nail holes in his hands, watching you and speaking your name to the Father in prayer.

These women in Scripture were always accurately seen by Jesus, and he allowed women to hear about his resurrection first.[33] Jesus validated their testimony in a culture where women couldn't be legal witnesses by telling Mary Magdalene to go back and tell the other disciples that she saw

31. Luke 13:10–17.
32. Luke 7:36–50.
33. Luke 24:1–10.

Jesus resurrected.[34] Additionally, Jesus doesn't take harm or insult to women lightly; he clearly takes it personally when his people are injured, as he held Saul responsible for directly persecuting him even though he persecuted Christians.[35] Remembering this is helpful in your healing process.

When I've hurt the most, this good news has been balm to my soul: Jesus is our high priest and intercessor. What a comfort to know that, right now in heaven, Jesus is not only seeing you but also praying for you.[36] Get that picture in your mind right now. Jesus is sitting on the throne, with the nail holes in his hands, watching you and speaking your name to the Father in prayer. Hallelujah!

What We Can Do as a Community of Church Girls

The previous sections were aimed at helping you and other Black women take steps to heal from church hurt personally. Now I would like to offer empowering and practical action steps we can take as a community of Black women to be helpers, influencers for good, and life givers in our churches. This story is a hard one of assault, but it provides a simple guide from Scripture that can help protect Black women from church hurt in the future.

Think It Over, Discuss It, and Speak Up

Judges 19:22–30 details the brutal gang rape of a concubine who was left for dead in the Benjaminite city of Gibeah. A Levite and his concubine were welcomed into the home of an old man. During the evening, "wicked men of the city surrounded the house and beat on the door," demanding that the owner bring out the Levite so they could have sex with him (verse 22). Instead, the woman was seized and given to the

34. John 20:17–18.
35. Acts 9:4–5.
36. Hebrews 7:25.

men, and horrific acts happened to her throughout the night. The next morning, she made her way back, collapsed, and died.

As if this woman being offered up was a lesser evil than the rape of the Levite man, he then took her dead body home, cut it into twelve pieces, and sent one piece to each of the tribes throughout all the territory of Israel. Verse 30 shows the shock and disgust of the people in the region: "Everyone who saw it said, 'Nothing like this has ever happened or has been seen since the day the Israelites came out of the land of Egypt until now. *Think it over, discuss it, and speak up!*'" The text tells us that the brutal rape, murder, and dismemberment of this woman was, at that time, the most egregious evil that anyone had ever seen among God's people.

This blew me away when I read it with church hurt on my mind. The final instructions to the people of God in Judges 19:30 should serve as a simple but powerful blueprint for our efforts to protect the most vulnerable Black women among us. In response to this horrific act committed against the concubine woman, God's community recognized their need to "think it over, discuss it, and speak up." Get in community with other Church Girls, follow those instructions, and encourage the larger body of the church to do so as well.

Think It Over

This is a call to meditate on the hurt Black women have endured in the church. Don't dismiss it. Thinking something over requires time and invites us to connect our heads and hearts. This invites us to be empathic listeners, learners, and feelers, which helps us be doers. We can't pretend the pain doesn't exist. When we think it over, we are asking God to show us his heart, his solution, his indignation at how one of his daughters has been treated in his house. Church Girl, what have Black women endured in your home and in God's house that you can encourage your sister friends and the church to think about?

Discuss It

The church must also talk about what Black women have experienced. This conversation needs to happen in community, such as small groups, town hall meetings, Bible study, and men's and women's ministry, and as a normal part of seeing and caring for Black women. Instead of turning a blind eye and a deaf ear, we must face the truth of Black women's lived experiences in communities of faith. This is a project for both men and women. Encourage the community of faith where you belong to come together and talk about what's really going on and what the church can do about it. Church Girl, use your voice and influence to bring people together to share their stories and encourage others to listen.

Speak Up

This is a call to action for you and the church. The church must use her voice, power, and influence to do something about the hurt Black women have suffered, and you can help lead the way. Speaking up demands that the church isn't silent, inactive, or complicit. The church must not only be vocal but also overtly declare that it won't be a place that tolerates the harming of Black women and that when harm does occur, the church will be the first to forcefully defend God's daughters and bring accountability. Speaking up also means the church must tell on itself. Speaking up demands that no victims are silenced and cover-ups are nonexistent. It isn't good enough for people to know about sin happening against women and the abuse of power but do nothing. Be empowered to issue an even stronger challenge to the church leadership and yourself—stop minding your business and speak up.

"Open your mouth for the mute, for the rights of all who are destitute. Open your mouth, judge righteously, defend the rights of the poor and needy" (Proverbs 31:8–9, ESV).

A Gospel Vision for Your Healing

A gospel vision for Black women's healing from church hurt begins with acknowledging that God is a loving father and he cares about any harm that happens to his daughters, especially in his house. There is no more protective and compassionate father than God. The gospel reminds us that Jesus came not only to heal our disease of sin but also to heal our broken hearts. Healing is possible, but not without opposition. The devil doesn't want us to have freedom from pain, have faith in God, reconcile with offenders, or have abundant life in Christ. Healing looks different for each woman, takes time, and is vital for our flourishing. God has given us the grace of healthy community, tools and strategies in Scripture, counsel inside and outside the church, and ultimately the presence and prayers of a loving, protective, and compassionate savior who hears and sees us.

Discussion Questions

 LIGHT: The promise and proclamation in Luke 4:18–19 is that Jesus came to bring liberty, healing, and favor.

1. Why are so many tempted to walk away from the faith when they experience church hurt?

2. What can you do to set healthy boundaries and heal without walking away from Jesus? What truth about God can you recall and rehearse to help you stay connected to him?

3. Why is spiritual warfare a part of church hurt and healing? What is Satan's agenda, and what can we do to prevent him from winning?

👓 **LENS: Having a right perspective when we are healing is important.**

1. Can you relate to having had seasons when you carried baggage, times you were in healthy bandages, and others when you were in bondage? How did those seasons each look different in your life?

2. Why could mischaracterizing your church hurt worsen the situation? What can you do to patiently but proactively help yourself have a healthy perspective on your experience?

3. Why is it important to speak up when something wrong or something unfair happens among the people of God? How can you implement making healthy appeals like the daughters of Zelophehad?

❤️ **LOVE: God is a loving father who cares about the hurt you've experienced in his house.**

1. What healing strategies have you tried and what strategies from the chapter would you like to incorporate into your journey of healing from church hurt?

2. How instrumental is the love of community when healing from church hurt? What do we learn from the story in Mark 2 that we can implement in our lives?

3. Why is it important to be heard and seen, and how does Jesus demonstrate love by hearing and seeing women who are hurting?

4. How can you implement the simple call to action issued in Judges 19:30 in your own life and community?

CHAPTER 5

I'm Not Your Superwoman

A Gospel Vision for Black Women's Rest

Come to me, all of you who are weary and
burdened, and I will give you rest.
—**Matthew 11:28**

"You are the youngest patient I've ever treated with shingles." Those were my doctor's words to me after she lifted my shirt and saw the constellation of red blisters wrapping around my mid-back and across my lower abdomen. I didn't know what shingles were, but I had debilitating fatigue and a strange intense pain that felt like someone was stabbing my back. If I'm honest, I went into the doctor's office with a "patch me up so I can go" plan, and it never crossed my mind to consider how unwell I was. I was just looking for a prescription to help me keep going, because I had so many things that hadn't been crossed off my to-do list and there were so many people depending on me.

My doctor's second question stopped me in my tracks: "Are you under a lot of stress?" Stress, for many Black women, seems to be baked into our DNA. It's an unwelcomed birthmark that we learn to call a beauty mark because we might as well accept and make peace with it. "Stress . . . Mmmm? No more than usual," I answered. Returning her attention to my shingles, I asked, "How do I get rid of it? What can I take? I have forty people coming to my house tomorrow for a baby shower that I'm hosting for a friend." The truth was, like many of you may understand, I had been under a lot of stress, but I considered it normal life. I was raising four children who needed constant attention and chauffeuring for academics, social events, and sports. My husband traveled for work, which left me with the lion's share of day-to-day care, cooking, cleaning, and parenting when he was gone.

> Our bodies will rebel and yell at us through pain and fatigue and all other forms of dysfunction when we refuse to listen to God's voice in us.

On top of family life, I was serving and leading multiple ministries at the church, teaching biweekly Bible study for women's ministry, working in a private practice counseling more than thirty clients a week, teaching as an adjunct professor at a medical school, working through the heartache of extended-family conflict, traveling for consecutive ministry speaking engagements, discipling multiple women, and walking with a friend through a painful divorce, and to add to that, my mother's cancer had returned. Just typing that list out makes my chest tight even today, but more than that, seeing it in writing makes me feel sad for the woman I was. I encourage you to come face-to-face with the daily demands of your life by simply writing them out. It's sobering to see what you do. It can be convicting, but I pray it helps you have empathy for yourself and inspires you to reevaluate.

"You need to rest," my doctor said, and I responded, "Okay," but in my mind I was really saying what every Black woman's famous words are when we decide to say yes to everything but rest: "Ain't nobody got time for that." That statement, though a humorous meme in our culture, unfortunately is often used to help us Black women laugh when we really should pause and cry. Have you been there, saying you don't have time to rest?

That statement helps us defend and deflect instead of paying attention to the deep cry of the soul begging for rest. That statement helps us communally agree that our out-of-control behavior and weariness are our normal lot in life. It disconnects us from ourselves. What exactly are we communicating that we don't have time for anyway? Are we saying we have no time to live well, to enjoy life, to sleep, to stop, to exercise, to eat healthy, to breathe, to be happy, to let someone else do it, to ask for help, to say no? We treat "Ain't nobody got time for that" like a scripture that we must obey instead of letting the actual words of God inform how we work and rest.

As much as I knew I needed to change, I was so embarrassed. As someone who had earned a PhD in psychology and was getting paid to help other people's lives get better, I was failing miserably at my own self-care. Shingles was snitching on me. Our bodies will rebel and yell at us through pain and fatigue and all other forms of dysfunction when we refuse to listen to God's voice in us. Unfortunately, I didn't cancel the baby shower, but I covered the shingles area to follow the counsel from my doctor that no one would be at risk if they didn't touch my blisters. I cleaned, cooked, and decorated my home. I greeted the guests and lied many times that day when I said I had to use the bathroom, only to go upstairs, lie across my bed, and cry my eyes out in agony. Then I'd wash my face and head back downstairs to continue my performance as a good host.

I smiled and cringed as a young lady who was admiring the floral-infused ice cubes I'd made said to me, "Dr. Sarita, how do you do it? With all you have on your plate, you are also killin' the game as the hostess with the mostest." Her next words, though meant as a compliment, cut me because they were so untrue: "Dr. Sarita, you are a *superwoman.* I want to be just like you when I grow up." I wanted to grab her hand and sing Karyn White's 1988 hit song: "I've got my pride, I will not cry, but it's making me weak. I'm not your superwoman."[1] But unlike Karyn White, I didn't need to sing those words to an unappreciative and neglectful man; I needed to sing those words to myself.

Superwoman. If ever a compliment could cut, it's one that is a big fat lie. We all have self-image lies that we project to the world, our idealized selves[2] that we meticulously curate when we believe that we aren't good

1. Karyn White, "Superwoman," track 4 on *Karyn White,* Warner Records, 1988.
2. *The idealized self* is a psychological term that represents the person you want to be. It's who you envision yourself to be—your hopes, desires, and wishes—and can be a healthy motivator. However, according to therapist Michael Schreiner, it can also become a neurotic or unhealthy version of healthy high self-esteem. Schreiner says that we sometimes create an idealized self as a strategy to resolve the inner conflict of not being who we wish we were; we create a sort of fantasy

enough or perhaps that God couldn't love us just the way we are. We often lead with a version of ourselves that we believe is our best shot at securing respect, admiration, and love. There is nothing more exhausting than pretending and believing you don't have another choice.

I wish I could say I learned my lesson and confessed my sin of idolatrous work and disobedience around rest. I wish my testimony was that I studied Scripture on work and rest, started counseling about why I was so out of balance, read books, and set up healthy boundaries, but that isn't the case. In fact, I did what I think a lot of Black women do—we promise ourselves that we will do better, and we ask our girlfriends to hold us accountable (but they often have the same problem, so it's the blind leading the blind). I may have even made a hypocritical post on social media about what the Lord was showing me through this trial and had the audacity to offer a lesson for someone else that I hadn't learned for myself. The truth is, when I did lie down to rest, it was only because my body couldn't take another step, paralyzed by the pain.

> Learning and living a gospel vision of rest is the call and cure for the "superwoman stronghold" that's imprisoning us.

It was unfortunate that I obeyed the vice grip of pain more than the voice of God. Can you relate? I knew the truth, but I didn't live it, and the consequence was that I continued to suffer, which is exactly why I had a second diagnosis of shingles the next year. My doctor was right. I needed to rest. Learning and living a gospel vision of rest is the call and cure for the "superwoman stronghold" that's imprisoning us.

How we think about ourselves and what we were taught about our identity and value have greatly affected our ideas and behavior pertaining to rest. How we've been socialized in this culture, which praises

---

world where we ascribe to ourselves traits, abilities, and accomplishments that are exaggerated beyond reality. For more details, see Michael Schreiner, "Idealized Self-Image," Evolution Counseling, February 24, 2015, https://evolutioncounseling.com/idealized-self-image.

production over people, has made us sick. We must honestly survey our lives and unpack our minds.

It's an Epidemic

What Black women are experiencing is an epidemic of dramatic proportions—an epidemic that I'm diagnosing as endless work and elusive rest. Let's look at some statistics and testimonials highlighting the epidemic we as Black women continue to experience.

Burnout

- Black women are increasingly experiencing burnout, and it's taking a toll on our health. According to data from the Study of Women's Health Across the Nation, "Black women are 7.5 years biologically 'older' than white women [and] perceived stress and poverty account for 27% of this difference."[3]

- Black women report that they are "not only experiencing burnout—but exploitation as well." A survey showed that "nearly 40% of Black women have left their jobs due to feeling unsafe."[4]

Sick and Tired

- Blacks and Latinos are more likely to get less sleep (fewer than six hours a night on average) and are more at risk for cardiovascular disease, diabetes, depression, obesity, and other chronic illnesses.[5]

3. Arline T. Geronimus et al., "Do US Black Women Experience Stress-Related Accelerated Biological Aging?," *Human Nature* 21, no. 1 (March 2010): 19–38, www.ncbi.nlm.nih.gov/pmc/articles/PMC2861506.

4. Amira Barger, "POV: Is It Burnout or Exploitation? For Black Women, It's Often Both," Fast Company, September 29, 2023, www.fastcompany.com/90955852/pov-is-it-burnout-or-exploitation-for-black-women-its-often-both.

5. Niema Jordan, "Why Black Women Need More Sleep, ASAP," *Essence,* last updated October 23, 2020, www.essence.com/lifestyle/why-Black-women-need-more-sleep-asap.

- Qualitative research with Black women suggests they often suffer from having a superwoman schema based on five characteristics: "a perceived obligation to present an image of strength, a perceived obligation to suppress emotions, a perceived obligation to resist help or to resist being vulnerable to others," along with "motivation to succeed despite limited resources" and "prioritization of caregiving over self-care."[6]

Racism and Microaggressions

- "A 2020 study published in the journal *Sleep* found that higher levels of perceived racism were associated with increased odds of insomnia among middle-aged and elderly Black women."[7]

- Racquel P. Jones, founder of Transforming Lives Counseling Center, said, "If you're always trying to survive, you can't think about resting. You feel like no one is going to take care of you."[8]

The research and testimonies are staggering, but the gospel offers another way. A gospel vision for Black women's rest leaps off the pages of Scripture in the Old and New Testaments. Let's take a moment to examine several examples that can improve how we view rest:

- "My presence will go with you, and I will give you rest" (Exodus 33:14).

    This truth is a game changer. Rest can be a gift of God and an outgrowth of being in his presence; the best rest is connected to both. My encouragement for you is to stop more frequently to attend to the presence of God. Acknowledge that he is right there with you, giving you rest.

---

6. Ana Sandoiu, "'We Must Educate Healthcare Providers' About Black Women's Experience," *Medical News Today*, July 31, 2020, www.medicalnewstoday.com/articles/we-must-educate-doctors-about-black-womens-experience-says-expert#1.

7. Alisha Acquaye, "Why Is Exhaustion So Normalized for Black Women?," *Allure*, June 12, 2022, https://allure.com/story/black-women-rest-self-care.

8. Quoted in Acquaye, "Why Is Exhaustion."

- "I will both lie down and sleep in peace, for you alone, LORD, make me live in safety" (Psalm 4:8).

  This verse connects feeling safe with the ability to sleep in peace. Consider why you may feel unsafe in the world, and apply Scripture to those areas to build your confidence that it's the Lord alone who provides safety and rest.[9]

- "Rest in God alone, my soul, for my hope comes from him. He alone is my rock and my salvation, my stronghold; I will not be shaken" (Psalm 62:5–6).

  The promise of rest is rooted in our willingness to see God as the ultimate source of our rest. Is your rest elusive because you've tried to rest in financial stability, a relationship, a job, material possessions, shopping, food, or drugs and alcohol? Anyone or any place we are seeking as the ultimate source of our rest outside God will disappoint.

- "Return to your rest, my soul, for the LORD has been good to you" (Psalm 116:7).

  There is an implied instruction from the psalmist—do you see it? We are encouraged to remember that the Lord has been good. Returning to rest requires us to remember the goodness of God toward us.

- "Come to me, all who labor and are heavy laden, and I will give you rest. Take my yoke upon you, and learn from me, for I am gentle and lowly in heart, and you will find rest for your souls. For my yoke is easy, and my burden is light" (Matthew 11:28–30, ESV).

  To find rest, we are first told to come to Jesus with our burdens. Second, we are told to have a "yoke exchange." It's implied that we all, like working livestock, have yokes around our

---

9. Here are a few scriptures that remind us that our lives are safe with the Lord: Joshua 1:9; Psalm 37:3; 41:2; 55:22; 91:3–16; 121:3–8; Proverbs 1:33; 18:10; Isaiah 41:10–13; Jeremiah 32:37; 33:16; Ezekiel 34:27; Philippians 4:6–7; 2 Thessalonians 3:3; 2 Timothy 4:18.

necks, being driven and directed by our "farmers" to accomplish their desired tasks. Your farmer may be your boss, your own will and ambition, sin, or the devil himself. Jesus says, Wear my yoke; submit to me; be driven and directed by me. Last, we are called to learn about Jesus. Coming to Jesus, taking on his yoke (which is easy and light, not burdensome), and learning his ways—these are the keys to finding rest for our weary souls.

Other Factors

There is more to our elusive rest than the statistics. At least three other influences can affect us: slavery, spiritualizing overworking, and self-centeredness.

Effects of Slavery

The unfortunate paradoxical chorus of many Black women's lives is "If I don't work, I won't live; if I don't rest, I will die." Black women are prone to over-function and prematurely force recovery when sick or injured. The effects of slavery may have a lot to do with it.

American chattel slavery is a major factor when thinking about the maladaptive beliefs and "caught" lessons we've integrated into our attitudes and behaviors surrounding work.[10] Slavery was a direct attack on the dignity and humanity of African people through forced labor and abuse. Enslaved Black women were stripped of their femininity and humanity. The basic human rights and needs to rest and have their limitations acknowledged, respected, and accommodated were ignored and denied. Black women were forced to work after being whipped, being raped, and giving birth. Enslaved women were forced to cook and clean when they were injured, hungry, and sick. They were forced to nurse other people's children, even if their nipples were sore, cracked, and bleeding. Our ancestors had to work even if they had just witnessed their

10. For more information on the impact and psychological legacy of slavery, see Joy DeGruy, *Post Traumatic Slave Syndrome: America's Legacy of Enduring Injury and Healing,* rev. ed. (Portland: Joy DeGruy, 2017).

husbands sold off to new plantations or if their own children had been ripped from their arms and sold to other enslavers. Their worth was qualified only in terms of their ability to work and produce. When enslaved people were too sick to work, rather than receiving empathy or medical care, they were diagnosed with mental illnesses and accused of being lazy.[11]

This history has relevance for us today. Rest was often withheld from our ancestors, and their lives would be threatened if they tried. In many ways, the fear of receiving retribution for resting has been encoded into our DNA.[12] It's important to consider how a legacy of trauma from slavery has been passed down generationally. Consider these questions:

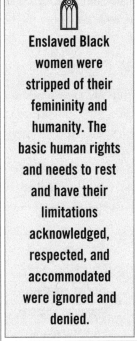

Enslaved Black women were stripped of their femininity and humanity. The basic human rights and needs to rest and have their limitations acknowledged, respected, and accommodated were ignored and denied.

- Do you believe that resting and taking time to care for yourself are forms of laziness?

- Do you believe that being sick means you are weak or damaged in some way?

- Are you seen as a producer rather than a person? Do you think asking for care and rest is viewed as complaining?

- Do you see taking a break to attend to your mental health as being weak?

11. This is supported by Dr. Samuel Cartwright's 1851 creation of a condition called dysaesthesia aethiopica that was rooted in racist pseudoscience. Samuel A. Cartwright, "Report on the Diseases and Peculiarities of the Negro Race," *The New Orleans Medical and Surgical Journal* (May 1851): 691–715.

12. Reba Peoples, quoted in Amanda Miller Littlejohn, "Black Professional Women Are Exhausted. They're Finally Claiming the Time to Rest," *Washington Post,* August 20, 2021, www.washingtonpost.com/business/2021/08/20/black-women-professionals-rest.

If you answered yes to any of these questions, perhaps you've been negatively influenced by the experience of our ancestors when it comes to work and rest. We know that Jesus can break chains and cycles of suffering, but if we are unaware of the influences we need deliverance from, we resist help from the Lord by normalizing unhealthy patterns of living.

Spiritualizing Overworking

From my experience in leading and teaching women, one of the more damaging influences on Black women's beliefs and behaviors involving work and rest is the misunderstanding and misapplication of Scripture. It has been clear to me that many Black women have been taught or have adopted faulty ideas of work and rest that they believe are biblical. Sometimes the most difficult unhealthy work and rest behaviors to change are those that fly under the radar as altruistic and Christlike sacrificing.

Dying empty shouldn't replace dying full of joy, full of love, full of hope, and full of the peace that is found in Christ.

Maybe we got the message to "die empty" wrong. In the 1990s, "die empty" was a catchy phrase many in the Christian community adopted from the teachings of the late Dr. Myles Munroe.[13] I remember loving the idea of dying empty, and I would often say it to others. Dr. Munroe challenged us to "go to the cemetery and disappoint the graveyard. Die like the Apostle Paul who said I have finished my course, I have kept the faith and I have been poured out like a drink offering. There is nothing left. I am ready to die."[14] I believe the heart of his exhortation was to die having lived a full life maximizing your time, fulfilling your call, and doing the will of God. But dying empty

13. Nyambega Gisesa, "Motivational Speaker Dr Myles Munroe Who Spoke of His Death at JKL Show Dies," *Standard,* accessed February 13, 2024, www.standardmedia.co.ke/article/2000140968/motivational-speaker-dr-myles-munroe-who-spoke-of-his-death-at-jkl-show-dies.
14. Quoted in Gisesa, "Motivational Speaker."

shouldn't replace dying full of joy, full of love, full of hope, and full of the peace that is found in Christ.

When Christ calls you to deny yourself,[15] that isn't a call to ignore pain and fatigue. When the Bible calls you to share in the sufferings of your savior,[16] that isn't a call to suffer because you have a savior complex.[17] When the Bible tells you, "You are not your own" (1 Corinthians 6:19), that isn't relieving you of personal ownership and responsibility over wise choices for your well-being. When the Bible tells you the Lord will keep you in perfect peace if you keep your mind stayed on him,[18] that isn't a call to invite chaos and disorder into your life and then shut down your mind to ignore the realities of your circumstances. Do you believe you must perform, serve, and labor continuously in the church to earn favor and love from God? It might be that you are motivated by fear instead of faithfulness.

> **Pouring out requires you to be poured into and learn the glorious gift of a pause. My dear sister, fill up and rest up. Selah.**

For most church leaders, a people-pleasing servant appears to be a breath of fresh air, but she's suffocating. This type of woman is rarely asked to stop working and never told that she works too much. Rather, she is depended on to keep the church afloat, but no one notices she's drowning. Make it your aim to serve from a healthy place where God is ordering your steps for work and rest. A sabbatical from serving or a mental health leave from work may reveal things that God wants to show you. Sometimes you must rest to receive.

Rest is so often avoided because when we get still, when we don't

15. Matthew 16:24.

16. 1 Peter 4:13.

17. A savior complex, also known as a messiah complex, is a state of mind in which an individual believes that they are destined to become a savior today or soon. The term can also refer to a state of mind in which an individual believes that they are responsible for saving or assisting others and that they must help others, no matter what the cost is to their own life.

18. Isaiah 26:3.

have something occupying our hands and minds, keeping our hands, feet, and minds busy, we begin to feel the hard and painful stuff we typically numb with the drug of work. Rest is an opportunity not just for a nap or vacation but to sit still, assess your life, tell the truth, and then begin the work with God to set things in order. Rest is an opportunity to reorder your life. Dying empty isn't a call to live empty. Pouring out requires you to be poured into and learn the glorious gift of a pause. My dear sister, fill up and rest up. Selah.

Self-Care or Self-Centeredness?

Self-care is vital to human flourishing and helps bring restoration so that we can function more healthily. Self-care can be defined as doing anything to improve or maintain a healthy mind, body, and spirit. I believe the Bible even supports a life of self-care as a means of cooperating with the comprehensive way God cares for us. Black women at times receive criticism from the world when their rest is seen as weak, incompetent, and lazy. In a bold attempt to resist unhealthy attitudes about Black women's work and to correct the anemic way in which we often care for ourselves, Black women have unapologetically kicked off our red-bottom heels, unlaced our Dunks, cornrowed our hair, started lifting weights, scheduled firm pressure massages, stamped our passports, and learned to say no in every language under heaven. We are here for it: Rest, Sis! Rest!

However, if we aren't careful—if we aren't guided by Scripture—we can easily be on vacation, floating on our backs in Jamaica, unaware that the enemy wants us to drift far from true Sabbath, becoming idolatrous and selfish in the name of rest. The problem I want to caution us about is when self-care becomes an idol instead of a tool for restoration, renewal, and reconnection to God. For many Black women, myself included, when burnout strikes, the concept of needing to be "a little more selfish" is applauded. We don't even notice it, but when we tell ourselves or our sisters it's time to "put yourself first," we aren't even thinking about the question "Where does that put God?"

Is it possible for self-care to become self-centered in a way that decenters Christ in your life? I think yes. Additionally, is it possible to take care of yourself, unapologetically rest, and keep Christ at the center of your rest? I also think yes. Here are ten reflection questions to help you assess whether your self-care and rest are becoming idolatrous rather than Christ honoring:

1. Are my self-care practices sinful or creating obvious temptation for sin? Am I engaging in syncretistic practices to rest?[19]

2. Am I going into debt or compromising my financial stewardship goals?

3. Do I schedule rest and self-care in ways that are faithful and honest with my place of work or church responsibilities? Am I lying when I call out? Do I give the proper notice and leave my work or church responsibilities in good standing when I'm gone?

4. Do I see rest and self-care as restorative for my kingdom calling, or do I not think about God's kingdom being connected to how, why, and when I rest?

5. How do I think and speak about self-care and rest? Do I see them as running away, escaping life? Is it difficult for me to transition back to regular life after a longer period of rest? Do I tend to negatively ruminate or complain about my life (work, family, friends, church, and possessions) while I'm resting?

6. Am I happy and easy to be around only when I'm resting?

7. Am I inflexible when I rest? Can my rest be interrupted? How do I respond if I'm interrupted or needed while I'm resting?

8. Am I an undercover Christian or "off" from being a Christian when I'm resting? Do I refuse opportunities to share the gospel or meet the needs of others I encounter? Do I engage in behaviors that don't glorify God?

19. Syncretism is the blending of multiple faith practices, adding incompatible religious or spiritual practices to our Christian faith.

9. Do I use my time of rest to find ways to connect with God more intimately?

10. Am I motivated by jealousy, envy, or comparison when I rest? Am I trying to re-create someone else's experience? If so, am I doing it from a place of admiration (I like what she did) or from a place of lust (I want what she has; I want her life; I want to be her)? Do I want others to see or know what I'm doing when I'm resting and hope they become jealous or envious of me?

As you answer these questions, I hope they will reveal your motivations for rest and help you pursue greater emotional and spiritual health in rest.

Christ-Centered Self-Care

To bring balance to our lives, some of us need to delete much of our to-do list. And some of us are skilled subtraction strategists. We look at our overfilled calendars, and we begin to cut things out that we deem threats to our rest, joy, peace, and happiness. Before you applaud the anointed cutters too quickly, I've noticed one unfortunate pattern in some Church Girls. I've noticed during seasons of my own life and while observing church culture that sometimes the first things we cut in the name of prioritizing rest are our church community, church commitments, and church presence. What if the secret to self-care isn't just about what we delete but about what we add? Is it possible that the angst, pain, trouble, or weariness of life is not because you are doing too much but because you aren't doing enough? That seems counterintuitive, right? But when we turn to Scripture, we often see words that encourage us to "take up" (Matthew 16:24–26), "put on" (Ephesians 6:11; Colossians 3:12–14), "run"

What if the secret to self-care isn't just about what we delete but about what we add?

(Hebrews 12:1), "share in suffering" (2 Timothy 2:3), "carry one another's burdens" (Galatians 6:2), "do the work [and] fulfill your ministry" (2 Timothy 4:5), and "add to your faith" (2 Peter 1:5–8, NIV). What if our solution to finding peace, rest, and self-care is in saying yes, not in saying no? Sometimes when we avoid things we should be doing, we feel even more tired, burdened, and frustrated. Here are some examples:

- Is there a person you have unresolved conflict with that you have been avoiding, even though God may be telling you to go to them to work it out?

- Is there a book the Lord told you to write that you haven't started?

- Is there some ministry vision that you haven't committed to pursuing?

- Did God tell you to go back to school, but you haven't moved in that direction?

- Is there some sin issue that you haven't confessed to God and your trusted community to get support?

- Every time the church asks for volunteers, do you feel conviction about not serving but you haven't offered to help?

- Is there a business or nonprofit God told you to start but you are avoiding?

- Is there someone God has called you to help practically, financially, materially, or relationally?

- Is there a home project, such as decluttering, reorganizing, or purging, that you are procrastinating?

- Should you be in counseling, but you haven't followed through with scheduling an appointment?

- Has God called you to adopt or foster a child, but you've avoided starting the process?

- Have you felt a burden to disciple someone or lead a small group, but you are avoiding it?

- Do you have a calling in ministry that is unshakable, but you haven't said yes?

Avoidance is weighty. Running from responsibilities and God will make you feel like you have lead feet and a military rucksack on your back. Sometimes we run from God in the name of self-care. A spa day, a vacation, a nap, crocheting, a girls' night out, wine, a Peloton ride, brunch, hiking, salsa, journaling, and painting are all good and restorative things we can incorporate into our lives, but they won't offer us the peace a "Yes, God" can provide.

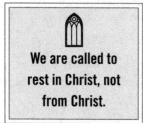

We are called to rest in Christ, not from Christ.

We are called to rest in Christ, not from Christ. While church (the building) isn't the be-all and end-all of rest or the only place where the presence of God is, he has indeed called us to fellowship with, do life with, serve with, learn from, grow with, love on, and be loved by his bride, the church. Certainly, some of us are biting off more than we can chew regarding our church obligations. Here are a few simple beginning steps to consider as you discern what is healthy to remove from your calendar:

- Pray. We should all start here and ask God to search us. There is no shame or condemnation to being honest about areas of needed growth. God isn't an unloving judge and angry father wagging his finger at us in disappointment; rather, he is a loving God who wants to be trusted to order our steps and invited to be Lord over our calendars.

- Ask a leader or friend who is serving faithfully in a healthy manner in your church community for feedback. It can be as simple as "Do you think I'm functioning as a healthy and committed member of the local church?" Ask for examples and suggestions for where you can improve.

- Ask yourself if you notice a difference in how you feel and are functioning in life when you are intentionally spending time with God—in his Word, in community, and in a weekly worship service. We can get used to being distant, but when we look back over more consistent seasons of connection, we notice a difference that we actually miss and long for. Sometimes it feels like we are starting over when we reengage, but the reality is, Jesus meets us wherever we are, and we are just continuing in our journey with him.

The Path to True Rest

We all may acknowledge that we want and need rest, but for many of us, rest is elusive and the path to achieving rest is unclear. In this next section, I want to guide you on the path to true rest that comes through Christ and explore the many ways we can begin to think and act differently to comprehensively experience rest right now.

Sabbath in Christ

Shabbat (שַׁבָּת) is the original Hebrew word for our English word *Sabbath,* and it represents "a day of complete rest from secular work following six days of labor. Established and modeled by God."[20] Though not all Christians agree on how to celebrate Sabbath,[21] it's my belief that the Bible describes Sabbath for the Christian to be less about Old Testament law keeping and more about remembrance, reverence, relationship, and rest

---

20. Bryan C. Babcock, "Sabbath," in *The Lexham Bible Dictionary,* ed. John D. Barry (Bellingham, Wash.: Lexham, 2016), accessed on Logos.com. See Genesis 2:3; Exodus 20:8–11; Leviticus 23:3; Ezekiel 20:12–24.

21. Romans 14:5.

in Jesus, now and eternally. Keeping Sabbath on a specific day isn't required for the Christian. The first day of the week, Sunday, is not a new Sabbath day but the Lord's day,[22] when Christians historically gathered to celebrate Jesus's resurrection.[23] Sabbath for us is no longer focused on a specific day but is a chance to delight in Christ, who secured our rest,[24] and it's an intentional shift away from the hectic grind of work life to focus on God and be renewed and refreshed in him. Sabbath is about resting in the finished work of Christ.[25]

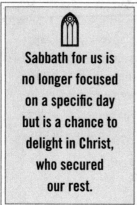

Sabbath for us is no longer focused on a specific day but is a chance to delight in Christ, who secured our rest.

When believers keep the Sabbath as a lifestyle and way of thinking versus a rigid day or rules to follow, we acknowledge the saving work of Jesus and cease from our own legalistic striving to earn righteousness, acceptability, and favor with God. We know instead that Jesus already completed the ultimate work on the cross to secure righteousness for us. We rest in knowing that though we work, and work is good, we don't work endlessly or anxiously, because our provision comes from God.

Rest Is a Gift of God's Grace

Rest is our agreement that we have limits; it reminds us that we aren't God and that we break down if we don't take care of ourselves holistically. We should first view rest as a gift from God—not something we have to manufacture, manipulate, or create but rather something we receive and enjoy. The Bible tells us, "Every good and perfect gift is from above, coming down from the Father of lights" (James 1:17). God gives us the grace of sleep, lets us lie down in green pastures, and leads us be-

22. Revelation 1:10.
23. Acts 20:7; 1 Corinthians 16:2.
24. Isaiah 58:13–14; Matthew 11:28; Colossians 2:16–17.
25. Hebrews 4.

side quiet waters.[26] He promises that our bodies will rest secure with him.[27] He promises rest in his presence.[28] All gifts must be received, opened, and enjoyed, or they are misused and wasted. "The Lord God, the Holy One of Israel, has said: 'You will be delivered by returning and resting; your strength will lie in quiet confidence. But you are not willing'" (Isaiah 30:15). I pray that we are willing to enjoy the gift of rest God is offering us.

Rest Can and Should Be Varied

In Scripture, we see people resting and being rejuvenated by eating, sleeping, praying, celebrating, meditating, healing, and being cared for by others. Even an angel of the Lord cared for Elijah when he was fatigued by fear and depression.[29] As you seek to find practical ways of resting, I don't think you need someone else to create your list. Think liberty, not legalism. Think delight, not duty. You may also want to think through Dr. Saundra Dalton-Smith's seven types of rest: physical, mental, emotional, spiritual, social, sensory, and creative.[30]

God has given us a beautiful earth to enjoy and family and friends, and through the ingenuity and wisdom of people, we now have numerous ways to rest. Some of the best rest is a full day of doing nothing, just being. Here are a few helpful parameters I advise:

- Rest should be righteous. We have liberty to do many things but not sin.

- Rest shouldn't be running away. Get honest about your propensity to label escapism *rest* because you haven't learned healthy ways of coping with stress and trauma. Going to a therapist for counseling may be a good start to that inner work.

---

26. Psalm 23:2; 127:2.
27. Psalm 16:9.
28. Exodus 33:14.
29. 1 Kings 19.
30. Saundra Dalton-Smith, *Sacred Rest: Recover Your Life, Renew Your Energy, Restore Your Sanity* (New York: FaithWords, 2017).

- Rest should be affordable. How you rest shouldn't break the bank in an unwise way, especially if it will propel you into more unhealthy work habits and stress.

- Rest should target aspects of your life that tend to be underused in your work. If you spend most of your life and job being sedentary, rest should include activity. If you are doing a lot of intellectual, heavy-thinking work, rest should include some activities that don't require high-level analysis and processing. If you are typically in a creative space for work, find rest options that activate other parts of your brain and heart, like reading, contemplation, and journaling. If your work requires you to spend a lot of time with people, rest should include alone time in nature or with animals—just make space for some limits on human contact. If you help people for a living, make sure you incorporate rest options where you are served and taken care of. If you work at home, include rest outside your home and workspace. You get the picture. Make sure to include balanced rest options and give yourself a break from the norm of work life.

Think liberty, not legalism. Think delight, not duty.

- Rest regularly. Rest before you are burned out. Doctors tell us that by the time we notice we are thirsty, we are already dehydrated. Regarding rest, it's important to drink from God's living water and the fountain of rest before our souls are parched. Be intentional about saturating your life with rest before you are thirsty. The goal is consistency and variety. Talk to your girlfriends and family, and have fun coming up with other options for one another's rest. The possibilities are endless.

  - Daily: You should do something restful every day, whether that's taking a walk, taking a ten-minute break to be still and sit in silence, journaling, reading a great book, or listening to some music and dancing.

- Weekly: You should do something more substantial every week, such as giving yourself a facial, doing something fun with friends, having select days to lift weights, seeing a therapist, getting your hair done, volunteering, working on a dream, or sleeping in.

- Monthly and quarterly: You should plan something more elaborate at least once a month or quarterly, such as going on a long drive, taking a trip, visiting the spa, finishing a book, investing in learning something new, taking a personal retreat, making appointments for health visits, starting a fast, or catching up with family and friends you haven't seen or talked to in a while.

• Rest reactively. The beauty of doing life with people is that when we miss the signs of our depletion, others won't. "You look tired" are often fighting words for women. I'm joking, but if you've ever been told this, you likely paused for a moment, and if you are sarcastic like me, you said something like "Thank you?" I think we get insulted when people say we look tired, but only because our clever tactics of trying to cover over functioning and fatigue haven't worked. Sometimes women can be sensitive about being seen as tired, because when we hear "You look tired," we hear "Girl, you look a mess." Let's consider how to be more gracious in our observations of our sisters' weariness. Instead of commenting on a woman's appearance, ask questions about how she is feeling and doing. Ask what's going on in her life; ask how you can help; ask about her rest. We can do better in how we notice one another's lack of rest, but when someone notices, see it as a gift, a call to action, a gracious nudge from God. Don't be offended; be reactive, and respond by making some changes or asking for help.

Rest Like Jesus

One of the primary ways we see Jesus resting in Scripture is in his alone time praying.[31] He also rested with his disciples and shared meals and fellowship.[32] However, one familiar story in the Bible I never heard taught in connection to rest grabbed my attention. In John 4, we read,

> When Jesus learned that the Pharisees had heard he was making and baptizing more disciples than John (though Jesus himself was not baptizing, but his disciples were), he left Judea and went again to Galilee. He had to travel through Samaria; so he came to a town of Samaria called Sychar near the property that Jacob had given his son Joseph. Jacob's well was there, and Jesus, worn out from his journey, sat down at the well. It was about noon.
>
> A woman of Samaria came to draw water.
>
> "Give me a drink," Jesus said to her. (verses 1–7)

Most of us are very familiar with this passage of Scripture. The story concludes with this Samaritan woman running back to her town as a witness for Jesus Christ. That's the typical focus of the passage, so we can easily miss the point here about rest. Verse 6 says, "Jesus, worn out from his journey, sat down at the well." I always missed it until I was writing on rest. What lessons can we learn from that short sentence?

First, Jesus didn't pretend to have energy when he felt tired. He stopped to rest. We know that he experienced life as fully human, which means, like us, he got tired. I love that the Christian Standard Bible says he was "worn out," because that's how Black women talk. Jesus models for us the doctrine of "sit yo-self down and rest." He honestly and appropriately responded to the condition of his human body, as we should. The next time you catch yourself yawning nonstop, your eyes getting heavy as you drive, or your brain getting foggy, take a minute and pause,

31. Mark 6:46.
32. Mark 2:15; 6:31.

acknowledge you are tired, and give yourself the gift of rest.

Second, Jesus didn't have FOMO, or the fear of missing out. As John 4 shows us, he left the area to head to Galilee after the Pharisees became angry. When he arrived in Samaria, he wasn't rushing to another ministry event and didn't ignore his weariness. He was settled and patient. Many of us have not only FOMO but also FOMMO—the fear of missing ministry opportunities or, in non-church work environments, the fear of missing move-up opportunities. Some of us don't rest from ministry or work because we are afraid that we will lose relevance or miss advancement, are insecure that someone will take our spot, or are desperate for the applause and attention of people. God didn't call

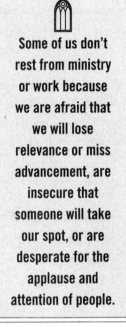

Some of us don't rest from ministry or work because we are afraid that we will lose relevance or miss advancement, are insecure that someone will take our spot, or are desperate for the applause and attention of people.

you to take on every project at work, volunteer to go on every out-of-town work trip, speak at every event you are invited to, or do all the labor of the church. There are other capable people who can teach the Bible in your church and run the event. You don't always have to respond to a post or make another reel; you don't have to say yes to every panel, podcast, or invitation. You can share some of the responsibility in the ministry you serve in, you can trust other people on the team and delegate, and you can go to a conference that you don't speak at to receive. Sometimes we need to recognize we are worn out and sit down and rest.

Ironically, Jesus's wisdom to pay attention to his humanity and sit when tired opened the door for the ministry with the Samaritan woman God, his Father, had ordained for him that day. We think we are missing out when we don't rest, but rest can be a vehicle through which God sends your next assignment. We like to say, "What God has for me is for me," but our FOMMO proves we don't always believe that. Resting is an act of trusting God with your fatigue and your future.

Rest in Peace

It's always struck me how we say "Rest in peace" to people who are deceased. While "Rest in peace" sounds nice and thoughtful, it really doesn't have much meaning. Instead, we should speak this to ourselves and others who are living. Let peace, not anger, be your motivator for

Resting is an act of trusting God with your fatigue and your future.

rest. Too many of us won't take care of ourselves until we reach a breaking point. Thoughts like *I'm tired of being sick and tired, I'm sick of this,* and *I'm sick of them* and feelings of being used, abused, and taken for granted are often the sparks that light a flame under us to act. Don't get me wrong—anger is a real and righteous emotion. At times, anger can be a powerful attention grabber, as it sounds the alarm that something is wrong, alerts you when justice is threatened, and warns you that something needs to be addressed or changed. Anger can help you course correct and motivate you to refuse to stay in unhealthy situations.

However, my encouragement and caution for you is to not *depend* on anger to be the impetus for you to act. I can testify that, in my attempt to take the high road, be diplomatic, and follow a biblical model of being slow to anger, I would take on more than I felt comfortable with, allow myself to be used, live without boundaries, and ignore offenses against me in the name of being patient, long-suffering, and Christlike. Overlooking an offense[33] isn't the same thing as ignoring an offense. Many times, I was overworked and burned out and I had only myself to blame. I said yes when I should have said no, I stayed late when everyone else left early, I gave to friends who didn't reciprocate, I charged less for services when people were paying others more with-

33. Proverbs 19:11.

out batting an eye, and I allowed myself to turn into an EMT when someone else's life was in crisis even if I didn't have the energy to show up and help them.

I noticed that sometimes I would have to get angry just to make better choices for myself. I can't tell you how many staycations, expensive dinners, massages, and shopping sprees happened in the name of "It's time for me to take care of myself, because nobody else will." I didn't make the time, spend money on myself, or do ordinary healthy things until I felt like no one else cared about me (which wasn't true, by the way). Have you been there? Can you think of a time when anger was the catalyst for your self-care? The reality is, much of the stress and weight we carry to the doorstep of anger is related to not living with consistent boundaries, not having consistent healthy rest, not engaging in clear communication and confrontation about small issues before they become big problems, and consistently saying "Yes, I'll do it" beyond our capabilities. Sacrificial giving of oneself is like a special offering beyond your normal ability,[34] which God honors.[35] However, to habitually sacrifice means you have made that level of giving a way of life. If you aren't clear that God called you to that level of consistent sacrifice, your "yes" may be motivated by something other than cheerfulness. "God loves a cheerful giver" (2 Corinthians 9:7).

Love, not anger, should be the fuel for rest.

Love, not anger, should be the fuel for rest.[36] Every time I "got away" to rest when it was fueled by anger, I wasted that time, ruminating over the precipitating events. I rehearsed what I would say when I got back and "put my foot down." I took showers, distracted by

---

34. See "What Is Sacrificial Giving," *The Stewardology Podcast,* Life Group Financial, accessed March, 5, 2024, www.thelifegroup.org/what-is-sacrificial-giving. This article quotes Randy Alcorn as saying, "There are three levels of giving—less than our ability, according to our ability, and beyond our ability." Randy Alcorn, *Money, Possessions, and Eternity,* rev. ed. (Wheaton, Ill.: Tyndale House, 2003), 202. If we are constantly giving of ourselves beyond our ability, I believe sacrificial giving is no longer the appropriate term, as we have made it a way of life that is harmful to us in the long run.

35. 2 Corinthians 8:2–4.

36. "Let all that you do be done in love" (1 Corinthians 16:14, esv).

my hurt and disappointment at people, and I never really talked to God during my so-called rest, because I was talking to the perceived ghosts of the enemies of my peace.

How you start your rest will influence your rest. Have you ever been angry and said, "I'm not going to work today" or "I'm not going to church today"? If I were a betting woman, I'd bet your day off or rest day wasn't as restful or joyful as you would have liked. God can meet us in our

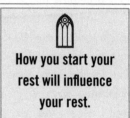

How you start your rest will influence your rest.

anger—he still invites us to bring our whole authentic selves to him—but we don't need to get angry to rest; we just need to get clear about things that are frustrating us and causing us to blame others for our lack of boundaries and healthy choices.

- We need to get clear on what God has called us to do and not do.

- We need to get clear on who fuels us and who drains us.

- We need to get clear on our strengths and limitations.

- We need to get clear on spiritual warfare and how it shows up in our lives and ministries.

- We need to get clear that rest must be a normal rhythm of life.

- We need to get clear that it's no one's job to speak for us; we must communicate our needs and concerns for ourselves.

- We need to get clear that we teach people how to treat us.

- We need to get clear that the cost of "yes" must be carefully considered and that "no" is a whole sentence that not everyone will like.

Let God's love for you fuel your rest. Let God's love walk with you while you work, comfort you when you're stressed, and give you peace in places of chaos. Let God's love for you be the gentle alarm clock frequently stirring your soul, beckoning you to come to him and rest.

De-Glamorize Your Rest

In her article "Why Rest Is So Important for Black Mothers," Erin McIntire insightfully pointed out that, "a lot of times, we have Instagram images of luxury in our heads when we think of 'rest.' We think that we aren't resting unless it looks like it belongs on a magazine cover."[37] While Instagram photos and the like can offer great visuals and vacation ideas for us to consider adding to our bucket lists, the potential danger is that they become the perceived standard of rest, which may not be realistic.

De-glamorizing your rest may begin with decolonizing your beliefs about self-care. "Decolonizing self-care separates self-care practices from the act of colonization that is perpetuated through the exclusion of marginalized communities from the standard picture of self-care. This standard picture turns self-care into a symbol of status and class rather than a varied practice that can take many different forms and can be practiced by anyone in an effort to care for oneself."[38] It is imperative that Black women not equate luxury with rest. For many Black women, rest may feel unaffordable if their finances are strained, they have housing issues, or they carry the pressure and responsibility to take care of others.[39] Rest that is billed as an unaffordable luxury and not an affordable necessity is counterproductive for Black women. The media's portrayal of self-care as a white woman's practice has unconsciously taught some Black women to view their right to rest and self-care as, like one young woman de-

37. Erin McIntire, "Why Rest Is So Important for Black Mothers," The Everymom, April 17, 2023, https://theeverymom.com/why-rest-is-so-important-for-Black-mothers.

38. Lauren Harrell, "Decolonizing Self-Care," Melanin Muse, accessed March 5, 2024, https://melaninmuse.com/decolonizing-self-care. Melanin Muses's tagline is "We believe in the genius and magic in every Black woman! Our vision is a world where all Black women are safe and own their narratives."

39. Paris B. Adkins-Jackson, Jocelyn Turner-Musa, and Charlene Chester, "The Path to Better Health for Black Women: Predicting Self-Care and Exploring Its Mediating Effects on Stress and Health," *Inquiry* 56 (January–December 2019), www.ncbi.nlm.nih.gov/pmc/articles/PMC6728668.

scribed, "images of wealthy White women taking bubble baths."[40] The Black Rest Project in New York aims to change the visual perception of Black rest through artistic depictions of Black people not doing anything glamorous other than being still. They note, "Rest and self-care practices can represent leisure and luxury, but for Black women, it's so much more. Rest is resistance."[41] Rest is resilience building and spiritual; it is necessary for physical, spiritual, and psychological health and a way of confronting and reprioritizing one's life.

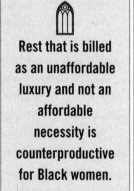

Rest that is billed as an unaffordable luxury and not an affordable necessity is counterproductive for Black women.

Let me be clear: If Black women want to vacation at expensive, exclusive resorts and travel the world, we should. I love that kind of vacation. De-glamorizing our rest isn't an admonishment for us to stop dreaming, wanting more, or having nice things and experiences. But the lengths we go to and the money we spend in the name of rest don't have to break us or exclude us from resting. We can rest in simplicity. Although, I'm kind of chuckling because I can't help but picture my friends and family reading this, thinking, *I know Sarita did not just tell those women to de-glamorize their rest when she is the bougiest among us!* I confess, I like ascetically pleasing experiences and exquisite travel, but even I have had to adjust my perspective of resting from an all-or-nothing mindset to a realistic one. I love to go away for a week, but if I can't, now I'm grateful for an overnight staycation at a nearby hotel. I love to go to the spa, but if I can't, I make time to give myself a facial at home. I'd rather go for a walk on the beach, but if I can't, I take my hips to the neighborhood high school track. I have three children in college and one headed that way shortly and sometimes money or time con-

---

40. Angelica Puzio, "Have We Been Doing Self-Care All Wrong?," *Washington Post,* October 1, 2021, www.washingtonpost.com/lifestyle/wellness/self-care-meaning-history/2021/10/01/c4f8a1ea-2232-11ec-9309-b743b79abc59_story.html.

41. Tricia Hersey, author and founder of the Nap Ministry, said, "Rest is a form of resistance because it disrupts and pushes back against capitalism and white supremacy." Tricia Hersey, *Rest Is Resistance: A Manifesto* (New York: Little, Brown Spark, 2022), 7.

straints make it impossible for me to rest in all the bougie ways I'd like to rest. But I have found great joy in accepting my limitations, adjusting my expectations, and not letting anything stop me from resting.

De-glamorizing your rest is the call to accept that there is more than one way to rest.[42] Rest can be and is communal and diverse when we take into account the different socioeconomic categories we all fall into. No one's bank account excludes them from proper rest. Additionally, many of us are waiting to have a grand experience of rest, saving money to do something big in the years to come, all the while denying ourselves the opportunity to do something that brings us rest on a smaller scale now.

Rest and care can be pursued in a variety of ways. It can be picking up painting, meditating on Scripture, playing instruments, going to counseling, dancing, spending time with friends, journaling and writing poetry, going on prayer walks, going to the gun range, riding motorcycles, climbing rocks, jumping out of planes, playing sports, gardening, knitting, crocheting, hiking, swimming, following our passions, and taking risks by trying new things. And for those of you who find cleaning relaxing, you can come to my house—I'll cook (lol). The list of ways to rest, relax, de-stress, and cultivate joy is endless and as diverse as we are. And let's not forget, one of the most important things we can reclaim is sleep. You should make your own list, and I dare you to start off by thinking of what you can do for free, what you can do alone, what you can do with others, and what you can do to commune with God. Be creative and have fun planning your rest! Study the Bible and travel with friends. Go as far as Fiji and as close as the farmer's market.

Many of us are waiting to have a grand experience of rest, saving money to do something big in the years to come, all the while denying ourselves the opportunity to do something that brings us rest on a smaller scale now.

42. McIntire, "Why Rest."

As rest is so meaningful to all of us, consider other Black women who value rest and have dedicated their lives to making sure we are healthy and living and resting well. Seek out other Black women who are trained and committed to the thriving of Black women. We have a wealth of knowledge and skill among Black women in the Christian community

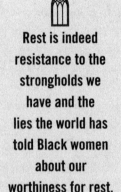

Rest is indeed resistance to the strongholds we have and the lies the world has told Black women about our worthiness for rest.

that is aimed at helping women rest, get healthy, gain margin in their lives, and assist them with normal life loads that can weigh them down. There are Church Girls who are aestheticians, dermatologists, medical doctors, cosmetologists, bodywork practitioners, natural body care product creators, travel agents, mental health therapists, life coaches, business strategists, financial planners, house cleaners, laundry servicers, short-term-stay property owners, dance instructors, herbalists, naturopaths, essential oil business owners, tour guides, in-home chefs, conference and retreat organizers, virtual assistant staffing business owners, ministers, disciple makers, Bible teachers, writers encouraging rest and flourishing in our community, and so much more. Black women's thriving is a group project. We all should be invested in helping Black women rest and care for themselves better. If you have a skill that can help Black women, consider how you market your skill set, specifically aiming at a comprehensive picture of health and rest for Black women. Church Girls, seek out other Black women in your family, community, and church, and together begin to prioritize rest and self-care.

As we close out the important discussion of rest, I want to talk about social media. Since it puts pressure on how we imagine rest, take notice of how you feel when you see photos of other people's vacations, honeymoons, and retreats. Next time you look on social media and feel something uncomfortable, close your eyes and say, *God, thank you for my life.* Repeat that simple prayer as many times as you need to lift your attention from someone or something else to the One who truly deserves your gaze and gratitude. Instead of us saying, "I wish I could go there or do this or have that," or quickly searching out the resort and looking for the cost of the stay, may this be the new prayer and confession of our hearts:

God, show me how you want me to rest. Help me notice and be grateful for the options for rest and renewal I don't often use because I have a habit of paying too much attention to someone else's life and not my own. Quiet my restless mind; heal my broken heart; crush my tendency to compare and compete to my own detriment. Teach me how to live well; ease my anxiety, which makes me prone to wander and seek satisfaction outside you. Help me, Lord, to trust you and prioritize rest in your presence. In Jesus's name, amen.

Rest is indeed resistance to the strongholds we have and the lies the world has told Black women about our worthiness for rest. The good news is that ultimate rest isn't something you have to plan, pack, or pay for. Just enter in. Jesus has already prepared a place where he will make you lie down in green pastures, where he will lead you by still waters, and where he will restore your soul and lead you on a path of righteousness for his name's sake.[43]

A Gospel Vision for Your Rest

A gospel vision for your rest begins with knowing that true rest is found in Christ. There is an epidemic of Black women finding rest elusive and working in maladaptive ways that come from slavery, spiritualizing overworking, and self-centered versus Christ-centered thinking. There are a variety of ways we can improve our rest practices, and making simple changes in our perspectives about what rest should look like can provide new opportunities for us to prioritize rest in our lives. We serve a God who walked the earth as a man and experienced human limitations like fatigue. Studying Jesus's life and rest practices in Scripture provides a

---

43. Psalm 23:2–3, esv.

beautiful model for rest that we can follow. Jesus is inviting Black women to come to him and learn his ways so we can find the rest we all crave.

Discussion Questions

 LIGHT: True rest is offered through a relationship with Jesus.

1. How does Jesus offer you ultimate rest?

2. What does the Bible teach about rest that helps you think about it in a new way?

3. How did Jesus model rest on earth, and how can we learn from his example?

👓 **LENS:** Many things affect how we view work and rest, but God's Word should be the greatest influence.

1. What are some unhealthy views you have been taught or have caught about work and rest, and how does the gospel free you from those unhealthy beliefs?

2. What are some practical changes you can make in your life to improve how you rest? Consider one thing you believe you should stop doing and one thing you should start doing.

♥ **LOVE:** God demonstrates his love for us by providing rest for us now and in the life to come.

1. How do you see God's love for you in his care and provision for your rest?

2. How have you struggled to feel worthy of rest? How has a gospel vision of rest brought you perspective and healing regarding your right to rest?

3. What is one thing you want God to help you with so that you can better rest? Write out a prayer about your desire for rest.

CHAPTER 6

Blooming in Babylon

A Gospel Vision for Black Women's Flourishing in a Decaying World

*Seek the peace and prosperity of the city to which
I have carried you into exile. Pray to the LORD for it,
because if it prospers, you too will prosper.*
—Jeremiah 29:7, NIV

The first time I remember being curious about Babylon was in 1995, during my sophomore year at Florida A&M University. I was listening on repeat to the Fugees' lead single "Fu-Gee-La" from their second album, *The Score,* and the lyrics arrested my attention. The lyrics seemed to juxtapose Babylon and Mount Zion, and I was curious about where Babylon was and its significance in Scripture.

I wasn't exactly sure what Mount Zion was either, but I assumed it had something to do with being a Christian, because, in Philly, many churches had *Zion* or *Mount Zion* in their name. I've since learned that Mount Zion is a physical place and is symbolic of so much more. Modern Mount Zion is the highest point in Jerusalem outside the Old City walls, but long before Mount Zion got its name, Scripture revealed a rich heritage of God's redemptive work. The word *Zion* is used more than 150 times in Scripture and means "fortification." *Zion* can refer to the City of David, the city of God, the city of Jerusalem, the land of Judah, and the nation of Israel.[1] In a theological sense, *Zion* is also figu-

---

1. 2 Samuel 5:7; Psalm 74:2; 87:2–3; Isaiah 8:18; 24:23; 40:9; Jeremiah 31:12; Zechariah 9:13.

ratively used to refer to Israel as the people of God[2] and to God's eternal spiritual kingdom or heavenly Jerusalem,[3] where Jesus is the precious and honored cornerstone.[4] For you as a Christian woman, Zion represents the assurance that because you put your faith in Christ, you have

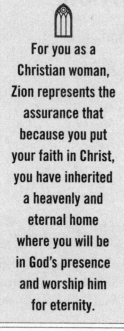

> **For you as a Christian woman, Zion represents the assurance that because you put your faith in Christ, you have inherited a heavenly and eternal home where you will be in God's presence and worship him for eternity.**

inherited a heavenly and eternal home where you will be in God's presence and worship him for eternity. In this present life, we have Christ as our hope, spiritual foundation, and protection. Jesus is our spiritual fortress, bringing us deliverance and defense from the attacks of the enemy.[5]

Where Zion represents a spiritual home and refuge in the presence of God, Babylon, similarly, represents both a physical place and a figurative spiritual condition. Babylon's ruins are located within modern-day Iraq, approximately fifty-nine miles southwest of Baghdad along the Euphrates River.[6] This small port town became one of the superpower cities within Mesopotamia. Babylon became a wealthy trading center under the sixth Amorite king, Hammurabi, who ruled from 1792 to 1750 B.C. and is credited with creating a comprehensive legal code known as the Code of Hammurabi.[7] After Hammurabi's death, the empire fell and a new line of kings took over and ruled what became known as the Neo-Babylonian Empire. Many historians regard the Neo-Babylonian Empire for their lavish buildings,

2. Isaiah 60:14.

3. Hebrews 12:22.

4. Isaiah 28:16–17; Romans 9:33; Ephesians 2:19–21; 1 Peter 2:4–6.

5. Psalm 3:4; 20:2; Joel 3:16; Luke 4:18.

6. William R. Osborne, "Babylon," in *The Lexham Bible Dictionary,* ed. John D. Barry (Bellingham, Wash.: Lexham, 2016), accessed on Logos.com.

7. D. J. Wiseman, "Babylon (OT)," in *The Zondervan Encyclopedia of the Bible,* ed. Merrill C. Tenney and Moisés Silva, vol. 1, rev. ed. (Grand Rapids, Mich.: Zondervan, 2009), 475.

art, statues, mythical gardens, and the cultural renaissance that was brought to the Near East.

While our history books don't describe Babylon, whose name is derived from the Akkadian word *babilu* and means "gate of god," quite like the Bible does, this city and its leaders theologically represent the counterfeit to God's eternal city, Mount Zion, under his divine rulership.

Nimrod, a mighty hunter, the son of Cush and the great-grandson of Noah,[8] founded the Babylonian Empire. His name ironically means "rebellion" or "let us revolt,"[9] and this remarkably represents the story of his descendants and the spirit of Babylon, renowned for its worship of false gods, pride, immorality, and rebellion.[10] Babylon's name has its roots in the narrative from Genesis 11:1–9 of the Tower of Babel, a symbol of Babylon's pride and opposition to God. "Babylon is one of the dread images of the Bible, stretching from OT history to the apocalyptic vision of Revelation."[11]

Babylon certainly doesn't have a glowing reputation in Scripture. The prophet Habakkuk lamented that God would use the evil Babylonians to discipline his own people for their rebellion.[12] Isaiah prophesied to King Hezekiah the coming judgment against the people of God (Judah): " 'Look, the days are coming when everything in your palace and all that your predecessors have stored up until today will be carried off to Babylon; nothing will be left,' says the LORD. 'Some of your descendants . . . will be taken away, and they will become eunuchs in the palace of the king of Babylon'" (Isaiah 39:6–7). Jeremiah also prophesied about the coming captivity of God's people.[13]

Like some professing Christians today, the people of God resisted

---

8. Genesis 10:1–10.

9. David C. Grabbe, "What the Bible Says About Nimrod's Arrogance," BibleTools.org, accessed February 16, 2024, www.bibletools.org/index.cfm/fuseaction/Topical.show/RTD/cgg/ID/22802/Nimrods-Arrogance.htm.

10. Genesis 11; 1 Peter 5:13 (likely a code word is being used to compare the evil of Rome to Babylon); Revelation 17:5.

11. Leland Ryken, James C. Wilhoit, and Tremper Longman III, eds., *Dictionary of Biblical Imagery: An Encyclopedic Exploration of the Images, Symbols, Motifs, Metaphors, Figures of Speech and Literary Patterns of the Bible* (Downers Grove, Ill.: IVP Academic, 1998), 68.

12. Habakkuk 1.

13. Jeremiah 20–22; 24–29; 32; 34–38.

God's call to repent and be holy. Instead, they acted like the pagan people they were supposed to point to God.[14] For many years, through prophets, God told his people to turn from their evil idolatry, but they refused to obey. Their disobedience angered God, so he declared that he would send King Nebuchadnezzar of Babylon to take them into captivity for seventy years. God promised to bring his people deliverance and, after their captivity, allowed them to return to Jerusalem to rebuild the temple, which had been looted and destroyed. God also promised to punish Babylon for their iniquity.[15] What is clear about this captivity and exile is that it was God-ordained.[16] God even called the king of Babylon "my servant" (Jeremiah 25:9).

When we are acting like Babylon instead of the people of God, we rarely think about the consequences of our disobedience. But God won't be mocked.[17] We must guard against the drift that leads to enemy captivity so that we aren't like the people of Judah, sitting by the waters of Babylon, weeping and remembering that we rejected the life God offered us in exchange for a decaying world that overpromises and underdelivers. "By the rivers of Babylon—there we sat down and wept when we remembered Zion" (Psalm 137:1).

The Drift Away from God Happens Slowly in Babylon

Can you imagine the irony and sadness of a horribly sinful nation known for violence, idolatry, and pride being used by God as a tool of judgment for his people? God's people were called to live differently from the world, showing the pagans what it looked like to be the people of God, but they were just as sinful as the Babylonians. Even today, it's a disgrace for an unbelieving world to be an arm of rebuke against the church, bringing

---

14. Warren W. Wiersbe, *Be Resolute: Determining to Go God's Direction* (Colorado Springs: David C Cook, 2000), 18–19.

15. Isaiah 13:19; Jeremiah 25:12–14.

16. 2 Chronicles 36:21.

17. Galatians 6:7.

rightful charges against God's elect, such as legal discipline for sexual abuse and perversion, fund misappropriation, and other ungodly conduct. God's people now, as they did then, are turning their backs on God, worshipping idols, losing their Christian distinction, violating his commands, and ignoring God's prophets' warnings, and instead of pushing back the darkness, some of us in the church are adding to it. It happened then and it's happening now. This can even happen to us as Church Girls. Some women who readily identify as Christians are sadly indistinguishable from the world, but we don't start out this way.

> **As Black Christian women, we must be aware that the influence of living in Babylon can cause us to drift away from the faith, and it doesn't happen overnight.**

In 2023, my pastor, Dr. Eric Mason, preached a sermon series from the book of Hebrews called Anchored: How to Be Secure in a Drifting World.[18] One important point he highlighted is how the drift away from the faith happens slowly. As Black Christian women, we must be aware that the influence of living in Babylon can cause us to drift away from the faith, and it doesn't happen overnight.

We don't go from worshipping God to worshipping influencers and entertainers overnight.

We don't go from reading our Bibles to reading tarot cards and astrological signs overnight.

We don't go from serving the one true God on his terms to practicing witchcraft overnight.

We don't go from walking in humility to being prideful overnight.

We don't go from faithfully serving and worshipping in church to attending "bedside Baptist" or being perpetual online members without just cause overnight.

---

18. Eric Mason, "Anchored: How to Be Secure in a Drifting World," video, 1:47:52, February 26, 2023, www.youtube.com/live/VKS9M94Izaw?si=KlL_3x3k4JommQ4r.

We don't go from being content in Christ to feeling entitled to personal preferences overnight.

We don't go from regarding our bodies as the temples of the Holy Spirit to calling immodesty, body positivity, and sexual sin sexual freedom overnight.

We don't go from resting in the provision of Jesus to hustling and killing ourselves in grind culture overnight.

We don't go from singing songs of praise to using profanity overnight.

We don't go from waiting on the Lord and trusting his plan to taking control of our own lives overnight.

No, my sister, in Babylon, in secular culture, the drift is slow. Our descent away from God's standard and intimacy with Christ isn't like the first drop on a roller coaster; rather, it's like a slowed-down elevator ride in the Burj Khalifa building in Dubai with its 163 floors. When the enemy lures and seduces you away from God's commands, it's like being in an elevator with soothing music and wall-to-wall mirrors so all you can see is yourself. You don't even notice you're dropping, because it feels so good, it's so much fun, you're the center of attention, and your sense of independence, pleasure, and ambition is the soundtrack for your ride. The scariest part about Christian drift is not that you've openly and boldly renounced faith in Jesus but rather that you believe you can live in opposition to God and have him still be good with you.

The chorus of this ungodly remixed and mixed-up form of Christianity is set to a beat that rocks us into folly and pride; its lyrics are "Do you," "God knows my heart," "Only God can judge me," and "The church is so judgmental." These lyrics give rebellious women the courage to stiff-arm Scripture, suck their teeth at truth tellers, and dis disciple makers who call for lives of holiness and submission to God. This New Age version of Christianity isn't Christianity at all.

Church Girl, we aren't called to be Christians in name only. You don't want to be an empty shell of real Christianity. You must decide. If you aren't going to live fully devoted to God, if you don't have any intention of getting off the throne of your life so Christ can rule, you ought to take off the Church Girl label or bring revival back to the house. The work of the kingdom is too important and time is too short to play church. Jesus is coming back![19]

How is it that you and I can go from devotion to disobedience? It's when we begin to question the authority of Scripture, isolate ourselves from Christian community, give ourselves permission to sin with no conviction, adopt the world's ideologies as truth, mock God's prophets, glory in our shame, and laugh at memes about the church instead of being the church. As a Church Girl living in the world, you are in a type of Babylon. We live in a decaying world of occultism, pride, idolatry, sexual perversion, bigotry, ungodly leaders, political unrest, and violence. As Church Girls, "we are the visiting team,"[20] and the crowd of the world around us is hostile to us. Jesus warned, "If the world hates you, under-

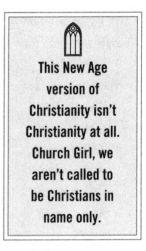

This New Age version of Christianity isn't Christianity at all. Church Girl, we aren't called to be Christians in name only.

stand that it hated me before it hated you. If you were of the world, the world would love you as its own. However, because you are not of the world, but I have chosen you out of it, the world hates you" (John 15:18–19). But there is hope! "The world and its desires pass away, but whoever does the will of God lives forever" (1 John 2:17, NIV).

We Are the New Exiles

What is the fate of a Christian woman in the world? Is it possible for the Church Girl to not only survive being an exile in Babylon but also thrive in her ability to represent God while living in hostile territory? Can a Black Christian woman flourish while having Christian convictions in a

19. Matthew 24:42–44; 1 John 2:28; Revelation 22:12.
20. Tony Evans, "Unapologetic—Divine Reset," video, 27:40, March 21, 2021, www.youtube.com/watch?v=6ZAh1i_OeE0.

decaying culture? The answer is a resounding yes, but it's not easy. Living unapologetically and faithfully for the Lord is so countercultural that you

It's imperative that while we are in our own type of Babylon, we stay authentically on brand as Black Christian women, maintaining Christian distinction by faithfully living differently from the world.

know you are doing it in the right way when you stick out like a sore thumb, people hate you for saying no to things, you can't do everything the world is doing, and people think you are a fool for trusting in a God you can't see and standing on a book you believe is the breath of God.[21]

It's a narrow way, and honestly, it can be lonely. The good news is, we don't have to do it alone or in our own strength. Christ is with us and protecting us, the Holy Spirit is empowering us, and we aren't the first to have to depend on God for the wisdom, power, and grace to live well in Babylon. Church Girl, there are other serious Christian women like you who fearlessly sing the hymn of a martyred Indian Christian: "I have decided to follow Jesus—no turning back, no turning back."[22]

We are the new exiles. We aren't in Babylon as a direct consequence of our rebellion like the nation of Judah, but we are free disciples in Christ and commissioned by God to spread the gospel and represent him as he accomplishes his plan to save humanity. It's imperative that while

21. 2 Timothy 3:16–17. The Greek word for "inspired by God" is *theopneustos,* which literally means "God-breathed" (NIV).

22. "'I Have Decided to Follow Jesus' is a Christian hymn originating from India. Some believe the lyrics are based on the last words of a man in Garo, Assam," whose entire family was publicly killed by angry villagers for converting to Christianity. It's thought that as he and his family were attacked, he composed these lyrics. Even as his sons were killed in front of him and he was asked if he would deny the faith, he continued to sing, "Though no one joins me, still I will follow." Shirley Murphy, "The True Story Behind the Song 'I Have Decided to Follow Jesus,'" Rev Shirley Murphy (blog), August 22, 2020, www.revshirleymurphy.co.uk/post/the-true-story-behind-the -song-i-have-decided-to-follow-jesus. Here also is an article that offers another perspective on the origin of the song: C. Michael Hawn, "History of Hymns: 'I Have Decided to Follow Jesus,'" Discipleship Ministries, June 10, 2020, www.umcdiscipleship.org/articles/history-of-hymns-i-have -decided-to-follow-jesus.

we are in our own type of Babylon, we stay authentically on brand as Black Christian women, maintaining Christian distinction by faithfully living differently from the world. God forbid the Church Girl becomes an unfortunate remix of the Fugees' lyric, because we don't want to be Church Girls siding with Babylon "fronting," as the song says, like we're "down with Mount Zion."

Daniel Bloomed in Babylon and So Can You

When we think of the book of Daniel, our minds tend to rush to the story of deliverance in the lion's den and the protection of the other three Hebrew boys from the fiery furnace. However, there are more gems to be mined. Daniel and his three friends, all teenagers in Babylonian exile, are models of what to do in Babylon. God has much to teach us Church Girls through just the book of Daniel's first chapter about how to navigate the culture, remain faithful, and flourish in a decaying world.

God Is in Control Even When It Looks Like the World Is Winning (Daniel 1:1–2)

Today many biblical scholars support the traditional view that Daniel authored the book in the sixth century B.C.[23] If this is true, one of the first things Daniel reveals to us about his ability to be faithful in Babylon is his perspective on who was in control of the Babylonian conquest and capture of Jerusalem. Daniel announced in the beginning of his account,

In the third year of the reign of King Jehoiakim of Judah, King Nebuchadnezzar of Babylon came to Jerusalem and laid siege to it. *The Lord handed King Jehoiakim of Judah over to him,* along with some of the vessels from the house of God. Nebuchadnezzar carried them to the land of Babylon, to the house of his god, and put the vessels in the treasury of his god. (1:1–2)

23. Wendy L. Widder, "Daniel, Book of, Critical Issues," in *Lexham Bible Dictionary.*

This is an important acknowledgment. Too often when bad things happen in our lives—particularly when terrible people seem to get away with doing horrible things, especially to Christians—we might ask, "Where is God?" But not Daniel. For many Black Christian women, we may see the promises of God in Scripture and hear the unlimited power of God preached to us from pulpits while also wrestling with a tearstained history of rape, abuse, abandonment, sexism, racism, and unjust treatment by law enforcement, politicians, and the other Nebuchadnezzars in our lives. In this world, Black women have to survive Harpos and Nebuchadnezzars. We might be tempted to question whether there is a limit to God's power. You may have wondered, *If God has all power, why couldn't he stop that evil from happening to me?* Conversely, if we don't question God's power, we often question his love, specifically his love for us. We think, *Maybe God does have all power; he just chose not to use any of it to help me. Maybe God loves, but perhaps he has his favorites and I'm not one of them.* We see men and other women doing much better than we are. We look in the mirror and think, *Maybe God loves men or white women more than me, because he doesn't seem to intervene to stop the injustice and trauma to my Black life.*

Bad times can tempt us to wonder about our acceptability and whether we have approval from God. That isn't far fetched. But Daniel's story helps us better understand God when bad times come. The main theme of the book of Daniel is God's sovereignty.[24] He is sovereign over the big things, like international powers and rotating planets, and sovereign over the smaller things, like getting a promotion or getting a good parking space at the grocery store. The old saints used to say, "God can do whatever he wants to do, whenever and however he wants to do it." However, it's important for us to remember that just because God is in control doesn't mean God is cold. His love, compassion, and, many times, promise of vengeance on our behalf[25] are fully present when he allows difficult things into our lives.

24. "The sovereignty of God is the fact that he is the Lord over creation; as sovereign, he exercises his rule. This rule is exercised through God's authority as king, his control over all things, and his presence with his covenantal people and throughout his creation." John M. Frame, "The Sovereignty of God," The Gospel Coalition, accessed February 14, 2024, www.thegospelcoalition.org/essay/the-sovereignty-of-god.

25. Romans 12:19–21.

We like to sing "God did" when something good happens to us, but do we have enough faith to say "God did," or, rather, "God allowed," when something hurts us? Though it isn't expressly mentioned in Scripture, it would be safe to infer that not only was God's power not questioned by Daniel but neither was his love. Without having the benefit of the entire Bible, like we have, Daniel knew God well enough to know that being sent to a metaphorical hell called Babylon didn't diminish God's character. Even in a hard place, dealing with hard people and hard circumstances, Daniel continually offered prayers and praise to the God who *put* him in Babylon.[26] It's imperative for us to remember that God does allow bad things to happen to his children and often it will look like the wicked are winning.[27] Sometimes we are suffering the consequences of our own choices, like the people of Judah, and other times we are suffering from the sinful choices others make that negatively affect us.

We like to sing "God did" when something good happens to us, but do we have enough faith to say "God did," or, rather, "God allowed," when something hurts us?

Not only did Daniel know the prophecy of the siege of Jerusalem, the destruction of the temple, and the seventy-year exile in Babylon, but he also knew of the judgment that would come upon his captors—he understood their destiny. Babylon the Great would fall by the will and power of God, the same God that handed the people of Judah over to a pagan nation.

Daniel is lauded in Scripture for his faithfulness to God in an anti-God land, but Daniel was faithful because he knew his God was faithful. When the world wants you to believe that our God is impotent, distant, or uncaring, meditate on God's Word to study his character, rehearse his promises, and see the fate of the wicked. When life feels hopeless and the

26. Daniel 2:19–23.
27. Psalm 73.

world feels victorious, do what the psalmist Asaph did: He entered God's sanctuary and understood the destiny of the wicked.[28] Enter God's sanctuary, make your way to God's presence, and like Asaph and Daniel, remember you know the end of the story. Trouble won't last always, and God is in control.[29]

Remember Who You Are (Daniel 1:3–7)

I remember as a child, one of the most difficult movie scenes to watch was from the 1977 TV miniseries *Roots,* based on Alex Haley's family history. The main character, Kunta Kinte, was captured from his African village, sold into the slave trade, and taken to America. Upon his arrival on the plantation, the enslaver had him hoisted up by his arms and mercilessly whipped until he would accept his new name: Toby. However, he refused, and with each determined "My name is Kunta Kinte," his body was split by the whip. As a young Black girl watching that scene, what started as pride in his unwillingness to take on the captor's forced identity quickly turned into fear and horror. As tears streamed down my little face, I remember trying to whisper to LeVar Burton, who played Kunta Kinte, through the television screen, "Just say 'Toby' so you can live." Eventually, we see the bleeding and exhausted teenage Kunta Kinte utter his captor's slave name, Toby, not out of submission but out of survival. To survive, Kunta Kinte surrendered his African name, but he never forgot who he truly was. Watching *Roots* taught me about the horror of slavery. Slavery didn't just isolate our ancestors from their homeland and people; enslavers wanted to take their identity and brainwash them so that they would forget the truth of how they were created to live and who they really were.

There is no whipping scene in the book of Daniel, but what we do know is that many people captured from Judah were castrated and made

---

28. Psalm 73:17.

29. Here are some scriptures to meditate on that reinforce God's sovereignty: 1 Chronicles 16:31; Psalm 115:3; Isaiah 14:24; 25:8–9; 41:10; 45:6–7; Jeremiah 29:11; 32:17; Matthew 19:26; Romans 8:28; 11:33; Ephesians 1:4–6; Colossians 1:16; Revelation 4:11.

eunuchs.[30] It isn't clear from the biblical text whether Daniel was made a eunuch; however, it is clear from Daniel 1:3–7 that the Babylonians had their own form of assimilation and brainwashing into their culture to strip God's people of their identity. There are a few important points to highlight about how Babylon and today's secular culture work to get you to forget your identity and your God.

Exploitation

Babylon always wants the best and brightest from God's people. The world will always take notice of the gifts, skills, and wisdom that God has blessed you with and will want to use them to further its agendas, businesses, ideologies, institutions, and spiritual practices and build its kingdom. The gifts we have been given are to be used for God's glory and the furtherance of God's kingdom agenda. Church Girl, the world would rather give you credit for your gifts and skills than ascribe that glory to God. Our egos must be ready to surrender the glory back to God. Whether we say it with our mouths or tattoo that truth on our hearts, we must be clear: We are nothing without God. Babylon is always interested in exploiting the vessel, taking the gifts, and robbing

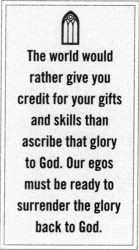

The world would rather give you credit for your gifts and skills than ascribe that glory to God. Our egos must be ready to surrender the glory back to God.

God of glory. Never let the devil use you to help him rob God of glory by recruiting your pride to be the getaway driver.

Indoctrination

It's interesting to me how many Christians have become weary of consistently attending Bible study, look at their watches during sermons,

30. 2 Kings 20:18.

avoid men's and women's ministry like the plague, show up late for worship, or view small groups and discipleship as a waste of time. These and other means of equipping and edifying in the church should be available arenas to help you grow to spiritual maturity, provide healthy biblical community, and teach you the fundamentals of your faith. These things shape your worldview, develop you spiritually, stir your gifts, sharpen you, train you in righteousness, and indoctrinate you into kingdom culture. How do we expect to skip Christian boot camp and still win the war that is being waged for our minds, allegiance, and identity?

The world wants you to forget who you are in Christ and also wants to give you a new identity. The world wants to put you in its own similar training and indoctrination program to get you ready to serve—but not serve Jesus. Whether through the universities, social media, entertainment (edutainment), the occult, New Age practices, gender redefinition, sex, marriage, or Black Religious Identity Cults (BRICs),[31] the world is constantly indoctrinating people into its beliefs, values, behaviors, and culture.

> The world's process of brainwashing involves attacking or erasing biblical truth with an overwhelming pollution of lies over a long period of time.

Unlike what happened to Daniel and the other captured people of God, who were forced to be indoctrinated into the Babylonian culture, many of us Black Christian women today voluntarily get indoctrinated. The world's process of brainwashing involves attacking or erasing biblical truth with an overwhelming pollution of lies over a long period of time, or it looks like minimizing and bemoaning what the Bible teaches about Jesus and his kingdom. The goal is to deceive you into believing the world has offered you something better than what Jesus offers.

---

31. Eric Mason, "Black Christians Are Confronting Black Lies About Christianity," *Christianity Today,* December 13, 2021, www.christianitytoday.com/ct/2022/january-february/urban-apologetics-eric-mason-black-christians.html.

Jesus gave us new hearts—new identity in him—and renews our minds through his Word. As Church Girls, we must know the fundamentals of our faith, grow in our ability to discern lies,[32] "contend for the faith,"[33] and, with the help of the Holy Spirit, guard the deposit that has been entrusted to us.[34] While the local church is called to have a hand in equipping you and building your faith, you must take personal responsibility for combating the indoctrination of the world. You must commit to doing such things as prioritizing your study of God's Word, practicing spiritual disciplines like fasting and prayer, surrounding yourself with godly friends, being discipled by wiser women, gathering for worship with the saints, submitting to godly leadership, participating in and supporting ministries of the local church, sacrificially serving and giving, and exposing (not enjoying) the fruitless deeds of darkness.[35] This is how you grow as a Christian. This is how you protect yourself from being indoctrinated by the world.

Identification

The enslavers in the movie *Roots* changed Kunta Kinte's name to Toby, and the Babylonians changed Daniel's and the three other Hebrew boys' names as well. Their Hebrew names honored the one true God, Yahweh. "The name Daniel means 'God is my judge,'... Hananiah means 'the Lord shows grace'... Mishael means 'Who is like God?' and ... Azariah means 'The Lord is my help.'"[36] A name change in the ancient world was significant and went to the identity and core of who a person was. The new names Daniel and his friends were given all honored the false gods the Babylonians worshipped. Daniel's name was changed to Belteshazzar, or "Bel protect his life," Hananiah's name was changed to Shadrach, or "Command of Aku" (the moon god), Mishael's name

---

32. 1 John 4:1–6.
33. Jude 1:3.
34. 2 Timothy 1:14.
35. Ephesians 5:11–12.
36. Wiersbe, *Be Resolute,* 21.

was changed to Meshach, or "Who is as Aku is?" and Azariah's name was changed to Abednego, or "Servant of Nego."[37]

For Black Christian women today, we may not experience a radical name change by the culture, but the world is inviting and influencing us to live as if we've been stripped of the identity God gave us to instead be identified with a false god of this world. We've heard it said, "It's not what you are called; it's what you answer to," and let it be known that this world is trying to get us to answer to all kinds of names and identities that don't reflect what God has already said about us. To bloom in Babylon as Black women, we need to know what God has already called us. These false names, worldviews, and dispositions of the heart can cause us to answer to lesser callings and begin to function beneath the inheritance we have in Christ.

- *God calls us new creations in Christ,*[38] but the world wants us to answer to our old selves—unchanged and slaves to the flesh as if we haven't been redeemed.

- *God calls us his adopted children and heirs,*[39] but the world wants us to answer to *orphan,* with no parent, future, or hope.

- *God calls us his sheep* who know his voice and follow him,[40] but the world wants us to follow the voice of the father of lies, like Eve did in the garden.

- *God calls us former foreigners* in the land of Egypt,[41] which should sensitize us to the command to not exploit or oppress foreigners in any way, but the world wants us to answer to xenophobia and nationalism.

- *God calls us "a chosen race, a royal priesthood, a holy nation"* (1 Peter 2:9), but the world wants us to answer to witches,

---

37. Wiersbe, *Be Resolute,* 21.
38. 2 Corinthians 5:17.
39. John 1:12; Romans 8:17; Ephesians 1:5.
40. John 10:27.
41. Exodus 22:21.

mediums, divinators, and psychics, as if we need a human to mediate for us. Christ is our mediator, and we offer praise to him for calling us out of darkness into the marvelous light. As Christians, we shouldn't play with dark magic by "illegitimately accessing the spirit world."[42]

- *God calls us friends of Jesus,*[43] but the world wants us to answer to *enemy of the cross, despiser of Jesus, accuser of Jesus, distant from Jesus,* and *distrustful of Jesus.*

- *God calls us temples of the Holy Spirit,*[44] but the world wants us to answer to our passions, our egos, and our flesh and submit our bodies as members of unrighteousness.[45] The world wants us to believe that our bodies belong to us, not God, and therefore we can do whatever we want with them.

- *God calls us members of Christ's body,*[46] but the world wants us to answer to autonomy, individualism, isolation, and disunity.

- *God calls us ambassadors for Christ,*[47] but the world wants us to answer to tolerance, universalism, "to each his own," and "go along to get along" as we engage the culture.

- *God calls us "his workmanship, created in Christ Jesus for good works"* (Ephesians 2:10), but the world wants us to answer to the fruitless works of darkness and just sit down on our gifts and do nothing.

- *God calls us chosen,*[48] but the world wants us to answer to *rejected, alone, unloved, unwanted,* and *discarded.* The world doesn't want us to remember that he chose us in Christ before the foundation of

---

42. Leviticus 20:6; Deuteronomy 18:9–15; 1 Samuel 28:7–20; Acts 19:19; Galatians 5:19–20; "illegitimately accessing the spirit world" is a phrase I've heard my pastor, Dr. Eric Mason, frequently use to describe why these pagan practices are sinful.

43. John 15:15.

44. 1 Corinthians 6:19.

45. Romans 6:13.

46. 1 Corinthians 12:27.

47. 2 Corinthians 5:20.

48. Ephesians 1:4.

the world, he loves us with an everlasting love, and Jesus pursued us for relationship and salvation.

- *God calls us citizens of heaven,*[49] but the world wants us to answer to *citizens of the earth* and submit to the ungodly dictates and kings of the world.

- *God calls us free,*[50] but the world wants us to answer to *slaves* and submit to being bound emotionally, spiritually, and physically.

- *God calls us to be prophets like Amos and apply the gospel mandate to social justice issues,*[51] but some, including segments of the church, want to identify us as *Marxist* or *CRT thumpers* and say, "Just preach the gospel," as if calling out racism, seeking justice, protecting the marginalized, preaching liberation, and defending the oppressed aren't mandates of the gospel of Jesus Christ.[52]

Resolve to Be Faithful (Daniel 1:8–16)

Daniel determined that he would not defile himself with the king's food or with the wine he drank. So he asked permission from the chief eunuch not to defile himself. (verse 8)

Daniel was a rising star in Babylon. He and his three friends were among those recruited as the best, brightest, and most beautiful that the Judean exiles had to offer. They came from Judah's aristocracy, and they were exactly what the king of Babylon wanted in his inner circle. Daniel was matriculating through the three-year training program to serve the king, which afforded him some access, privilege, and luxuries that were reserved for the king, like food and wine. Commentators have speculated on various reasons Daniel refused the king's food and wine, citing that

---

49. Philippians 3:20.
50. Galatians 5:1.
51. Amos 5.
52. Matthew 23:23.

the kinds of food or the methods of preparation likely would have been a violation according to the law of Moses[53] and that the food being given may have first been offered sacrificially to the Babylonian gods, which would have been associated with idolatrous worship forbidden by Jewish law.[54]

Another commentator proposed an interesting consideration on why Daniel would have wanted to be resolute, saying, "Babylon was simply smothering Daniel and his friends. Daniel may well have thought, 'There is a real danger here: I could get sucked up into this and neutered by it all.' He recognized that if Babylon [the world and its values] gets into you, the show is over."[55] While refusing the food and wine seems simple and not as sacrificial as the things we often feel called to refuse, it's important to note that this was a courageous and bold act of faithfulness.[56]

When we refuse something to honor Jesus in our context, it requires boldness and faith. When we refuse things from our bosses or friends that appear to be gifts or opportunities but don't align with our values, it could be taken as insulting and may jeopardize promotions and friendships. When we experience pressure from peers, even other Christians, to do the wrong thing because "everyone is doing it," it takes boldness to say no and stand on our convictions. Last, there is no doubt that the king's food was quality and delicious, which made the temptation to partake even more challenging.[57] Whenever we sacrifice something for our Christian convictions, it isn't easy; we may really want to go along and enjoy it, but the Lord promises to provide a way of escape[58] and to reward us for doing good if we don't give up.[59]

We get offered many things by the world, and sometimes saying no is difficult, seems trivial, or feels unfair. The offer can be a person, place

53. Leviticus 11; Deuteronomy 14.

54. Stephen R. Miller, *Daniel,* The New American Commentary, vol. 18 (Nashville: B&H, 1994), 66–67.

55. Dale Ralph Davis, *The Message of Daniel* (Downers Grove, Ill.: InterVarsity, 2013), 32, note added in Daniel L. Akin, *Exalting Jesus in Daniel* (Nashville: Holman Reference, 2017), 10.

56. Miller, *Daniel,* 67–68.

57. Miller, *Daniel,* 67.

58. 1 Corinthians 10:13.

59. Galatians 6:9.

(status/position), thing, or a mindset you choose to adopt. Like a legal contract, the world makes the offer and wants us to accept with rationalizations like these:

- You'll save more money; just cheat on your taxes—everyone is doing it.

- You can be the boss at work and climb the corporate ladder; just be willing to step on people and be unscrupulous on your way to the top—all the winners do it.

- Steal from your job; it's only supplies. Swipe that company card for yourself; they don't pay you enough anyway.

- You deserve pleasure and a stress release. God made you a sexual being. Just watch porn, use vibrators, or go ahead and have sex with someone who isn't your husband.

- Put yourself first, take care of your tribe, look out for your own, be in the in crowd, secure the bag, and enjoy the spoils of a capitalist grind culture; you don't need to speak up against injustice, fight for the poor, care for the oppressed, or see your neighbor as an equal image bearer.

- You need to be treated well and go on a date, and none of the men on these dating apps or in the church are your type. So just date this married man; he said he's waiting to get his divorce finalized. Or just date the "spiritual" dude who believes there is more than one way to get to God; so what if he isn't a practicing Christian? He said his grandmother used to take him to church. He's fine; he has a good job; he has a car; he owns his own house; he has a tight fade; he has a pulse; he just doesn't have Christ.

- You can get a lot of attention because you're beautiful. Don't let patriarchy and the churchy Holy Rollers police your body. Just show off your breasts on social media; turn sideways in your pictures so people can see the shape of your butt; flaunt your sexuality loud and proud—let 'em know whatchu working with.

- Let them know you aren't the one to be played with; show your strength: "Fool me twice, shame on me." You'll feel better after you cuss them out and give them a piece of your mind. The cool Christians are hood and holy, right?

- Enjoy a blast from the past; just meet your ex for lunch, flirt with them in the DMs, send that picture, and remind them what they let get away. It's not sex, and your husband doesn't have to know.

> Live your life for applause from heaven, and walk the stage of life for an audience of one—the Lord Jesus Christ!

Some Christian influencers begin functioning in the church (our preaching and platforms) in ways that look not like a faithful brand of Christianity that honors Scripture but rather like a version of Christianity smudged with fingerprints from the world. Like me, you may have noticed the church compromising in various ways and taking "food and drink" from the world for personal comfort, money, connections, prominence, and acceptance. For instance, I've seen the following disturbing trends:

- If you want more social media followers, more speaking engagements, more books sold, and more access to religious power and fame—just make church feel like Hollywood and be partial to celebrities. Just exalt people's personal preferences above the Word. Teach love is love; lead with sensuality as a leader, preacher, and Bible teacher; make it cool to curse and get high as a Christian; ignore leaders who are living in sin; and stop preaching about holiness and hell.

- If you don't want to rock the boat on New Age syncretism in the church, start talking about the universe, energy, the law of attraction, vibrations, manifesting, and chakras.

- If you want to blow up as a Christian influencer and leader, rebrand Christianity as the faith that brings prosperity and makes you, instead of Christ, the center of everything. Start preaching "It's your season," "Name it and claim it," "Get money," "Get boaz," "Get loose," and turn Christianity into a Burger King slogan: "Have it your way." If you want to be admired, show the world the property deal you closed, the clothes you wear, the car you drive, but not the cross you carry.

We don't have to sacrifice righteousness for relevance. Live your life for applause from heaven, and walk the stage of life for an audience of one—the Lord Jesus Christ! If you notice these trends among your influencers or similar ones at the church you attend, maybe you should consider the impact they are having on your life, evaluate whether these patterns have been so normalized that you are desensitized to the behavior, and pray about how you can be better encouraged to live out your Christian distinction. If you are a woman who can honestly admit that you've slipped into some of these trends, there is grace and time to change. People are watching you, and we have a responsibility to represent the Lord in a manner that gives him all the glory. We can't give God all the glory if we are reserving some for ourselves.[60]

God Rewards Your Faithfulness (Daniel 1:14–21)

We've heard it said in our culture, "No risk, no reward," and certainly, Daniel and the other faithful Judean exiles took great risks. Babylon wants us to believe it's a waste of time, it's too costly, and we'll end up with nothing and no one if we are faithful to God. But those are lies from the pit of hell. God rewards faithfulness. The reward may not be

60. Isaiah 42:8.

what we think or on our time schedule, but God doesn't ignore the faithfulness of his servants, as these scriptures remind us:

- "The LORD will repay every man for his righteousness and his loyalty" (1 Samuel 26:23).

- "Blessed is the one who endures trials, because when he has stood the test he will receive the crown of life that God has promised to those who love him" (James 1:12).

- "Let us not get tired of doing good, for we will reap at the proper time if we don't give up" (Galatians 6:9).

- "Look, I am coming soon, and my reward is with me to repay each person according to his work" (Revelation 22:12).

These few passages about God's rewards for faithfulness may feel so futuristic in scope that you might wonder if you can expect a reward in this present life. While it's true that some of the greatest rewards we'll receive will be given at the second advent of Jesus, Daniel shows us that God rewards, in real time, the faithfulness of his children.

God Rewards Your Faithfulness with Favor

Immediately following Daniel's decision to not defile himself, God granted him "kindness and compassion from the chief eunuch" (Daniel 1:9). This is important because the chief eunuch was assigned the responsibility to prepare the trainees for their service to the king and to make sure they had the proper food for nourishment.[61] Daniel had resolved to not eat the king's food, but he knew he had to get the support and permission of the pagan authority figure to do it safely. Notice, we see Daniel not circumventing the pagan authority structure but humbly working with it. Our attitudes and dispositions in the world can cooperate with God's desire to give us favor or work against it. Daniel

61. Daniel 1:3–5.

asked, and a pagan official was filled with kindness and compassion toward God's child in exile. Scripture tells us, "When a person's ways please the LORD, he makes even his enemies to be at peace with him" (Proverbs 16:7).

> Don't cut corners, show respect and humility when working in the world, do your job with excellence, and stay faithful, and then watch God work and grant you amazing grace.

God can give you favor with people who don't seem to like you or love God. One time I needed a simple signature from someone on my campus for scholarship paperwork. The woman I needed to see had a history of being very difficult and nasty and making every request feel like you asked for the life of her first grandchild. So many of my friends said, "Just sign her name and be done with it." I knew that was wrong, and even though everyone was doing it and it seemed to work for them, I didn't want to forge her name. I remember before I walked into the office to get her signature, I prayed and asked God to go before me. Long story short, I walked into the office and was greeted with the warmest smile and "Hey, baby, what can I do for you?" I almost passed out. Even though I had just prayed, I was shocked. But why? I asked God for favor, and sometimes favor comes fast with a signature and a smile. But that day it came with so much more. Not only did she sign my papers, but she also helped me complete the next sections of my paperwork, made a phone call to the bursar's office, and got a refund check processed. Anyone who matriculated through an HBCU is taking a lap and about to speak in tongues right now, because they know this miracle was on par with the splitting of the Red Sea!

When you are determined to obey God, when you are determined to be faithful, God will use those in authority over you to give you compassion and kindness. Some say "Favor ain't fair," but it is God's reward for faithfulness. You want to do business and your job in a way that honors God, but you may find yourself with a difficult boss or co-worker, or you may need approval from a loan officer, the green light from a grant reviewer, a building inspection to go successfully, or help with your taxes. Don't cut corners, show respect and humility when working in the world, do your job with excellence, and stay faithful, and then watch God work and grant you amazing grace.

God Rewards Your Faithfulness with Mental and Spiritual Gifts

We love to say things like "Your gifts will make room for you,"[62] even though, contextually, that passage is referring to said room being made for you when you bring a bribe to the king. However, as a broader application point, the good gifts God gives us will open doors for us with people and in places we couldn't have made it to without the help of God. God's gift giving is good like that. In Daniel 1:17–21, we see Daniel being presented to the king for an evaluation after his years of training. The king promoted Daniel and his friends to attend to him and consulted them "in every matter of wisdom and understanding [and] found them ten times better than all the magicians and mediums in his entire kingdom" (verse 20). The gifts God gave led to their exaltation in Babylon. Daniel was faithful to God, God favored Daniel with gifts, and then Daniel was promoted.[63]

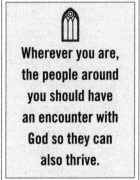

Wherever you are, the people around you should have an encounter with God so they can also thrive.

God has given you gifts and talents that will unlock doors of opportunity in your life, not just so you can benefit personally but also so you can be a light in a dark world. Regardless of what industry, organizations, schools, affiliations, social networks, or families you have access to, wherever you

---

62. Referring to Proverbs 18:16.
63. Daniel 1:8, 17, 19–21.

are, that place should get better because you are there. The world will want you, like the king wanted Daniel, because of the grace you have when you are operating in faithfulness to God, even if they don't know it or care.

Daniel used his gifts and took advantage of his promotion for God's glory, and so should you. After Daniel's promotion, he honored God before the king, didn't take credit for his gifts, used his influence to get promotions for God's people, counseled the king to change his ways, and showed allegiance to God in the face of death,[64] and before the end of the book, the king was giving praise to Daniel's God.[65] Daniel was given gifts and promoted to attend the king because God was trying to reach the king. God has gifted you and placed you in some area of the world because he's trying to reach someone in your sphere of influence. You are called to flourish with your gifts in the place God puts you. Wherever you are, the people around you should have an encounter with God so they can also thrive. "Seek the peace and prosperity of the city to which I have carried you into exile. Pray to the LORD for it, because if it prospers, you too will prosper" (Jeremiah 29:7, NIV).

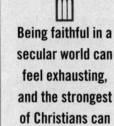

Being faithful in a secular world can feel exhausting, and the strongest of Christians can experience *faithfulness fatigue.*

Being faithful in a secular world can feel exhausting, and the strongest of Christians can experience *faithfulness fatigue.* The truth is, sometimes we get tired of doing the right thing all the time. We are exhausted with denying the flesh, loving our enemies, being the oddballs among peers, fighting demons, defending the faith, serving in church, saying no to sin, and waiting for Jesus to come back. All while the world

---

64. Daniel 2:27–28, 30, 49; 4:27; 6:10–12.
65. Daniel 4:34–37.

seems to be having a grand ole time living it up, unbothered by sin and unconcerned about God.

To combat faithfulness fatigue, it's important to be honest when we are feeling weak and tired. Fatigue is a symptom, not a sin, but unaddressed symptoms can quickly turn into a sin sickness. Being honest, confessing our weaknesses, living in community, having healthy outlets for self-care, and abiding in Jesus are key. Even soldiers on the battlefield take breaks to get restored. We can't live on the front lines of Babylon indefinitely; we all need rest, or we will be in danger of getting injured by the opposition or injuring someone on the same team with friendly fire.

We may be in Babylon, but Babylon doesn't have to be in us.

We may be in Babylon, but Babylon doesn't have to be in us. The paradoxical call of a flourishing Christian woman in secular culture is to "come out from among them" (2 Corinthians 6:17) yet be among them. We must have standards, thinking, affections, and actions that are different from the world yet live, work, and build relationships with the world in hope of them having a relationship with Christ. Many people in Babylon will never read a Bible, but they will read you. Church Girl, you are the living epistle being read by the world,[66] and a key to your flourishing and theirs is making sure you are telling an accurate story about God's kingdom while living in another kingdom. Will your life tell God's story right?

We may be exiles for now, but one day our Christus Victor will crack the sky and come back for his bride, and there will be no more suffering, no more persecution, no more fear, no more temptation, no more pain, no more trauma, no more enemies, no more Babylon. We are going home with our King to a building not made by human hands.[67] Church Girl, one day this life will be over, and we will enter his rest from our la-

---

66. 2 Corinthians 3:2–3.
67. 2 Corinthians 5:1.

bor.[68] We will walk all over the New Jerusalem with the other saints of God, and any rewards God gives us for our faithfulness to him? We will cast those crowns at his feet. Just stay faithful a little while longer, run your race with endurance, keep the faith, and don't quit. In the words of an old Negro spiritual—"Before I'd be a slave, I'll be buried in my grave and go home to my Lord and be free." Keep blooming in Babylon, Church Girl.

Be faithful until death, and I will give you the crown of life. (Revelation 2:10, NKJV)

A Gospel Vision for Your Flourishing

A gospel vision for your flourishing in a decaying world starts with understanding that when Christ saved you from the world, he sent you back into the world to be his ambassador and representative. The book of Daniel provides a great model for us as Black Christian women on how to flourish in secular culture. It's important to remember that God is in control, even when hardship and suffering come. While you are an exile in the world, you aren't without hope and power, and you know the end of the story. You also must remember who you are, because Babylon wants you to forget your identity in Christ. And last, you must resolve to be faithful and trust that God will reward your faithfulness.

Discussion Questions

 LIGHT: Jesus saved us from the world to send us back into the world.

1. What is the difference between Babylon and Mount Zion in Scripture, and what did you learn about your true citizenship as a Christian?

2. Why are we saved from the world to be sent back into the world?

---

68. Revelation 14:13.

👓 **LENS:** Babylon (the world) wants us to lose our Christian distinction, but God has called us to remain faithful as his representatives in the world.

1. How can you recognize when you begin to drift from the Lord?

2. What hardships have you experienced as a Black Christian woman in Babylon that have tempted you to distrust God, especially as you watched the wicked win and prosper?

3. How has the world tried to exploit your gifts, indoctrinate you with its values, and get you to embrace a subpar identity rather than the one given to you by God?

4. What are things that you can do to help you remember God is in control, remember who you are, and resolve to be faithful while living in a secular world?

💜 **LOVE:** God will help us bloom in Babylon. He has placed us in the world not to be crushed by it but to be a light to it. His love and power will keep us.

1. What fears do you struggle with as a Christian as you seek to live faithfully? What do you fear will happen if you don't eat the king's food or take his gifts (e.g., loss, rejection, missed opportunities)?

2. Do you ever get faithfulness fatigue as a Black Christian woman? How can God and community help you when you feel weak?

3. What are worship songs and scriptures that you meditate on to help you in Babylon? Write a prayer of resolution to be faithful in Babylon, and share it with another sister.

CHAPTER 7

Have You Seen Her?

A Gospel Vision for Missing Black Women in the Church

What do you think? If someone has a hundred sheep, and one of them goes astray, won't he leave the ninety-nine on the hillside and go and search for the stray? And if he finds it, truly I tell you, he rejoices over that sheep more than over the ninety-nine that did not go astray.
—Matthew 18:12–13

When I was four years old, I went missing for three hours. While it was a common occurrence for my parents to not be able to find me because I was hiding between the racks of clothes at the Strawbridge & Clothier department store, this wasn't the case. No, I was taken. A neighbor who lived up the street asked my mother if she could take me "around the corner," which is just a hood way of saying "not too far," to buy me ice cream. Up and back, it should have been a thirty-minute trip, but after more than an hour passed, my mother knew something was wrong. There were no cellphones back then, so I can only imagine the horror, the guilt, and the fear my mother must have felt. The entire neighborhood was searching for me, including the woman's own family members, who, my parents said, "had that uncomfortable look on their faces." People were worried because everybody knew Sandy meant no harm but her mental disability at times prevented her from appreciating the gravity of her actions.

Eventually, I was found, grinning from ear to ear, with dried ice cream around my mouth and Sandy holding tightly to my hand. Sandy had done exactly what she told my mother she would do: She took me around the corner to get ice cream, but then she walked with me two more miles to the mall. I have no memory of this event, although I do remember Sandy. Praise God, I was found, and I was fine. That's the way you want all missing stories to end—missing, searched for, found, and with no memory of anything terrible happening in between. But that's not how all missing stories end, especially for Black women.

Not too long ago, God led me on a path to learn about missing Black women in the world. To my surprise, he used that education to set in motion a series of events to open my eyes, sensitize my heart, convict my soul, and invite me to be burdened for the missing Black women in the church. This is a burden I'm inviting you to share. We need to care about Black women we don't know who go missing in the world, as well as Black women we do know who go missing from our congregations.

This chapter is an invitation to consider how the power of sisterhood, friendship, and discipleship among Black women can be leveraged to help missing Black women. I believe our collective eyes, ears, and empathy are the tools we need to make sure Black women aren't invisible, ignored in the church, or unnoticed and unfound when they depart. Whether you are a Church Girl in leadership or a lay parishioner in the pews, we each have a part to play in helping one another stay rooted where God plants us so we can flourish in our lives and local churches.

I believe our collective eyes, ears, and empathy are the tools we need to make sure Black women aren't invisible.

Despite Black women historically being considered the backbone of the church and earning the distinction of outnumbering men in the pews, there is a disturbing trend that we must address. Though we as Black women are among the most religious groups in the United States,[1] there is an exodus of Black women from churches for a variety of reasons, and some of us aren't just leaving a specific congregation; we are leaving the faith completely. Aswad Walker of the *Defender* wrote about the top reasons Black millennials say they are leaving the church: (1) The church is too judgmental, (2) they are choosing traditional African spiritual practices, (3) the church is too anti-intellectual or closed to new information, (4) the church is too apolitical, and (5) not enough of their peers attend.[2] Additional thoughts include the impact of patriarchy in the church and Black women not being able to adequately see themselves as image bearers of the triune God.[3]

Do these conclusions surprise you, or are you familiar with what is being sourced as the reason for Black women leaving our churches? As Black Christian women, it's imperative that we investigate and become sensitive to these realities so that we can better serve as apologists and be sisters and friends to other Church Girls whom the enemy is trying to isolate and sift. Being sensitized to missing Black women in church was a game changer for me. God gave me an unexpected but beautiful lesson on what it means to die to yourself so that another Black woman can live.

How My Heart Became Hardened

Our church had a hard season of post-pandemic member exoduses that culminated in disappointment, confusion, sadness, and loss as several members left the church without warning, conversation, or explanation. Or if there was some communication, it was rooted in "God told me to leave" with no room for discussion, like a Do Not Disturb sign on a

1. Theola Labbé-DeBose, "Black Women Are Among Country's Most Religious Groups," *Washington Post,* July 6, 2012, www.washingtonpost.com/local/Black-women-are-among-countrys-most-religious-groups/2012/07/06/gJQA0BksSW_story.html.

2. Aswad Walker, "Top 5 Reasons Black Millennials Are Leaving the Church," *Defender,* September 20, 2023, https://defendernetwork.com/news/opinion/top-5-reasons-Black-millennials-are-leaving-the-church.

3. Claudia Allen, "For Colored Girls When Christianity Isn't Enough," *Message,* March 5, 2021, www.messagemagazine.com/articles/for-colored-girls-when-christianity-isnt-enough.

hotel door. Do not disturb, do not come in, do not engage, do not ask me any other questions, because "God told me to leave" and that should insulate me from your curiosity and care. Not all former members left this way, but when people you love, pastored, served with, discipled, prayed with, comforted, and enjoyed laughs and meals with leave suddenly, it's difficult; it was for me, especially when it was women I knew well from our women's ministry.

Admittedly, many thoughts that often swirled through my head were very me-focused, especially if the leaving was quiet and the person was unwilling to talk. I would wonder, *Did I do something wrong? Did I miss something? Did I love them well enough?* I personalized things that probably didn't have anything to do with me. At the root of it was that leaving without a proper goodbye just didn't feel good.

Conversely, if my thoughts weren't me-focused, then they would be them-focused: *They are selfish. They just left as a leader and didn't care about how that would affect the ministry,* or, *They were takers and not givers, and when they were done taking, they ghosted everyone.* Maybe, *This is immaturity. They resisted the truth, they wanted to live the way they wanted, and they blame everyone else and take no responsibility for (whatever may have happened),* or, *If something bad happened, why didn't they care to tell us so we could address it and work to make things better together?* The thoughts were mostly negative self-talk. It hadn't always been that way. The reality was that, after the pandemic, there was a shift in me. I've since processed it and realized that the shift was due to cumulative loss over several years, unreconciled issues with people (which I hate leaving unaddressed), God's purging, and grief. Nothing can be more disorienting or damaging than unrecognized and unmanaged grief. I didn't even realize that grief had changed me until God began to speak.

I want to share a story with you that happened over three days around that time. Much like the death, burial, and resurrection of Jesus, God did something miraculous in my life. In three days, he taught me what it means to go after the lost, die to yourself, and be used as an instrument to save. It's a story about being courageous enough to not mind your own business and to think of others above yourself. I believe this is an important lesson God wants to teach Church Girls so we can better protect Black women from going missing and go after one another when we do.

Day One

It was an ordinary day in the office. When I arrived at the church building to work, our office manager casually informed me, "Dr. Sarita, I'm not sure if you knew, but Tammy filled out the church's exit interview form stating that she would be leaving the church." *What!*

"When did this happen?" I asked. I was told that, a few weeks before, Tammy had completed the church's "I'm leaving" form but her answers for why she was leaving were vague. This may not seem like a big deal as you read this, but for me, it was a bit of a gut punch. Tammy was a young woman whom I was building a relationship with. She was a life group leader, a serious Bible student, and instrumental in reporting a case of abuse of power by one of our male lay leaders that opened the door to a necessary intervention, discipline, and restoration plan. She was a consistent participant in women's ministry; she was someone I prayed with and talked to on numerous occasions, and I generally felt like we had a healthy relationship. I liked her; she had spunk and was a faithful servant. It was very shocking that Tammy, a leader and respected member of our congregation, would just decide to up and leave without talking to anyone.

My initial thought was to wonder if something had happened, but the office manager said Tammy didn't indicate on her exit interview that anything nefarious had occurred. I tried to recall the last time we spoke. I was sure we had smiled and said hello with a hug. I tried to recollect whether anything had seemed off or wrong with her, and I couldn't. Her leaving without communicating just didn't make sense to me.

What I know to be true today, which I wasn't aware of at the time, is that the tidal wave of emotions that I felt had less to do with Tammy and more to do with the countless other women before her who just left the church without saying anything. When this had happened before, my first thought was always to give the person a call, to check in and see if they were leaving because of some hurt that didn't get addressed. However, this time, I immediately canceled that plan. For the first time, I said something in my heart that I'd never said before: *I refuse to call her. I'm tired of chasing after women who just up and leave the church and don't say anything.* I felt justified in my anger. I felt annoyed by her apparent casualness. I felt abandoned by someone I thought cared about me like I cared about her. At the very least, I assumed that even if she was planning to leave, she would have at least told me. I was done feeling this responsibility to call, text, and meet with women who didn't appear to care.

If you serve in the local church or are a leader, I'm not sure if you can relate to my feelings. My response wasn't right, but it was real. I'm sharing this unflattering expression of raw frustration for a few reasons. First, I don't think people who leave churches always know that it may make others sad to see them leave without a conversation. Second, I believe my response is one of the reasons so many Black women fall through the cracks when they leave—because people give up on them. And last, a response or heart like mine may be one of the reasons Black women decide to leave.

My role in ministry isn't just about planning events, teaching, creating curriculum, organizing ministries, or providing counseling. Rather, I'm the person who often intervenes when I have knowledge about a problem another woman has at the church. My unspoken role is to take concerns to leadership, to help translate and communicate church members' pain, and to work with the pastors to see how we can help. But in this instance with Tammy, I was different. I'll admit I didn't pray and I didn't take a moment to look at it from another perspective. I was in my feelings, and I let my feelings lead me instead of the Lord. I didn't call as I normally would. I'd already said to myself, as if I was talking to God, *I refuse to call her.*

Day Two

I was scrolling on Facebook when I saw "Please share—my friend's daughter is missing." I clicked on the shared post to get more details and realized we were all mutual friends. In fact, the mother of the missing teen had been a member of our church with her family. My heart began to race as I realized I knew this family. As terrifying as it would be to know that a Black teen couldn't be found, it was doubly painful to have had a relationship with the family. I read through the details of when she was last seen, whom to contact, and the request for prayers. I immediately picked up my phone and contacted the mother. I'm sure she had received hundreds of messages from concerned family, friends, and church members, but I just had to reach out. I expressed my sadness and concern and asked how the church could help. I'd never personally known anyone who was missing, so this felt surreal. Apparently, the mother believed her daughter had run away from home, but I wasn't given many other details, nor did that matter. I just wanted to help, and I knew our church family would want to help too.

I quickly sent her a monetary donation, hoping it could help with food, printing flyers, or whatever was needed. Later that day, the mom reached out to me, grateful for my concern and love gift. She informed me she and her family had moved and were no longer at our church. I told her that them no longer being members didn't matter; I still wanted to be a blessing. She said she would let me know if she could think of anything and just asked for prayer. Ironically, while I was praying for the missing child, my heart was still hardened by the experience the previous day, and I didn't make the connection with Tammy. But that would soon change.

Day Three

Something (someone) told me to open my Audible app on my phone the next morning. Under the suggested titles on the app, one caught my eye right away because I recognized the name of my old teacher's assistant from Freedom Theatre. Actress Erika Alexander, perhaps best known as cousin Pam on the hit sitcom *The Cosby Show* or Maxine on the sitcom *Living Single,* was the demonstrator for my dance and acting class at the historic Black theater training school I attended in Philadelphia. Erika was the narrator for a neo-noir true crime drama documentary called *Finding Tamika,* produced by Kevin Hart and Charlamagne tha God's SBH Productions.

This story detailed the search for Tamika Huston, a twenty-four-year-old Black woman from Spartanburg, South Carolina, who went missing in 2004. Sadly, Tamika's remains were found fifteen months later. An ex-boyfriend confessed to murdering her and disposing of her remains in the woods. Unfortunately, disappearances like Tamika's are more common than we typically hear about. According to Federal Bureau of Investigation reports, statistics from the National Crime Information Center's missing and unidentified persons files suggest that nearly one hundred thousand Black females went missing in 2022.[4] Additionally, the series highlighted gross disparities in our nation between missing white women and missing Black women. The late Gwen Ifill, the first African American woman to host a national news program on PBS,[5] coined the term "Missing White Woman Syndrome" to describe the disparity in media coverage that white women receive over missing Black and Brown women.

The Audible documentary sent me down a rabbit hole looking up missing Black women. One article I stumbled upon mentioned an HBO documentary series called *Black and Missing*. I quickly began to watch. There were two things I heard in the HBO special that God used to rock me to the core and allow me to see Black women like I'd never seen them before. Natalie Wilson, co-founder of the Black and Missing Foundation, said, "According to FBI stats, there were more than six hundred thousand people reported missing in the US in 2019. Close to 40 percent of those were people of color . . . but if you ask anyone to name three missing African Americans, I guarantee you they would come up short."[6] She went on to describe that police officers frequently label Black children as runaways when in fact they were kidnapped. When children are labeled as runaways, it puts them in a special category

4. "2022 NCIC Missing Person and Unidentified Person Statistics," FBI, accessed February 15, 2024, www.fbi.gov/file-repository/2022-ncic-missing-person-and-unidentified-person-statistics .pdf/view.

5. "Gwen Ifill," The HistoryMakers, accessed March 8, 2024, www.thehistorymakers.org/ biography/gwen-ifill-6.

6. Natalie Wilson, in *Black and Missing,* episode 1, directed by Geeta Gandbhir, Samantha M. Knowles, and Yoruba Richen, featuring Derrica Wilson and Natalie Wilson, aired November 23, 2021, on HBO Max, www.hbo.com/black-and-missing/season-1/1-episode-1.

"where they're responsible for whatever happens to them on the streets because they left."[7] It signals to the police that they don't have to put too much energy and effort into looking for these Black children.

I was listening to a message from the world that was stirring me about Black women in the church. There is a difference in how the system is set up and willing to respond to people who are seen and labeled as missing versus those labeled as runaways—those who are believed to have willingly left home aren't searched for the same. A white child who is classified as missing often triggers an Amber Alert, the national missing child alert that secures local and national law enforcement resources and attention to find the missing person. But when you are labeled a runaway, there is no Amber Alert and very little, if any, media coverage. In fact, when a person leaves and is labeled a runaway, the belief is that whatever happens to them out on the street is their fault and they deserve whatever happens to them. We have empathy for those we label missing, and we have contempt for those we label runaways.

> We have empathy for those we label missing, and we have contempt for those we label runaways.

Whew! I thought I was just watching a documentary about missing Black women in the world, but God said to me, *Sarita, that is what is going on in the church.* The Holy Spirit was revealing that when Black women disappear or leave the church, for whatever reason, too often they are labeled runaways instead of missing. We treat them differently when they leave. There is no church-wide Amber Alert. There is no search party. There is no phone call, visit, care, concern, or grace. They just vanish, and too many adopt the attitude "They left, so they deserve whatever they get." The next thing the Lord said to me was *Call Tammy!*

Look at the amazing grace and mercy of God, who pursued me through a Facebook post about a missing girl all the way to an HBO documentary just so he could get my attention, snatch my edges, snatch

7. Wilson, in *Black and Missing.*

me up out of my feelings, and get me back on kingdom mission. The setup, the love, the sovereignty, and the providence of God overwhelmed me. I cried, I repented, and instead of refusing to call, I rushed to call Tammy. If you're reading this, maybe God is using this story to grab your attention like he did mine. Before we go on, let me ask you, Is there someone you need to call? Is there a church member, former church member, family member, or friend who left the church, left the friendship, left the job, left the faith? Someone who ran away, and you decided, *I'm not going after them.* Maybe God wants you to make a call. Before the end of this chapter, you'll see why you should make the call.

When I called Tammy, she answered very quietly and reservedly. This wasn't how I was accustomed to hearing Tammy, who is typically jubilant, is full of energy, and laughs loudly. She was pleasant, but I could feel the tension through the phone. I proceeded to tell her that I'd heard she submitted a form stating she was leaving the church and I wanted to follow up with her to see if she was comfortable sharing why she made that decision. She was short and vague. "I just feel like it's time. I'm even considering leaving my job, maybe even moving out of state. I just need a change. I have a lot going on," she said.

I heard so many things in those words, but I was reluctant to ask too many probing questions. I don't remember exactly everything that was said, but I do remember at some point asking if she needed anything and if her reason for leaving had to do with something that happened at the church, which she assured me wasn't the case. She even confirmed that she told a few friends who were in her life group. Then I asked her the question that I probably should have started with: "Tammy, are you okay?"

"No." Tammy said that one word as if it was the only word left in the world. It came up quickly, and it was the loudest thing she'd said on the phone in our entire twenty-minute conversation.

"I'm sorry, Tammy. Do you want to talk about it?"

"No. Not right now." Her voice was quieter.

"Okay, I understand. I just want you to know that I love you and I'm here for you if you change your mind. Give me a call anytime. I love you," I said.

She responded, "Okay, thank you. I appreciate that. I'll pray about it and let you know. Thanks for calling, Dr. Sarita."

I asked if I could pray for her, we prayed, and that was it . . . for the time being.

Deploying a Search Party

After ending the call with Tammy, I prayed again. "Lord, something is not right, but what else can I do?" Soon after that prayer, I remembered that Tammy had mentioned talking to two of her friends from life group. I reached out to both women, who affirmed that Tammy had mentioned to them months ago that she was planning to leave, but because she hadn't made the move, they didn't feel compelled to act and assumed she was no longer considering it. I expressed a concern for her and asked if they could just touch base with her to make sure she was okay. I was gathering help, deploying a search party, to go after Tammy. No one person has it all, and God calls his church a body with many members and functions.[8] As a church family, we must work together to help one another in times of need. I knew Tammy needed God's help, but she also needed community to extend love, concern, and care.

One of the women told me that calling her was confirmation regarding a dream she'd had about Tammy. In her dream, Tammy had appeared homeless on the street and in a desperate situation. The other woman I contacted said Tammy's leaving had slipped her mind. She graciously apologized, even though she didn't need to apologize to me, and said she wanted to get better at not letting things slide when they require uncomfortable conversations. Both ladies said they would reach out to her and keep me posted. I decided that I wasn't going to keep asking Tammy to talk to me and that I would trust the Lord and be patient with his process. I periodically sent scriptures via text and just said things like "Thinking of you" and "Hope you have a great day." I wanted to have contact, to show love, but to minimize any pressure to talk about what she was dealing with. And I kept praying.

8. Romans 12:4–8.

In the following weeks, Tammy was invited by one of the sisters to attend a fellowship for young ladies organized by an older saint at her home. I was told that Tammy had a great time and said she needed that fellowship. Three weeks later, I saw Tammy back in church. I didn't say anything, just gave her a hug and told her I was so happy to see her. The next week, Tammy was back in church again, and all the weeks following, I saw her worshipping in her normal spot. She seemed to be doing well and spending time in community. Praise the Lord. I thought that was the good ending of the story, but there was more to come.

Unexpected Discipleship

That December, during the men's and women's ministry joint Christmas party, Tammy and another young lady asked me if I would disciple them. I told them, "Let's set up a time to discuss it." I needed that time to pray and ask the Lord if this was something he was calling me to. This felt like God was up to something, so after meeting with both individually, I agreed to a yearlong formal discipleship relationship. Initially, Tammy and I never talked about why she'd been planning to leave the church several months prior.

I wondered if she would ever tell me what was going on with her when she left, but I put it out of my mind and continued to meet with her. Two months after agreeing to disciple Tammy, I invited her and the other young lady to go shopping with me for supplies for our Equip U Christian education classes. I certainly could have ordered everything online, but for the sake of spending some time together and getting to know the ladies better, I turned it into a field trip. After we shopped, we ended the day the way all shopping trips should end: We went to dinner. I'll tell you more about that dinner at the end of the chapter. It was dinner, but it was a divine revelation that tied this entire story together.

The Ecclesial Gone Girl

I learned many lessons going through this experience. First, organizations like the Black and Missing Foundation should be applauded but also supported. I pray that sharing this story shines a light on a dark reality of our world regarding the numerous Black and Brown people who go missing every year. These are our people who don't have the media attention, manpower, or assistance they need from law enforcement to be found. Consider donating and finding a way to be an advocate for change in your community.

Second, the epidemic of missing Black women was a vehicle through which God opened my eyes and burdened my heart for another type of missing Black woman. It's important to not be too quick to assume you understand what each woman is going through and what contributes to her falling out of sight or leaving a church.

Some Black women may not have been abducted by men, but they have been taken captive by false teaching and men who deceive.[9] They may not have been lured away from their homes by predators, but they may have left the church because the predators were in the pulpit. Black women may not have run away from abusive parents, but maybe they ran from abusive leaders. They may have left because they didn't have the tools to resolve normal conflict with other believers. Over time, some go unnoticed and fade into the shadows of insignificance, because they don't feel like they belong, they struggle to connect with other women, and they are weary of trying. Some Black women may have been easily wooed away by the culture. But instead of people caring to intervene, these women may be seen as irritants, unserious Christians, and problems to be rid of instead of people to be reached, rescued, and restored.

The Black women God showed me may not be missing from their biological families, but they are missing from the family of God. They are the ecclesial gone girl, or one of the forty million "dechurched,"[10] and no matter the reason they go missing, I believe God is clear that we should care.

The third important lesson I learned is that it's our responsibility to

---

9. 2 Timothy 3:6–7.

10. Approximately forty million adults in America who regularly attended Christian worship services have decided they no longer desire to attend church at all. These are what are called the dechurched. See Jim Davis and Michael Graham, *The Great Dechurching: Who's Leaving, Why Are They Going, and What Will It Take to Bring Them Back?* (Grand Rapids, Mich.: Zondervan Reflective, 2023).

consider how we as women may unknowingly contribute to other women going unseen and missing, and we should care enough to intervene. I pray that you will become a vehicle to start this conversation among your Christian friends, in your churches, among leaders, and with other Black Christian women. I pray Church Girls will be burdened to ask the question the 1970s group the Chi-Lites asked in their song "Have You Seen Her."[11]

How You Can Help Missing Black Women

As a Black woman, you can commit to building relationships more intentionally, caring more consistently, and practically living out your God-given identity as an *ezer* (helper), an influencer for good, and a life giver. You can use your voice and experience as a Church Girl to help move the church in a healthier direction and to help the family of faith become more sensitive to Black women who go missing. Below are suggestions for how you can begin to better address the issue of missing Black women in the church.

Act like Family

There are three relationships with women in the family of God that I believe will help protect Black women from leaving: sisters, friends, and spiritual mothers/aunties. We all should be occupying these roles over the course of our spiritual lives. One of the beautiful things about being a Christian is that you automatically get adopted into the family of God.[12] You get a family of siblings, spiritual parents, and friends. Through these relationships, we are called to grow with one another and influence one another's growth from spiritual infancy to spiritual maturity.[13]

11. The Chi-Lites, "Have You Seen Her," track A4 on *(For God's Sake) Give More Power to the People,* Brunswick Records, 1971.

12. Romans 8:15; Ephesians 2:19.

13. Proverbs 27:17; 1 Corinthians 4:26; 12:27–31; Galatians 6:10; Ephesians 4:11–16; Philippians 2:1–4; Colossians 3:12–16; Titus 2; Hebrews 10:24–25.

We get the benefits of protection, accountability, knowing and being known, spending time with like-minded people, discipleship, spiritual nurturing, prayer partners, and friends to worship and celebrate with in a community of diverse and intergenerational wisdom that helps us develop holistically as women.

Social media has famously coined the hashtag #squadgoals to accompany posts and pictures of our closest friends, but no one should represent squad goals better than Church Girls. We should be an example for the world of what friendship should look like because we have Christ, the greatest model of friendship. "It's just me and God" is a lie from the pit of hell, because God made us for relationship. Relationships, even among family members, require work. They won't always be easy, feelings will get hurt, and undoubtedly, we will be closer to some than others, but at the end of the day, we ride with one another. If Church Girls stick together, love one another, cheer for one another, lift one another, wipe one another's tears, pray together, and tell one another truth, we can be an unstoppable force in God's kingdom.

Reprove and Restore Black Women Struggling with Sin

Words like *reprove* or *rebuke* are often frowned on in our current climate, which quickly labels things as spiritually abusive when they are merely biblical correction and accountability. To reprove is to correct or criticize someone with the intent of amending some fault. It can also be defined as "to scold or correct usually gently or with kindly intent."[14]

God is shown in Scripture as a loving parent who brings discipline to instruct and correct his children. However, as Christians we don't always do this well. We can pick people apart with constant rebuke that is crushing instead of redemptive, or we can avoid reproving our sisters because we don't want them to get upset or run away. However, the

---

14. *Merriam-Webster,* s.v. "reprove," accessed March 8, 2024, www.merriam-webster.com/dictionary/reprove.

psalmist said, "Let the righteous one strike me—it is an act of faithful love; let him rebuke me—it is oil for my head; let me not refuse it" (Psalm 141:5). Many times, women go missing when they are led away by sin because no one had the courage to offer a word of correction or warning. God calls you to do this for your sisters in Christ.[15] Proverbs 27:5–6 emphasizes this point: "Open rebuke is better than love carefully concealed. Faithful are the wounds of a friend, but the kisses of an enemy are deceitful" (NKJV). We weaken the church when we don't cooperate with God in confronting sin—after examining our own hearts first,[16] then gently correcting[17] and, when necessary, rebuking sharply.[18]

As members of a local body, this is an act of love. Love isn't punkish. Love isn't politically correct; it's biblically correct. Love isn't silent when you run out in the street like a child playing in traffic. One of my favorite quotes is "Experience isn't the only teacher, but it's the only school a fool will attend."[19] Your sisters need the wisdom of your testimonies that say, "I've been there, done that, got the T-shirt," and "Sis, you don't want him." We need to tell one another, "Don't go down this path," "That's not a good look," and "You need to pray about this." We need older church mothers to say, "Baby, that's not wise; that's not right. You need to repent." The goal of Church Girls loving other Church Girls this way is not just to call women out but to call them up into Christ.[20]

Sometimes in the church you will see women running, leaving, hiding out, or ghosting to avoid God's conviction. Let's love other Church Girls enough to give them truth with grace.[21]

15. Ephesians 4:25; 1 Thessalonians 5:11; Titus 2:15.
16. Matthew 7:3–5; 1 Corinthians 16:14.
17. Galatians 6:1.
18. Galatians 2:11–14; Titus 2:15.
19. I remember Crawford Loritts saying this at an I Still Do marriage conference more than twenty years ago. It's probably an adaptation of a popular quote originally from Benjamin Franklin: "Experience keeps a dear [costly] school, yet Fools will learn in no other." Benjamin Franklin, *Poor Richard's Almanack*, 1743, https://founders.archives.gov/documents/Franklin/01-02-02-0089.
20. Ephesians 4:15.
21. James 5:19–20.

Supporting Black Women

Women are so often stereotyped as being highly relational that we can assume building healthy relationships comes easily and doesn't have to be taught. That isn't the case. We all need our understanding and practice of relationships upgraded by the gospel. Here are a few helpful ways to make that happen:

1. Take the lead in relationship building. Jesus's mission was about initiating and restoring relationship with us;[22] therefore, we need to lead the way in initiating loving relationships with others.[23] When Black women are new to the church, it's important that we remember what it was like to be in their shoes. As an established church member, it's your responsibility to pursue relationship, start the conversation, and offer to connect. Be consistent in reaching out and following up to invite women to activities and events at the church. Certainly, new members can and should pursue relationships, but current members should take the lead. Everyone wants to be loved by being chosen. Jesus modeled choosing us, though we're unworthy of his friendship, so let us also choose others.[24]

2. Introduce and integrate new members into your friendship group. Jesus loved friendship, and we are called to follow his example.[25] Research reveals that the dechurched who are Black, indigenous, and other people of color (BIPOC) between the ages of eighteen and thirty-nine said that the number one reason they left the church was that "I struggled to fit in or belong in church."[26] Conversely, the top three reasons given for this group being willing to return to church were all related to wanting

22. Matthew 4:19; John 6:44; 2 Corinthians 5:19.
23. John 15:12.
24. John 15:16.
25. Mark 10:45; Luke 10:28–42; John 3:22; 12:1–3; 13:15; 15:12–15.
26. Davis and Graham, *Great Dechurching*, 90–91.

friends.[27] It's imperative that we all see friendship as a major factor in whether or not someone might leave the church or return. Friendship is a context where the love and power of the gospel can be extended to Black women who feel isolated and alone.

3. Show up for other women. Jesus spent time with people, and we should too. We can show up for Black women in several ways, such as celebrating Black women's successes; saving birthdays, anniversaries, or important death dates on our phones; sending cards; attending funerals, sporting events, or recitals for children; visiting people in the hospital; and supporting businesses and launches (without asking for a hookup). Sometimes you can coordinate help for women through the church, and other times it may be something you personally can offer to do.

4. Find ways to connect outside of Sunday mornings and planned church events. Jesus modeled doing regular life things like eating meals and celebrating with others.[28] Seek opportunities that are fun and laid-back to connect with women. Every interaction doesn't have to be a Bible study or serious to be spiritual and valuable.

Pursue opportunities to experience laughter, enjoyment, creativity, physical activity, and fun. Invite women to your home or outings with small groups, since smaller groups make it easier to connect.

5. Ask questions and share stories. Jesus modeled asking questions and sharing himself with others.[29] People love to talk about themselves, and nothing shows kindness like curiosity. Get curious and ask questions, especially of those from

An easy starting point that builds connection is "Tell me your story."

27. Davis and Graham, *Great Dechurching*, 94.
28. Luke 9:10–11; John 2:1–10; 12:1–3.
29. Matthew 8:26; 11:16; 16:15; 26:38; Luke 6:46.

different generations, cultural backgrounds, abilities, and statuses. An easy starting point that builds connection is "Tell me your story." Sharing one's story isn't an invitation to just share the horrors of life. Encourage story sharing that is more comprehensive and inviting. You should be willing to share your story too. Paul's words revolutionized not only how I lead and teach women but also how I show up with women willing to share my story: "We cared so much for you that we were pleased to share with you not only the gospel of God but also our own lives, because you had become dear to us" (1 Thessalonians 2:8). Additionally, ask how you can pray for women, and when possible, pray with them in person. My friends Mary Johnson and Dannet Mitchell are just amazing at stopping everything to pray with you. There is nothing more loving and intimate than hearing another sister call out your name before the Father.

6. Cultivate a culture that models healthy expectations. Jesus taught and modeled kingdom culture,[30] and we should model healthy expectations of the Christian experience. We must teach and model kingdom principles such as biblical peacemaking, mercy, and humility. Kingdom culture teaches that we save our lives by losing them, the greatest is the servant, and the foolish are chosen to shame the wise.[31] Jesus also promises we are blessed when we mourn and when we are insulted and persecuted.[32] With the rise of the self-centered prosperity gospel and the propensity to view God and the church through a pain hermeneutic,[33] many times our faith is rattled when we have unmet expectations of God and the Christian experience and when we aren't rooted in contentment in Christ.[34] It's imperative that other women see us being healthy members and setting an example for things such as

30. Matthew 5–7; 16:24; 18:15–20; 28:19–20; Mark 10:21; John 5:19; 16:7–16.
31. Matthew 16:25; 23:11–12; 1 Corinthians 1:18–31.
32. Matthew 5:4, 10–12.
33. A pain hermeneutic is the practice of interpreting Scripture through the lens of your painful experiences and feelings.
34. Philippians 4:11–13.

committing to service; meeting needs; submitting to and supporting leadership; showing mutual respect between men and women; defending truth; enduring hardships; engaging in spiritual warfare; walking in holiness with grace, not legalism; and creating a gossip- and slander-free community of women where sisterhood is the norm. Finally, don't let the popular but unhealthy mindset of "I don't get along with other women" keep you from pressing into women's ministry, building new relationships with women, and making yourself vulnerable in relationships. Our kingdom values and expectations are not of this world.

Engaging Missing or Drifting Black Women

Missing Black women deserve to be sought after. Jesus coming to earth was a literal rescue operation motivated by his love.[35] This is a key point for us when we seek after other Church Girls, because love must precede any seeking actions.[36] Below are a few suggestions for you to be a healthier engager and seeker of missing Black women.

Reach Out

Don't underestimate how powerful a "thinking about you" text, email, handwritten note, or phone call can be. Sometimes just knowing someone thought of us and took the time to reach out makes all the difference in the world. You can even take it a step further and invite physical connection. Being able to lay eyes on someone makes relationship and people more real. Try not to accomplish too much in the initial invitation to connect, and don't get into anything too heavy via text, as that could be overwhelming and turn the person off. Focus on being present, pleasant, respectful, gentle, and a good listener.

35. John 3:16.
36. Isaiah 62:12; Ezekiel 34:11; Matthew 18:11–14.

Discern If They Are Deconstructing Their Faith or Having a Faith Crisis

I've heard countless stories of women who left churches because they had questions about Christianity that no one answered. If you know someone in this boat, if they are willing to share, ask them questions so you can understand where they are coming from. Has there been a life stressor that has caused anger or disappointment toward God (a death, unanswered prayers, job loss, etc.)? Are they willing to share about their recent curiosity about other religions or ideologies and who has captured their attention?

Additionally, we must be prepared to counter and truthfully respond to doubts such as "Is Christianity the white man's religion?" "Are God and the Bible sexist against women?" and "Is Christianity a safe place for the flourishing of Black women?"[37] Validate, empathize, and normalize that having questions is good and that God can handle our questions. Be open to hearing their viewpoints, even if you don't agree, and do your best to provide answers. Be humble and honest if you don't know something; showing a willingness to help find someone who can answer their questions is helpful and an opportunity for you to learn. Resist the urge to just send videos or other resources without engagement or follow-up. You don't have to know everything to help Black women who are questioning or drifting.

Discern If Emotional Issues Are Responsible for Their Disengagement

We have to prayerfully appraise the signs of depression, stress, grief, trauma response, or other psychological issues. You don't have to be a psychologist to trust your instincts and concern. We can also ask people

---

37. These are common questions that Black women have given about the way Christianity has been used against Black people, the centering of whiteness in evangelical spaces, and the patriarchy and misogyny that Black women have experienced in the church. It's vital that you educate yourself and be equipped to provide a factual, empathic, and robust defense of the faith.

how they are doing and lovingly share that we noticed a change. Often people will be grateful and willing to share. Don't feel pressure to fix their situation or emotional stress; rather, simply say, "Tell me more." Allow them to share as much as they want, and offer to help them figure out what they need. This may look like encouraging them to make an appointment with a therapist, encouraging them to talk to someone at church if there are counseling services or people who can do immediate crisis intervention, and praying with them. Sometimes women go missing or disengage and they haven't even processed why. Asking great questions, letting the person talk, showing care for their mental state, and normalizing the impact of mental distress are very helpful when someone feels overwhelmed or stuck emotionally.

Meet Pressing Needs; Don't Just Preach

Many times women disengage because life is really hard for them and they are overwhelmed. We are called in Scripture to "meet pressing needs" (Titus 3:14, NASB), but sometimes when we connect with disengaged or missing women, we lead with moral lessons, Christian platitudes, and biblical counseling. Not everything that causes a Black woman to go missing initially requires a Bible study or only a quick prayer. Some women need a sister who is willing to sit with them and help them figure out housing, find childcare, write an obituary, or find a lawyer. They need someone who will go with them to a doctor's appointment, help them with their aging parents, strategize how to get out of an abusive relationship, or just cook a meal, play games, sit with them, and let them eat, cry, and vent. Practice the ministry of presence so you can discern how best to help them. Address the immediate needs in their lives before you preach to their souls. Remember, Jesus often met physical needs and fed people literal food before he gave them spiritual food.[38]

38. John 6:5.

Go After the "Difficult" Missing Black Women

Like the dangerous mentality of law enforcement when responding to cases of missing Black children, we should be honest if we struggle with the same biases in the church. Are we seeing Black women as runaways or as missing women? Do we see Black sisters in Christ with eyes of grace and love or with judgment, contempt, and dismissiveness? Or, even worse, do we not see them at all?

We can't be naïve and think every Church Girl is going to be someone easy for us to get along with and to love. However, how we see some Black women in our congregations may result in us being less motivated to release an "Amber Alert" in our churches. Are there some women who have annoyed us so much that we say in our hearts that they ran away from the church, so they deserve whatever they get out in these streets? Do you see some Black women as troublemakers or as trauma survivors? Do you see a Black woman having an attitude or anxiety? Do you see failure or fear, disrespect or depression? What you see will affect whether you seek.

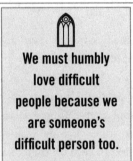

We must humbly love difficult people because we are someone's difficult person too.

I'm not suggesting that all Black women are completely innocent regarding their actions or attitudes. I've worked in the church long enough to know that "people are going to be people" and ministry is often difficult because people are difficult. I'm not looking at us as Black women with rose-colored glasses that show Black women as only victims and always blameless. However, what if innocence and blamelessness weren't the most important attributes when determining whether or not to go after Black women? What if we cared most about seeing each one as an image bearer, a complicated Black woman whom God fiercely loves and has called us to radically love too?[39] We must humbly love difficult people because we are someone's difficult person too.

39. Romans 5:6–8.

Receive Black Women When They Come Home

God lets us go when we want to walk away from him, and he is always willing to receive us with open arms when we return. Sometimes the return may be coming back to the church for membership, or it could be just coming back to visit, have a conversation, or repair a burned bridge; even more exciting, it may be a return to Jesus. I am a prodigal daughter. I didn't just walk away from a church, but I walked away from Jesus. However, I remembered my Father and went back to him.[40] Like Nebuchadnezzar, who lost his mind, when I looked up to God, my sanity returned to me, and I came back to the Lord.[41] By God's grace, I was received with open arms, just like the prodigal son.

You don't want to be like the older brother who was angry that his father received the prodigal son;[42] rather, you want to make sure your heart is prayerful for all the prodigal daughters and expectantly waiting to receive them with joy! Have your arms open to all the women who left hurt, lonely, deconstructing, sinning, or slandering. Be ready to listen, repent, forgive, and learn from Black women who left to heal their wounded hearts. Be ready to throw a feast and receive Black women when they come home or come back to the Lord.

I remember the day I shared my testimony at a prayer meeting. I knew the older church mothers had no clue about African spirituality, but they understood what it meant to be set free from satanic bondage. They didn't ask a lot of questions. They just hugged me, cried with me, and shouted praises unto God that I was back.

The Lord is not slow to fulfill his promise as some count slowness, but is patient toward you, not wishing that any should perish, but that all should reach repentance. (2 Peter 3:9, ESV)

40. Luke 15:17–18.
41. Daniel 4:34–37.
42. Luke 15:28–32.

The Icing on the Cake with Tammy

No one could have anticipated what God was going to reveal and teach during my dinner with Tammy and the other young lady I discipled. While at dinner after our shopping outing, they asked me how my book writing was coming along, and as I began to share, I had this deep sense to be extremely vulnerable. I began to share with Tammy about this chapter, which the Lord had told me to include. I began to confess my heart and attitude after initially hearing that she was going to leave. I told her how the Lord had convicted me for not initially calling her, and I shared the extraordinary lengths he went to in order to teach me about missing Black women in the world and church. I told her I was sorry for ever thinking something negative about her over first having concern for her. I told her how I felt when I saw her in church week after week and how I was so honored and humbled to watch how God turned things around and that I had the privilege to now be discipling her. I smiled wide and beamed with joy, but then I saw her pensive face. I noticed her leg begin to shake under the table and saw her stare off beyond me, as if she was afraid to make eye contact. I saw the other woman, who seemed to know something, and it was awkward. Her eyes filled with tears. *Oh no,* I thought to myself. My heart began to race. Had I shared too much? Had I hurt Tammy with my transparency? All I could think to say in the silence that seemed to be packed with pain was "I'm sorry."

After those words, she seemed to shake herself from the trance, and she looked me right in the eye and said, "Dr. Sarita, thank you for calling me. I was going to kill myself." I was paralyzed. Tammy continued, "I was very depressed when I decided to leave the church. I had a lot going on, and I just pulled away. I was suicidal." I will spare you the details of what happened next—just know that little Mexican restaurant was disrupted by our tears, hugs, and praise. I had no idea, but God did.

To the one reading these words right now, don't you ever think that God won't move heaven and earth to save you. He already did and he's still doing it. Oh my Lord! Look what God did to rescue Tammy. Look at the amazing, unlimited love of God. What a rescue mission. He used a concerned office manager, a weary, unwilling leader, a missing teen, an Audible documentary, an HBO special, loving friends, fellowship with Church Girls, discipleship, and probably many things beyond what I can even see. God used it all to come chasing after Tammy, and he will do the same for you.

Church Girl, this is why we need to love, build relationship with, see, seek, and rescue other Black women. This is why we can't neglect the missing Black women. This is why our hearts should be filled with truth and compassion and why we need to value Black women and build a church culture that creates systemic and organic means of following Jesus by leaving the ninety-nine to go after the one. Hallelujah. I thought the great ending of this story was that Tammy came back to the church, but the real icing on the cake was that God came after her to save her life, just like he's done for you and me! Thank you, Jesus! Let me say it like my mama used to say it to me: "You never know what people are going through." You never know. Almost a year later, and I found out the full scope of what was going on and what God was doing. We don't always have to know all the details except the most important ones: Black women are missing, and they are deserving of love, respect, and somebody to go after them. Will you enlist to be a part of the army that the Lord can deploy to rescue other Black women? My dear sister, if you are a hurting, doubting, drifting, or missing Black woman like Tammy was, just know that God hears your SOS and he's coming after you; he's sending an army of Church Girls to find you!

A Gospel Vision for Missing Black Women

A gospel vision for missing Black women is the heart of the gospel—a rescue mission. Jesus left heaven to pursue humanity, which was lost, broken, and taken captive by sin, and we should do the same for other Black women. There are several reasons Black women go missing, such as being invisible in the church, being captivated by false ideologies, having difficulty building relationships, and enduring emotional struggles and life stressors. Despite these challenges, there are many things you can do as a Church Girl to help retain and engage Black women. Of primary importance is going the extra mile to reach out, build relationships, and model healthy Christianity as a sister, friend, or spiritual mother or auntie. Jesus modeled that he will go to great lengths to come after his daughters, and like my story with Tammy, he will often recruit you to be a part of his rescue plan.

Discussion Questions

 LIGHT: The heart of the gospel is that Jesus performed the greatest rescue mission ever when he left heaven to come seek and save the lost.

1. What is your conversion story? How did Jesus come after you when you were lost?

2. Why should you as a Church Girl show care for missing Black women in the church?

3. Why is it sometimes hard to go after women who are drifting or missing from the church? Do you have a story that shows that you were helped because a woman cared enough to come after you?

LENS: God wants us to see other Black women the way he sees them. His lens is always full of grace and truth.

1. How do we identify other Black women who may be drifting from the church or the faith, and how can we respond?

2. What is the power of acting like family toward other Black women? What roles do you play (sister, friend, spiritual mother, auntie), and what relationships do you wish you had more of? What should the #squadgoals be for Black Christian women?

3. Do you view any Black women who leave the church without a trace as missing or runaways? How does the label influence how you respond?

4. Do you feel like a missing Church Girl? If so, what is your prayer to God? What do you need from other Church Girls?

💜 **LOVE: Everything God did to come after us was motivated by his love. He invites us to participate in his mission to seek out those who are lost, hurting, drifting, and missing.**

1. God showed great love for Tammy and me in how he providentially set things up to intervene. What did you learn about God's love through this story? Do you relate to this story in any way?

2. Is there anyone who may be a missing, drifting, or unseen Black woman that God is putting on your heart to reach out to? What are you going to do? What fears or apprehensions do you have? Will you commit to prayer and obedience?

CONCLUSION

T hank you for going on this journey with me to see the wonder and power of a gospel vision for Black Women. I hope that *Church Girl* has encouraged and challenged you in your faith. I want to leave you with a prayer:

Heavenly Father, I pray for the woman reading these words. You are her creator, savior, and redeemer. Thank you for her life. I pray that she will more deeply and intimately know you, abide in you, walk with you, and serve you. I pray that she will set her affections on you and that you will strengthen her to be the Church Girl you have called her to be. Father, help her root her identity in you, sense the "baby" of purpose kicking inside her, and push through every obstacle to bring it forth for your glory. Help her steward her gifts and assignments with wisdom and humility. Help her find sweet rest in you and walk in the grace and gift of rest. I pray that you would heal every broken area of her life. Touch the tender spots of church hurt, and bless her to experience the power of your restoration. God, help this woman live unapologetically and flourish as a Christian woman in this secular world. I pray for her to be rooted in the local church, to find healthy community, and to put her hand to the plow and serve your kingdom. Protect her from the evil one, who may be tempting her to drift from the faith and question your Word and goodness. Radically intervene in her life and call her back to yourself. Remind her that you are a patient, loving, forgiving God and you welcome her with open arms, if she would just come to you. If she is running, backsliding, or being captivated by false teaching, Lord, let the light of your Word shine brightly in her and around her that she would see the truth and surrender in obedience to you. Thank you for this woman. Bless her, keep her, heal her, fill her with your Holy Spirit, and stabilize her faith in you. If this woman reading hasn't confessed that she is a sinner, repented of her sin, and received the gift of grace to save her soul from eternal separation from you, I pray, God, that you would save her. Allow the scales to fall from her eyes. Allow her to receive spiritual sight that she might be declared righteous in you and receive everlasting life. Invade her life in a profound way. Lord, help her feel just how much you love her. Speak to her now in an undeniable way, and give her a deep sense that you are doing something new in her life. I thank you in advance for the testimonies of healing, deliverance, revival, revelation, and salvation that this woman will share because she had an encounter with you through reading this book. I thank you for being faithful to hear my prayer and to act on her behalf. To your name be all the honor and glory forever. In Jesus's name I pray. Amen.

A Love Letter to the Black Church

Bright Hope: The Black Church Raised This Church Girl

I love the Black Church, and she has loved me. I am a proud Church Girl—a Philly Church Girl to be exact. For as long as I can remember, I have always been a member of a Black church, and even now, I am on staff and serve at a Black church. I was raised in Philadelphia by my parents and by a Black Baptist church, but depending on how the service flowed, we may be what people jokingly call "Bapticostal." I got my start and introduction to the faith and church culture as a child, who, like many other Black Church Girls, spent multiple days at the church for choir rehearsals, youth group, junior usher meetings, junior trustees, Sunday school, Vacation Bible School, Bible study, Saturday enrichment, and a host of other events as the calendar demanded.

My Church Girl story might bring back a whole host of memories for you as well. Even if you have never been a member of a Black church, I would bet you have close relatives or friends who have. As a Black woman, you have undoubtedly been shaped, nurtured, and exposed to its traditions, culture, and history, which influence so much of Black culture today. Whether it's the gospel music, preaching style, community investment, missions, ministries, and auxiliaries or the exuberant worship that reminds us of our roots in Africa, we all can be inspired and encouraged by, and in some way connected to, the legacy of the Black Church.

I was raised at the historic Bright Hope Baptist Church in North

Philadelphia (pronounced by locals as "Norf Philly"), under the pastor-
ate of the late majority whip congressman Rev. William H. Gray III,[1]
whose father and grandfather also pastored the church. Years later my
own father, Rev. Dr. George F. Taylor, would become (and is still today)
the assistant pastor of the church. They, along with so many others, were
such an important part of my faith foundation.

The Black Church taught me many things and shaped who I am
today. Sundays were an all-day affair. I went to Sunday school, worship
service (we called that church), and sometimes the after-church service
if there was an anniversary for some auxiliary board or if a ministry was
having a service we had to attend. On these "special Sundays," we'd either stay at my church or travel to another church to support whatever
was going on, because we were like a second family. Even if no one in
my immediate family was personally involved, we still attended and
showed support. That's another great thing I learned from the Black
Church: Being a Church Girl meant being involved and showing up,
because everything happening at the local church was a family affair. It
didn't matter if you didn't personally serve in a given ministry; you
showed up and supported other ministries in the church because being
a member of the local church connected you to every aspect of the
church. Every event at church was your event. If all you did was sit there
and clap and pray and watch what another ministry had going on, then
march around the church and deposit your love offering in the wicker
baskets, that was worth your time and commitment. There was a sense
of unity in community that I loved.

Before I continue, I want to be honest and open about the Black
Church. It's not without its challenges. I want to be empathic toward the
many Black women who may not have fond memories. The Black
Church, like any other church or human entity, isn't exempt from willful
sin, but I believe there is far too much good to allow the foothold Satan

---

1. Rev. William H. Gray III (August 20, 1941–July 1, 2013) represented Pennsylvania's Second
Congressional District from 1979 to 1991. He also served as the chairman of the House Budget
Committee from 1985 to 1989 and as the House majority whip from 1989 to 1991. In 1991, he
resigned from Congress to become the president and chief executive officer of the United Negro
College Fund until 2004. Rev. Gray was the fourth pastor of Bright Hope Baptist Church, serving
for thirty-five years (1972–2007).

may have gotten in some churches to cancel out the faithfulness of so many more. I also am not writing about the Black Church as if I have been a Black girl and a Black woman unscathed. I, too, have been injured, disappointed, used, silenced, and preyed on during various seasons of ministry. I am not suggesting we silence our experiences of pain and not hold people accountable. However, what I am emphatically stating is that white supremacy and other forms of spiritual warfare have so consistently attempted to minimize, demonize, and scandalize the Black Church that we need to reclaim the whole story and tell it instead of letting Black Church adversaries tell us what to think, believe, and feel. But I still talk about the Black Church with gratefulness, joy, and hope. I speak as a woman who believes that we can hold all these truths, that there is some good, there is some bad, and there is always God.

It's essential for us Church Girls to commend the Black Church, especially now, as we live in a generation full of memes, jokes, tweets, and disparaging images of Black Church culture. It has even become popular for professing Christians to publicly shame and criticize the church more than they testify about the overwhelming good and mission of the church that Christ died for. My friend Dr. Tiffany Gill provides clarity on why we should celebrate and honor the Black Church and her survival:

> The Black church has survived against all odds. Its survival is quite possibly God's strongest apologetic for the power of the gospel within American Christianity.[2]

We can praise the Lord that "the Black church is a miracle,"[3] that we believed in God during a time when he was being weaponized against our freedom and humanity. We can praise God that the Black Church teaches and preaches Christian doctrine that edifies the church and builds our faith, even though racists said we had no scholarly theology to offer, reducing Black faith to emotionality. As Dr. Eric Mason has stated,

2. Tiffany Gill, "Black Church History and Urban Apologetics," in *Urban Apologetics: Restoring Black Dignity with the Gospel,* ed. Eric Mason (Grand Rapids, Mich.: Zondervan Reflective, 2021), 49–50.
3. Gill, "Black Church History and Urban Apologetics," in *Urban Apologetics,* 49.

Many [seminary] professors will only grudgingly admit that many of those who shaped western philosophy, rhetoric, exegesis, apologetics, missionary efforts, and our doctrinal understandings were people of color.[4]

The Black Church sings hymns of hope into the souls of Black folks when life isn't easy and offers a place to worship, belong, and be somebody of significance when the world has told us we have no dignity, we aren't worthy to worship with whites,[5] and our lives don't matter. The Black Church built their own, educated their own, equipped their own, fed their own, ordained their own, raised their own, and baptized their own when we were disowned by the world. It's this institution that raised me and many other Black women like you. It's the Black Church culture—the complexity, the community, the convictions, and the exaltation of Christ—that made me a Church Girl. It's important for us to celebrate how the Black Church has had a hand in reaching, rearing, and rescuing so many Church Girls for the glory of God.

In many ways, the Black Church has been my family, co-parenting with Rev. Dr. George and Etta Taylor in stewarding, maturing, and loving me. That's why, no matter what challenges we face, I'm grateful for their contribution to me and so many others in the earth.

When I was growing up, there was no children's church. Kids went to church with adults and listened and learned whether we wanted to or not, so I fondly remember sitting in the pews, listening to the pastor preach. I learned how to holler "Hallelujah," sing hymns, and watch Black people praise their way through. Sitting in the pews, we kids doodled on the church programs and learned self-control. We also

---

4. Eric Mason, "Restoring Black Dignity," in *Urban Apologetics*, 5.

5. One example of whites having a hostile attitude toward integration in worship happened at St. George's Methodist Church. The predominantly white church had held segregated all-Black services, but then in 1786, white congregants physically threw the Black members out while they were kneeling to pray. This experience encouraged Rev. Richard Allen and Rev. Absalom Jones to start the first African Methodist Episcopal church. Gill, "Black Church History," 41–42.

learned how to help our low blood sugar from hunger by sucking on hard candy our mamas stored for us in ancient plastic bags deep down in their purses. That plastic candy bag was tattered and worn and had candy you never saw sold in stores, but somehow Black mamas knew where to buy it, because they all had it. It held the secret to my church survival.

I would sit in church, smelling fried chicken waft through the air vents, and I couldn't wait to eat in the fellowship hall after service. I remember that before I understood and appreciated the significance of communion, I saw others taking it and it felt like they got to enjoy a pre-dinner snack that I couldn't have. I loved my Black church and thought we were cool because we served real wine for communion—Manischewitz, I later discovered, that was hand poured by the deacons every week. We didn't have the new fancy, convenient two-compartment communion containers everyone has today. You didn't move, talk, or walk during communion. There was no getting up to go to the bathroom. My church dimmed the lights during communion. The darkened, still room, I suppose, made it feel more contemplative, more sacred, and forced us to focus on the sacrifice that Jesus made for the world. When the Black Church wants to affirm something as sacred and holy, we know how to do it.

I didn't realize then how special it was, but the Black Church does everything with a level of dignity and sacredness. On communion Sundays, the ministers wear their white robes; the ushers, deacons, and deaconesses wear their white suits with white gloves and, like synchronized swimmers, pass out communion. There are unwritten rules on how you respectfully raise your hand if you are missed, and the organ plays as the choir sings softly so that the music saturates our souls in worship. I remember songs like "Power in the Blood"[6] and so many others. These songs played in the background as communion was being distributed, and sometimes someone would get happy and start shouting on a song that reminded us that the blood of Jesus not only gives us strength every day but Jesus's blood was also incapable of losing its power![7]

6. Lewis E. Jones, "Power in the Blood," Hymnary.org, accessed February 15, 2024, https://hymnary.org/text/would_you_be_free_from_the_burden_jones.

7. Andraé Crouch and the Disciples, "The Blood Will Never Lose Its Power," track B2 on *Take the Message Everywhere,* Light Records, 1968.

Living in a world where so many Black people didn't feel like they had a lot of power, or the little power they did have could be snatched from them at any moment, singing about Jesus's blood never losing its power was a song of hope whose significance was never lost on this Black Church Girl. And it still is today.

The Black Church has always played an integral role in identity formation and building the dignity of Black people, including Black girls and women. You may have similar experiences of not only your faith being grown but also your goals and hopes of a bright future being encouraged. As a young girl, I remember that the Black Church was great at spotting our gifts in a world where we don't often feel seen and fanning the flames of our dreams through exposure and opportunities we didn't have elsewhere. The Black Church taught me to memorize Scripture, gave me my first acting role in an Easter play, and allowed me to walk a catwalk in a church basement fashion show. It introduced me to men and women who were doctors, lawyers, politicians, teachers, journalists, police officers, seamstresses, and chefs who didn't own a restaurant in the city but owned the kitchen in a church in the hood.

I'm thankful for the faithful Black pastors whose names may never be known.

It was in the Black Church that I learned to honor my elders, to respect men and women who weren't respected or esteemed in the world. I honored older women as nurses who didn't go to nursing school but who took care of you if you shouted yourself into heart palpitations and cared for you if you felt ill in service. I heard Black men being called "Doc" who didn't even graduate from college, and people were "bankers" running credit unions without a finance degree. We didn't question credentials; we honored the faithfulness and skills of our elders who were unable to receive formal training and those the world had never affirmed or licensed. In the Black Church, you were and are somebody. It was not an act on Sunday but a safe place to be fully human, worthy, and loved. It was at the Black Church that I was given responsibility; I was told I was smart and could do anything I put my mind to; I was celebrated for good grades; my name, grade, and accomplishments were often printed in the Sunday bulletin. I was given a mentor; I had aunties and uncles. My church was my extended family. I was loved, corrected, encouraged, pushed, held, and cooked for, and doors opened to me through it. I even got a full Presidential Scholarship to Florida A&M University because a Black physician named Dr. Leonard Johnson personally called the president of FAMU, Dr. Frederick Humphries, and advocated for me.

The Black Church taught me to look out for others. Through the Black Church, I passed out Bible tracts and food. The Black Church taught me to pray and to unashamedly lift my hands and open my mouth to worship a God who could do anything but fail. The Black Church taught me I was a contralto, taught me how to harmonize and sing vibrato like Mahalia Jackson. The Black Church let me wear a nurse's uniform and taught this Church Girl how not to lock her knees when ushering to prevent me from passing out while standing for long periods of time.

It was through the Black Church that I received my first set of fine china, before I ever got married. Ms. Debbie Russel, who was an educator by profession and the superintendent of the Sunday school, found out I was moving out of my parents' home for graduate school, so she invited me to her apartment and gave me Lenox, Waterford, Corelle, and porcelain pieces. She gave me forks and knives and spoons from her own beautiful collection. At that age, I couldn't even appreciate the depth of her generosity and what she was doing for me, but I now understand that Ms. Russel broke up her china set to share with me. She gave her "good stuff" to a young woman moving into her first apartment who didn't have any dishes.

It was in the Black Church that I saw men and women lead and minister to God's people through preaching, Bible teaching, and Sunday school. I remember that Rev. Marcia Watkins was the first woman I ever heard preach a sermon. She was tall and had a booming voice, but in person, out of the preaching moment, she was so kind, a gentle giant who gave the best hugs. Seeing a preacher be powerful, kind, and a woman meant a lot to me as a little girl.

In the Black Church, I saw pastors leave their dinner tables or beds in the middle of the night to head to hospitals to pray over sick people or comfort grieving families when their loved ones went home to be with the Lord. Despite the proliferation of negative stereotypes and misrepresentations of Black pastors and ministers in the world, most of these men and women aren't rich, don't drive expensive cars, and don't fleece their congregations. I've seen men and women serve, teach, comfort, pray for, and forgive people who have treated them like dirt, because the goal was to truly be shepherds like Jesus, and getting hurt by the flock came with the job. I've known leaders who privately struggle with depression, anxiety, and suicidal ideation but never have a safe place to be human. While there are the unfortunate examples that live up to the negative caricatures of preachers and pastors in the world, that isn't everyone. I'm thankful for the faithful Black pastors whose names may never be known but who, week after week, preach the gospel, help people find jobs and housing, put food on people's tables, help kids get to college, reach into their own wallets to meet needs, pray cancer out of bodies, agonize as they prepare eulogies, and shepherd with integrity for the glory of Jesus.

That is the Black Church that I remember, and I am grateful. It taught me that Black is beautiful, and at my church as a kid, I never questioned what color Jesus was or if my color was somehow rejected by God, even if it was rejected by man. Because, at Bright Hope, unlike many other churches, our stained-glass windows had a wall-size depiction of Black Jesus, whom we just thought of as Jesus.[8] He had a thick 'fro, dark skin, a broad nose, and thick lips, and I saw him glow every time the sun beat against the panes. Every day in North Philly, where, like all over the world, Black people are told to believe Black is anything but beautiful and anything but powerful, there is a stained-glass Jesus who looks like a dark-skinned Jesse Jackson from the sixties looking out over abandoned Philly streets and forgotten people. That stained-glass Black Jesus was shining brightly over Black Christians, Black Church Girls, worshipping and relating to the One of whom it was said, "Can anything good come out of Nazareth?" (John 1:46).

Despite the trials and conditions of the community, I always wit-

8. You can see it on the Bright Hope Baptist Church website: https://brighthopebaptist.org.

nessed the Black Church show up and meet pressing needs. Beyond the limelight of photo ops and news vans, which many churches seem to relish as they serve the community, the church I was raised by, like many others, served in obscurity. They fed you if you were hungry, clothed you if you were naked, and provided character references and packed-out courtrooms when members had legal trouble. The Black Church prayed over sick people and not only visited the elderly in nursing homes but also started nursing homes, schools, food pantries, tutoring services, basketball leagues, and community centers. It offered in-house Girl Scouts and Boy Scouts, housed AA and NA meetings, and provided college scholarships.

I learned to share the gospel and preached my first sermonette, not in a pulpit but in a basement that served the homeless and hungry every weekday. I remember it like it was yesterday. The people coming to eat would line up outside for Bright Hope's Surviving to Thriving program. They would come in, take their seats, and be served a full home-cooked dinner. Ms. Maimie Roberts, Ms. Helen Moragne, Ms. Christine Baxter, and many other faithful servants would tirelessly work in the kitchen and cook food for the community. My father would typically provide an exhortation and devotional while the people ate, but this day, it was my turn to talk about the goodness of God to people whose lives were hard. I didn't know how to write a sermon; I didn't know anything about the use of alliteration or illustrations; I didn't know about the OIA method,[9] context, genre, or Greek and Hebrew, but my daddy said, "Just tell them about Jesus," and that's what I did. The Black Church is where I learned about Jesus and learned to talk about Jesus. It was nurturing my gifts and callings even when I didn't realize it.

I thank God for the Black Church. She is a mystery, a marvel, and a miracle. We may have to critique her, but we ought to love her, pray for her, support her, and value her. Any critique of the Black Church not flowing from love and respect, in my opinion, is suspect and dangerous. I love her, ultimately, because she's Christ's bride, and I'm going to love whatever Christ loves. Christ died for the church, and even from Calvary,

---

9. The OIA method is a Bible study technique—observation, interpretation, application.

he knew the Black Church would rise from the discarded ashes of the dismissed disobedience of the evangelical church. The Black Church would rise from the ashes of a demonic attempt to destroy her, to abort her life and her children's lives before she was ever born, and she will continue to declare her God-ordained dignity and destiny as an echo of Scripture. Jesus shed his blood for her, and if he loved his bride that much, the least we can do is love her too.

It's in the Black Church that many Black girls grew into Church Girls. The Black Church, for many Black Christian women, is evidence that, despite the challenges we have faced in the world, we serve a God who is no respecter of persons and he has invited all to be citizens of his kingdom and eat at his table in the time to come. The Black Church is an encouragement to Church Girls who at times need to be reminded of our strength, resilience, beauty, worth, and place in history and in the future. The Black Church can also inspire Church Girls to take up their crosses and follow Jesus daily,[10] lock in on the ultimate mission of the church to spread the gospel, make the name of Jesus famous, meet the pressing needs of our neighbors, care for the poor, fight for the forgotten, and ultimately bring glory to God despite the opposition we sometimes face. It was in the Black Church that many Church Girls were introduced to the *light, lens,* and *love* that gave us a glimpse of the gospel vision we should have of God and our own lives. For that, I am eternally grateful. I love the Black Church. Church Girl—our lives matter, our future is secure, and our hope is bright, because our great God is faithful.

> Strength for today and bright hope for tomorrow . . .
> Great is Thy faithfulness, Lord, unto me![11]

10. Luke 9:23.
11. Thomas Chisholm, "Great Is Thy Faithfulness," Hymnary.org, accessed February 15, 2024, https://hymnary.org/text/great_is_thy_faithfulness_o_god_my_fathe. Chisholm wrote the lyrics based on Lamentations 3:22–23.

ACKNOWLEDGMENTS

I first give honor to God, who is Lord and savior of my life (yes, I'm an old-school Church Girl). I would be nothing without Jesus. Thank you, Jesus, for saving me, loving me, and calling me to serve you. Thank you, Holy Spirit, for the help and conviction to write this book. When you spoke and said, *To not finish would be sin—ignoring a clear call,* that rebuke refocused me and called me to greater dependency on you. It is my highest aim to glorify Jesus and be faithful unto death.

Mark, my love. Your steady leadership, humility, wisdom, protection, and love have healed me, empowered me, and made room for me to be my full self. I couldn't have written this book without your prayers and enthusiasm. Thank you for loving me through this process by patiently listening to my ideas, reading chapters over and over, setting up writing retreats so I could get away to work and rest, and speaking life to me when I felt the weight of the assignment. I admire, respect, and love you. I wouldn't want to be on the journey with anyone else; you make life sweet and fun. Mark, you are my favorite pastor, pilot, and person in the whole wide world. I love you.

To my children, Malachi, Sophia, Olivia, and Gabriella. You are answered prayers and the pride and joy of my life! Thank you for celebrating each step of the journey, making me laugh, and hyping me up. Thinking of leaving you this book as a legacy and modeling that you can do hard things with God's help is what pushed me to keep going on days when I wanted to quit. You all are brilliant, beautiful, resilient, and called by God. Each of you will change the world in your unique way—I know this to be true because you've already changed me.

Mommy and Daddy. Your love, sacrifice, and faith have been my foundation. You are the first people to show and tell me about Jesus. You've always believed in me, prayed for me, and filled our home with joy. I appreciate the long rides in the car, talking for hours, every vacation, every extracurricular activity, the meals, the laughter, and even the correction. Your wise counsel to dream big, care about others, and work with excellence as unto the Lord continues to guide me. You filled our home with books, and now your daughter has written one—look at God. I love you.

Epiphany Fellowship family—pastors, pastors' wives, staff, leaders, and covenant community members. I'm grateful for your love and support. Pastor Mason, you are a rare gift as a pastor. I don't take being seen, affirmed, and loved in ministry lightly—thank you. It is an honor to lead and co-labor with my teams for EquipU Christian education and SALT Women's Ministry. I can't say enough about all the women of Epiphany and my spiritual daughters near and far—I love you; thank you for loving me too!

To my agent, Jevon Bolden of Embolden Media Group, your fierce support, wisdom, and willingness to go above and beyond gave me boldness as a first-time author. One night over dinner, you said, "Sarita, you are writing an anthology, a manifesto for Black Christian women. Your book will change lives." You don't know this, but your words caught me at a time when I was falling on the inside—weary from this writing process. You reignited a fire in me to go on. Thank you.

To my team at WaterBrook and Penguin Random House. Thank you for supporting the vision of *Church Girl*. To my wonderful editor, Jamie Lapeyrolerie. I learned a lot from you. I'm grateful for your expertise and encouragement along the way.

Many friends, family members, and sisters have supported by reading chapters and offering direction, stories, or encouragement and prayers. Thank you, Sister Martina Lambert, Dr. Tiffany Gill, Mary Johnson, Amanda Baker, Ladesha Albury, Brittany James, Dannet Mitchell, Rashida Winslow, Debra Butler, Daniella Colletta, Shonny Miller, Dr. Bridgette Rice, Karen Ellis, Pastor Jerome Gay, Dale Mobley, Daarinah Henry, Pascale Mobley, aunts, uncles, cousins, and extended family. Thank you to the Lyons, Taylor, and King families—I love you all. Special thanks to Sarah Lowney for being a faithful assistant and co-laborer in ministry. Sarah, you did an amazing job capturing my vision and designing my beautiful book cover.

Thank you, Jackie Hill Perry, for writing the foreword to *Church Girl* and for inviting me into your life and ministry; your encouragement and support in this process have been a blessing.

I'm grateful for my first church family, Bright Hope Baptist Church, who instilled in me a love for Jesus, community, social justice, the Black Church, and Church Girls all over the world.

ABOUT THE AUTHOR

Sarita T. Lyons, JD, PhD, is a wife, mother, speaker, Bible teacher, and psychotherapist. Her greatest joy in ministry is serving on the front lines in urban ministry in the local church. She is on staff at Epiphany Fellowship Church in Philadelphia as the director of discipleship and women's ministries. Prior to full-time ministry, Dr. Lyons was in private practice for eight years, where she provided counseling for a variety of psychological needs. She is passionate about improving the emotional and spiritual health of the church, making disciples, and developing women leaders. Dr. Lyons cares deeply about the church being equipped and rooted in Christ amid the changing tides and influence of culture. She is a highly sought-after speaker for conferences, churches, corporate organizations, and educational institutions. She consults with churches regarding ministry and leadership development, and she provides counsel, care, and crisis intervention for leaders and congregations after leadership failure. Dr. Lyons speaks, writes, and advocates about the intersections of faith, mental health, justice, culture, and women. She is a proud graduate from an HBCU, Florida A&M University, where she earned a bachelor of science in broadcast journalism. Dr. Lyons earned a juris doctor from Villanova University School of Law, as well as a master of science and a doctor of philosophy in clinical and forensic psychology from Drexel University. Dr. Lyons is married to Pastor Mark Lyons, and they are the proud parents of Malachi, Sophia, Olivia, and Gabriella.

You can find more information about Dr. Lyons here:

@drsaritalyons

SaritaLyons.com